INNER MONGOLIA: COLOURFUL AND MAGNIFICENT

微观内蒙古

（汉英版）

莫久愚 主编

商务印书馆
The Commercial Press
SINCE 1897

2017年·北京

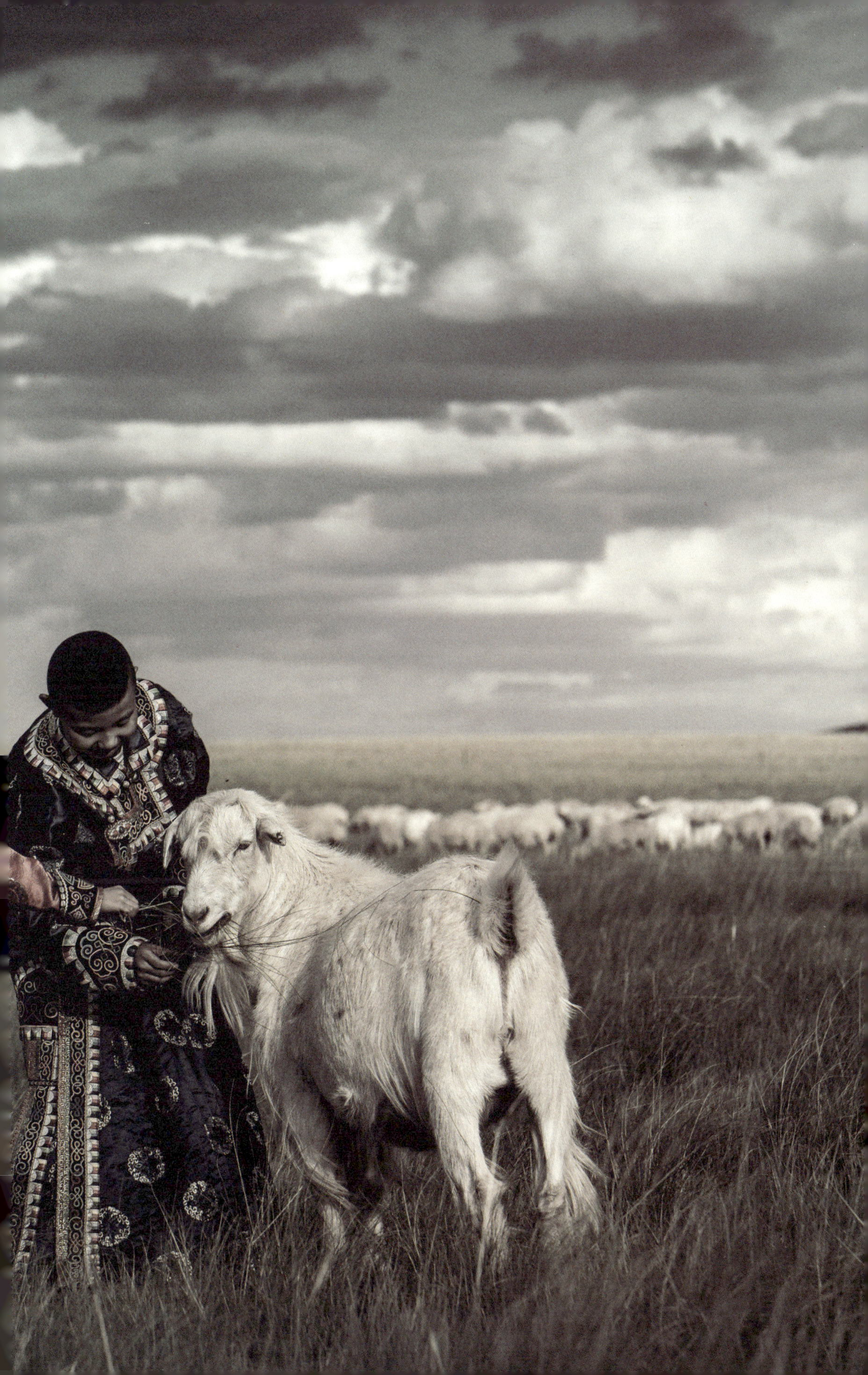

丛书策划　聂晓阳　周洪波

主　　编　莫久愚
副主编　　高雪峰
撰　　写　（按音序排列）
　　　　　敖继红　白江宏　班　澜　达　子　邓九刚
　　　　　郭雨桥　黄　蕾　姜　苇　李　倩　刘秉忠
　　　　　刘馥宁　刘伟建　莫　迪　莫久愚　娜仁托娅
　　　　　庞月莲　苏怀亮　王　芳　许　淇　殷向飞
　　　　　余佳荣　张阿泉　张弓长　张铁良

英文翻译　梅　皓〔美〕
英文审订　邢三洲

责任编辑　华　莎
装帧设计　东方美迪

Chief Producers　Nie Xiaoyang / Zhou Hongbo

Chief Compiler　Mo Jiuyu
Deputy Compiler　Gao Xuefeng
Compilers　Ao Jihong / Bai Jianghong / Ban Lan / Dazi / Deng Jiugang
　　　　　Guo Yuqiao / Huang Lei / Jiang Wei / Li Qian / Liu Bingzhong
　　　　　Liu Funing / Liu Weijian / Mo Di / Mo Jiuyu / Narentuoya
　　　　　Pang Yuelian / Su Huailiang / Wang Fang / Xu Qi / Yin Xiangfei
　　　　　Yu Jiarong / Zhang Aquan / Zhang Gongchang / Zhang Tieliang

English Translator　Mei Hao（USA）
English Reviewer　Xing Sanzhou

Executive Editor　Hua Sha
Art Design　EmDesign

序

宏观视野中的内蒙古

内蒙古位于我国陆地疆域的正北方，有着118.3万平方公里的面积，横跨东北、华北、西北三个地理单元，是一个对中外游客和商家充满诱惑力的地方。

地质时期的多次海陆变迁、气候变化，塑造了今日内蒙古的大地风貌，留下了瑰丽的自然风光。辽阔的草原，广袤的沙漠，平旷的田野，连绵的山林，纯净的蓝天，星罗棋布的湖泊，以及生活在这片土地上热情好客的人们，构成了"祖国北部边疆"的一道"亮丽风景线"。

内蒙古地处边疆，与蒙古国、俄罗斯接壤，拥有4000多公里的边境线。地理上的边疆并不意味着文明的边疆、文化的边疆。

内蒙古地区是中华文明的源头之一。五六十万年前，这里就有古人类生存，七八万年前鄂尔多斯萨拉乌苏河谷中的"河套人"，处于东亚大陆现代人类形成的关键时期。距今8000年至4000多年，新石器文化遍布内蒙古各地，在西辽河流域以红山文化为代表的发达的新石器文化遗址上，散布着远古先民的农业聚落，蕴含着中国古代文明形成的一些重要信息，是"中华文明的曙光"最初照耀的土地。

进入文明时代，生活在内蒙古地区的匈奴、鲜卑、柔然、突厥、契丹、蒙古等民族，创造了大规模的游牧经济，他们的历史活动在中国多民族国家的形成过程中留下了深刻的印记。内蒙古拥有全国最多、种类最全的长城遗存，从战国时期的秦、赵、燕长城到明代长城，不同时代的长城，犹如一条没有固定河道的长河，在内蒙古中西部地区南北移动。这个"长城地带"，可耕可牧，是农耕民族和草原民族交往最频繁的区域。随着气候、环境的变化，这里的文化景观也多次出现草场和农田的转换，是我国内地和边疆关系中的一个重要链条，不仅让中国历史的演进更加波澜壮阔，也把茫茫草原、广袤山林与国家核心区密切联系在一起，成为中国历史不可分割的部分。源自大兴安岭山地的鲜卑、契丹、蒙古民族建立的北魏、辽、元三个王朝，深刻影响了中国历史的发展轨迹。

在工业文明和近代交通出现以前，大范围游动的北方民族是东西方文化交流中的天然桥梁和媒介。内蒙古的古代民族是"草原丝绸之路"最早的开拓者、参与者。在近代"茶叶之路"的开通过程中，内蒙古地区是一个关键节点，沟通了我国内地与东欧乃至西部欧洲的交往。

传统的游牧经济和渔猎生活使这里的民族与大自然建立了一种特殊的依赖关系，他们普遍经历过漫长的萨满信仰时代。虽然生活方式早已变化，在蒙古、达斡尔、鄂温克、鄂伦春等民族生活中沉淀下来的萨满习俗却无所不在。他们敬畏苍天，敬畏大地，敬畏自然界的一草一木、一切生灵。生活习俗、日常行为中处处体现出爱护自然、珍惜环境的意识，是内蒙古民族文化中的宝贵遗产。这些民族历史上形成的朴素的生态理念，是"草原文化"的核心价值之一。

在漫长的历史时期，内蒙古是北方民族活动的舞台，但近代出现的以冀鲁民众为主的"闯关东"和以晋陕民众为主的"走西口"两个迁徙浪潮，以及中华人民共和国成立后随着内地支援边疆建设和林业开发而来的移民，逐渐改变了内蒙古的民族构成和人口结构。今天内蒙古2520万常住人口，是一个以蒙古族为主体，汉民族占多数，达斡尔、鄂温克、鄂伦春、俄罗斯、满族、回族、朝鲜族等各民族和睦相处的大家庭。人口结构的变化也带来了农耕文化与传统游牧文化、游猎文化的深层次交流，几百年的移民携着内地不同地区的文化基因，与不同民族、不同蒙古部族的文化艺术、生活习俗、语言习惯互相影响、交融，也衍生出一些新的文化形态，使内蒙古各地的地方民俗、区域性文化丰富多彩、灿烂百陈。

内蒙古是中国第一个实现民族区域自治的地方，自治区诞生于人民解放战争时期。她的建立使辽阔的内蒙古草原与东北解放区连为一体，成为中国共产党和军队建立"巩固的东北根据地"的侧翼屏障。内蒙古自治政府整编的内蒙古骑兵部队随即参加了东北、华北战场的战略决战，各民族子弟为共和国的建立做出了自己的贡献。

改革开放以来，特别是进入新世纪以来，内蒙古抓住国家实施西部大开发、振兴东北等战略机遇，经济实现了高速增长，发展速度连续多年居于全国前列。2016年，自治区年生产总值达到18632.6亿元，人均7.4万元。一般公共预算收入和城乡居民收入增幅均高于全国平均水平。

近年来国家的"一带一路"建设、京津冀协同发展战略等又为自治区提供了新的历史机遇，在可以预见的将来，内蒙古将会成为国家重要的能源基地、新型化工基地、有色金属生产加工基地、绿色农畜产品生产加工基地、战略性新兴产业基地和国内外知名旅游目的地。

随着经济社会的发展，内蒙古与内地及境外的交往，已经波及经济生活的各个领域，深入社会生活的不同层面，几乎每个内蒙古人都会遇到如何向内地及海外朋友介绍内蒙古的问题。商务印书馆主持策划的"微观中国"系列，为我们提供了一种新的讲述形式。

"微观中国"是商务印书馆主持策划的外宣读物，该系列首创"微博体"写作方式，强调从细微处观察、体验，用不到140字的篇幅独立呈现一个事实或传递一种情感。

我们这420多条"微博"，就是420多个话题，以看似无序的文字组合，述说内蒙古的大致面貌。宏观的视野，微观的视角，用细节构筑一个有温度的鲜活的内蒙古。"微博体"的容量、节奏和图文并茂的呈现方式，符合当代人的"微阅读"习惯。希望这些小细节能打动读者，让更多的人走进内蒙古，亲近和了解内蒙古。

本书部分条目引录了肖亦农、鲍尔吉·原野、席慕蓉、许淇、刘书润、敖长福、张泊寒等人的作品及一些新闻报道，实际上是借他们的视角、感受，来"微观"、体验内蒙古。个别条目囿于字数，无法注明姓名，在此向他们表达我们的敬意和谢意。

这部书的很大幅面是由图片构成的，很多摄影界的朋友慷慨提供了自己的作品，白兰、王大方、沃泽民、贾宝维、李阳光等人在图片征集中也提供了热情帮助。刘一玲、华莎女士自始至终指导着本书的编写，在此一并致谢。

适逢内蒙古自治区成立70周年，我们奉上此书，献礼大庆，希望能向中外读者展示一个真实而生动、兼具自然美和人文美的内蒙古。

莫久愚
2017年4月

| Preface |

A Wide View of Inner Mongolia

Inner Mongolia is located in the middle of China's northern land territory, and has a land area of 1.183 million square kilometres. It spans three geographical units—North-eastern, North, and North-western China, and is an attractive destination for businesses and tourists at home and abroad.

Changes in ocean coverage and climate over a number of geologic periods have formed the grand landscape of Inner Mongolia today, and left us with beautiful natural scenery. Broad grasslands, vast deserts, wide-open fields, and ranges of mountains and forests under clear blue skies, and landscapes dotted with countless lakes as well as the hospitable people who live on these landscapes have made Inner Mongolia a long strip of spectacular sight in China's northern territory.

At the north of the region is a border with the countries of Russia and Mongolia, which is over 4,000 kilometres long. The geographic border doesn't mean that it's a separator of cultures and civilisations, however.

Inner Mongolia is one of the sources of Chinese culture. About 600,000 years ago ancient humans lived here, and the "Hetao Man" of the Sara Usu River Valley, who lived around 80,000 years ago is evidence of a formative period of modern humans in East Asia. Between 8,000 and 4,000 years ago, Neolithic cultures existed all around the area, and the Hongshan Culture of the Xiliao River basin is a left behind representative cultural ruins of a well-developed Neolithic culture, with scattered ancient agricultural settlements. These remains provide important information about ancient Chinese culture, and evidence of the dawn of the Chinese civilisation.

Entering into the age of civilisations, people living in the area that is now Inner Mongolia, such as the Huns, Xianbei, Roen, ancient Turks, Khitans and Mongolians, created a large-scale herding economy, and made important impressions on China's long history as a multi-ethnic state. Inner Mongolia has the most and most varied remains of the Great Wall, from the Qin, Zhao and Yan Kingdoms of the Warring States Period to the Ming Dynasty. Different segments of the Great Wall exist like traces of a river with a variable path, moving north and south over the ages in central-western Inner Mongolia. This "Great Wall Zone" is suitable for both agriculture and herding, and is a place where farmers and herders came into contact with each other most frequently. With changes in climate and environment, there have been many changes between prairie and pasture over the ages in this area, which is an important link between inland areas and northern border of China. It not only added vigour and grandeur to the landscape of Chinese history, it also links the vast grasslands and wide forests closely with the core region of the country, and is an inseparable part of China in history. The Xianbei, Khitan and Mongolian people from the Greater Hinggan Range even founded the Northern Wei, Liao, and Yuan Dynasties, making huge impacts on the course of Chinese history.

Before the advent of industrial society and modern transportation, the peoples of the north, roaming a very large range of land, were an important natural bridge and link of cultural exchanges between the peoples of the east and west. The ancient peoples of Inner Mongolia were the earliest developers and participants of the "silk road on the grasslands". In the opening of the more recent "tea road", Inner Mongolia functioned as an important step, and a link between inland areas of China and Eastern and even the western part of Europe.

A traditional economy based on herding and a lifestyle reliant on fishing and hunting caused the people here to develop an especially reliant relationship with nature. They all have a long history of shamanist beliefs. Although their lifestyles have long since changed, among the Mongolian, Daur, Ewenki, Oroqen and other peoples these shamanistic customs still persist everywhere. They revere the sky, earth, grasses, trees, and all living spirits. Their living practices and daily behaviours show tendencies of protecting nature throughout, and they value the environment and knowledge about it—a precious aspect of the culture of the ancient peoples of Inner Mongolia. These peoples have formed some simple ecological concepts over the ages, one of the core values of the "grassland culture".

For most of its long history, Inner Mongolia's stage was dominated by the peoples of the north, but in more recent times people from Shandong and Hebei have come northeast and people from Shanxi and Shaanxi have come north into the area, with many more coming to support border development and forestry work after the founding of the People's Republic of China, gradually changing the demography of the area. Out of the population of 25.2 million residents, Mongolians constitute the core and Han Chinese the majority, with Daur, Ewenki, Oroqen, Russian, Manchu, Hui, Korean and other ethnic groups existing harmoniously, too. Changes in the makeup of the population have resulted in many interactions between agricultural and traditional herding, and hunting cultures, with centuries of migration from inland areas of China bringing new cultural genes to the area. Different ethnicities and Mongolian groups have come together exchanging styles of living, languages, customs, culture and art, forming a new culture that's rich in variety and wondrous to behold.

Inner Mongolia is the first place in China in which regional autonomy was established in an ethnic minority area, which happened during the People's War of Liberation. The vast Inner Mongolian grasslands were thus merged with the liberated areas of North-eastern China, and became a strong supporter for the Chinese Communist Party and its army to strengthen the foothold— the revolutionary bases—they had in North-eastern China. The government of the Inner Mongolia Autonomous Region organised riders to participate in the strategically decisive battles in North China and North-eastern China, and many of the sons of Inner Mongolia from all groups made contributions to the establishment of People's Republic of China.

After reform and opening up in China, especially in the 21st century, Inner Mongolia seized every opportunity for development by taking advantage of development planned for western regions in China, and participating in the rejuvenation plan of industrial base in North-eastern China, and experienced rapid growth, taking a place at the forefront in terms of development speed for several successive years. In 2016, the annual gross production for the region reached 1,863.26 billion yuan, or 74,000 yuan per capital. In general, public budget revenue and income of urban and rural residents increased faster than the national average.

In recent years, with the establishment of "Belt and Road" initiative and the cooperative development of the Beijing-Tianjin-Hebei region, Inner Mongolia was provided with further opportunities for development. In the foreseeable future, Inner Mongolia will become an important base for energy, new chemical industry, nonferrous metal production and processing, green agriculture and livestock production and processing, and strategic emerging industry, as well as popular tourist destination both among the Chinese and those abroad.

Along with the course of economic and social development, and increased contact between Inner Mongolia and China's inland provinces and foreign countries, effects have spread to all kinds of aspects of economic life in the region as well as different layers and aspects of society—this means that almost everyone in Inner Mongolia is faced with the task introducing their homeland to those from elsewhere. The "One-Minute China" series developed by the Commercial Press has presented us with a new format for exposition.

"One-Minute China" is a series of books aimed at promoting various areas in China to foreigners. Each book contains many short articles, each the size of a micro-blog entry. They emphasise careful inspection and experience, with each article, under 140 Chinese characters in length painting a picture or conveying an emotion.

Our 420 entries in this book represent 420 different topics. These 420 disparate pieces as a whole give the reader a general picture of Inner Mongolia. A wide view composed of narrow-angle snapshots makes for a fresh and warm total image. The size of the articles, the structure of the book, and the pictures included make the book suitable for readers who have become accustomed to "micro-reading". We hope that readers will be moved by this format and motivated to further understand and approach the region.

This book uses some text from writings and news reports by authors such as Xiao Yinong, Borjigin Yuanye, Xi Murong, Xu Qi, Liu Shurun, Ao Changfu, and Zhang Bohan. We show pieces of their perspectives and feelings to provide glimpses of their experiences in Inner Mongolia. As space is limited in the book, we can't mark the author for each entry. Thus, we'd like to express our respect and appreciation here.

A large portion of the content of this book consists of photographs. Many individuals, including photographers and curators, graciously contributed images, such as Bai Lan, Wang Dafang, Wo Zemin, Jia Baowei, and Li Yangguang. We very much appreciate their help. Mrs. Liu Yiling and Mrs. Hua Sha directed the compilation of this book from start to finish, and for that we are most grateful.

As the 70th anniversary of the establishment of Inner Mongolia Autonomous Region draws near, we present this book as a gift for the celebration, hoping to give an accurate and moving picture of the region to readers in China and abroad, a representation of this beautiful and cultured place for all to enjoy.

Mo Jiuyu
April 2017

目录 | Contents

历史·寻踪	1	History and Exploration
草原·印象	25	Impressions of the Grassland
城市·风情	55	Flavour of the City
传统·习俗	77	Traditions and Customs
地理·物产	95	Geography and Products
行旅·体验	119	Travel and Experiences
回望·轶事	145	Memories and Anecdotes
山林·沙地	163	Mountains, Forests and Deserts
舌尖·语言	191	Taste and Language
文化·交融	211	Culture and Interactions
附录	238	Appendices

摄影：达楞

历史·寻踪

History and Exploration

微观内蒙古
INNER MONGOLIA: COLOURFUL AND MAGNIFICENT

内蒙古博物院
Inner Mongolia Museum

文：莫久愚

中国民族地区最早建立的博物馆，藏品达 12 万余件（套）。拥有从 2.5 亿年前到 100 万年前的古生物化石标本，几乎没有缺环。馆藏查干诺尔龙是亚洲最大的白垩纪恐龙，中国古代北方游牧民族文物收藏是该馆特色，蒙古族文物的藏品质量、数量位居中国同类博物馆之首。认识内蒙古，可以从这里开始。

This is the earliest museum established in Chinese minority areas, with a collection of more than 120,000 pieces. It has fossil specimens from 250 million to 1 million years old, almost without a missing link. It also has a specimen of the Nurosaurus (N. qaganesis), the largest cretaceous dinosaur in Asia. Its real speciality is that of cultural collections of the nomadic herders of ancient northern China. Its specimens of Mongolian cultural artefacts are the most in number and best in quality in China. If you want to understand Inner Mongolia, this is a good place to start.

摄影：孔群

中华文明起源的地方
The birthplace of Chinese civilization

文：莫久愚

敖汉旗曾是远古先民活动最密集的地方。这个小县城里已发现古代遗址 4000 余处，敖汉旗博物馆拥有文物 6000 余件，揭取的辽墓壁画达 80 余幅，馆藏文物的级别和数量在中国的县级博物馆中位居第一。这里已经成为国内专家们寻找中华文明起源的重点区域。

Aohan Banner was in ancient times the home to the largest concentration of activities among the people. This small county-level city has yielded more than 4,000 archaeological sites, and the Aohan Banner Museum has more than 6,000 articles, more than 80 Liao tomb murals, and in regard to the quality and quantity, its collection ranks first among county-level museums in China. This place has already become a major point of interest for experts in China looking into the origins of Chinese civilization.

历史·寻踪
History and Exploration

河套人
Hetao Man

文：莫久愚

萨拉乌苏河两岸的砂崖，忠实记录着 50 万年来鄂尔多斯高原的气候变迁和地质变化。1922 年，法国神父桑志华、比利时学者德日进在这里发现了一枚晚期智人的铲形门齿化石，距今 7 万年左右，那正是亚洲现代人种形成的关键时期。铲形门齿是中国人独有的特征。这枚门齿的主人后来被我国考古学家裴文中命名为"河套人"。

The sand cliffs of the Sara Usu River faithfully preserve information about the climate and geological shifts on the Ordos highlands over the past 500,000 years. In 1922, French priest Émile Licent and Belgian scholar Teilhard de Chardin found a fossilized shovel-shaped incisor from a late Homo sapiens, from approximately 70,000 years ago, which was a critical time for the development of the modern Asian human species. The shovel-shaped incisor is a physiological trait unique to the Chinese people. Later, Chinese archaeologist Pei Wenzhong named the owner of this tooth "Hetao Man".

"中华第一龙"
"China's First Dragon"

文：张阿泉

1971 年，翁牛特旗牧民张凤祥在山上拾到一个"废铁钩"，给孩子当玩具，不想磨光后竟是一条碧玉龙。这块碧玉龙被旗文化馆花 30 元收购，存放在一个不起眼的地方。1984 年碧玉龙被选中进京参展，经沈从文、苏秉琦先生鉴定为"史前中华龙"，后被誉为"中华第一龙"。如今它展出的保金就高达 10 亿元人民币。

In 1971 in the Ongniud Banner, a herder named Zhang Fengxiang picked up a "broken iron hook" in the mountain and took it home to give to his kid as a toy. After he polished it, he discovered it was a jade dragon. The banner cultural relics authority bought it off him for 30 yuan, and stored it away nowhere special in particular. In 1984 it was selected to be exhibited in Beijing. Shen Congwen and Su Bingqi determined it was a prehistoric Chinese dragon, and it became famous as being "China's First Dragon". Now when it is exhibited, it's insured for as high as 1 billion yuan.

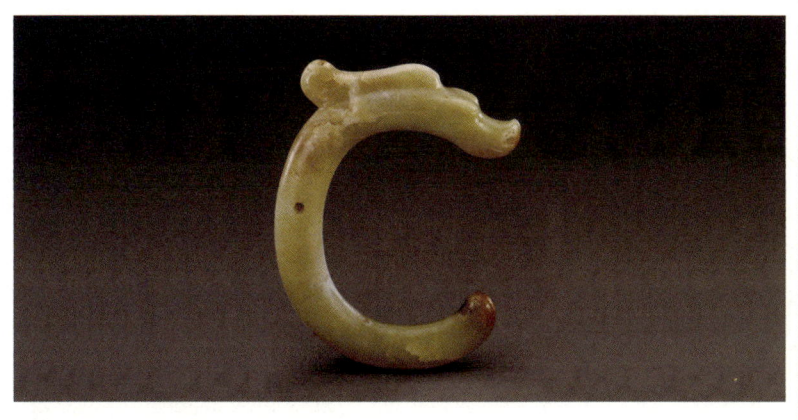

摄影：孔群

微观内蒙古
INNER MONGOLIA: COLOURFUL AND MAGNIFICENT

摄影：于海永

"华夏第一村"
"The First Village in China"

文：莫久愚

敖汉旗大窝铺村的一处坡地上，矗立着"华夏第一村"牌楼，只是"村民"早已远去。"村"内分布着兴隆洼文化、红山文化及以后的房屋遗址。距今8200年至3600年间，这里均有先民居住。在此发现过世界上最古老的玉器，出土的骨笛被认定为世界第一件乐器，"蚌饰裙"则是中国现存最早的服饰。

On a slope in Dawopu Village in Aohan Banner there is an archway that says "The First Village in China" upon it, even though the "village residents" had gone long ago. Within the village there are remains of the Xinglongwa, Hongshan and later cultures. From 8,200 to 3,600 years ago, people lived here continuously. Here, the oldest Chinese jadewares have been discovered, as well as a bone flute that is recognised as the world's oldest instrument, and a clamshell-made skirt which is China's oldest article of clothing in existence.

最早的牙科手术
Earliest dental surgery

文：张阿泉

2003年，赤峰市兴隆洼文化兴隆沟遗址发掘工作结束后，科研人员在M24墓主人头骨右侧两颗颌牙上发现有钻孔，系糙质人工钻磨，旨在减轻蛀牙疼痛。这表明在距今8000年前就已有牙医，这也是中国史前人类最早的一例牙科手术。

In 2003, at the Xinlonggou site in Chifeng City, which is an example of Xinlongwa culture, when excavations had finished, researchers noticed holes drilled into two teeth on the right side of the head of the owner of the M24 grave site. Roughly executed by a primitive drill, they would have been used to relieve the pain from a toothache. This shows that dentistry was being practiced 8,000 years ago, and is the earliest evidence of dental work by prehistoric Chinese.

历史·寻踪
History and Exploration

世界最早的人工栽培谷物
The world's first artificially cultivated grain

文：张阿泉

剑桥大学植物考古学家马丁·琼斯说："敖汉旗兴隆沟遗址谷子的出土，证明了谷子最早产于西辽河上游地区，同美洲的玉米、马铃薯一样，人工栽培的谷子对世界文化的发展有着同样杰出的贡献。同时，欧洲的谷子很可能就是由西辽河上游逐步西移而广为耕作的。"

Martin Jones, a researcher specialized in archaeobotany at Cambridge University says: "In the remains of the Xinglonggou site in Aohan Banner millet seeds were unearthed, which proves that the earliest millet was artificially cultivated near the upper reaches of the Xiliao River, which made a huge contribution to the culture and development of the world, just like maize and potatoes from America. At the same time, the millet cultivated in Europe are possibly the result of the gradual migration of tillage from this area westward.

匈奴金冠
Gold crown of the Hun

文：苏怀亮

1972年，76岁的鄂尔多斯老人王美子在杭锦旗阿鲁柴登沙窝子里挖土龙骨换零花钱时，挖出不少三棱形铜箭头和一根头上有金片的铁棍，接着又发现了更多的金银物件。王老汉认为这是庙宇上的东西，不可自留，就把这些器物交公。这一交，内蒙古博物院多了一件镇馆之宝——匈奴王金冠。

In 1972, when 76-year-old Wang Meizi was looking in the sands of Hanggin Banner for fossil fragments to sell for spending money, he found some triangular pyramid shaped copper arrowheads and an iron rod with gold plates on one end. He then found more gold and silver artefacts. Believing that these were from a temple, this old man knew it was ominous to keep them, and thus handed them over to the government. In doing so, he gave the Inner Mongolia Museum a most precious artefact—a gold crown of the Hun.

摄影：孔群

微观内蒙古
INNER MONGOLIA: COLOURFUL AND MAGNIFICENT

秦汉故迹
Traces of Qin and Han Dynasties

文：莫久愚

内蒙古可能是保有秦汉地面遗迹最多的省区。除了秦汉长城外，还有大批的汉城遗址。古诗文中的居延塞、鸡鹿塞、高阙塞、光禄塞等名称，在这里绝不只是象征边地的意象符号，而是真真切切的现实存在。在内蒙古西部沙漠至阴山、黄河间，可以寻找"秦时明月汉时关"的意趣。

Inner Mongolia may top other provinces and regions in China in possessing the most remains of Qin and Han Dynasties. In addition to the Qin and Han segments of the Great Wall, there are also a large number of ruins of Han cities. The Juyan, Jilu, Gaoque, Guanglu and other frontier fortresses, famous from ancient poems are not just symbolic here, but actually exist. From the deserts in the west to areas between Yinshan Mountains and the Yellow River, one can find many historical sites from these two dynasties.

摄影：莫久愚

两千年前的"高速公路"
2,000-year-old expressway

文：莫久愚

在鄂尔多斯漫赖草原上，可以看到很多被称作"古路豁子"的遗迹，那是2000多年前秦始皇修建的从咸阳至阴山脚下的"秦直道"孑遗，是连接关中和草原地带的快速通道。秦始皇死后，运载他遗体的车队经此路返回关中；司马迁曾陪侍汉武帝沿此道回到长安；远嫁匈奴的王昭君也是从这里出塞的。

On the Manlai Grassland of Ordos, "the remains of the old road" called by locals can be seen everywhere. This refers to the traces of the "Qin Express" built by the First Emperor of Qin Dynasty between Xianyang and the foot of Yinshan Mountains, a quick route connecting the central Shaanxi Plain with the grasslands. After the First Emperor died, his body was transported by cart along this road. Sima Qian accompanied and served the Emperor Wudi of the Han Dynasty upon this route to Xi'an, and when Wang Zhaojun married a Hun monarch, she travelled upon this route too.

历史·寻踪
History and Exploration

摄影：刘兆和

居延古塞
Juyan Fortress

文：莫久愚

额济纳河携带着历史的记忆，奔向沙漠中古老的居延海。沿河床散布着一百多座倾圮的古代烽燧，在夕阳的斜晖里，烽燧西侧残高只有十几厘米的古塞墙遗存若隐若现，这就是汉代的居延塞。这里出土的几万枚汉简是中国二十世纪四大考古发现之一，催生了我国学术界一个专门的学问——简牍学。

The Ejin River carries history upon it as it runs towards the Juyan Sea, a lake in the desert. Along the river bank there are more than a hundred ruined signal towers, and as the sun sets, the ruined wall of the fort, only over ten centimetres high, seems like it may be there and may not. This is the Han Dynasty Juyan Fortress. Tens of thousands of Han Dynasty inscribed bamboo slips have been unearthed here, one of China's four biggest archaeological finds of the 20th century, which sparked the development of a new academic field dedicated to the study of inscribed bamboo and wooden slips.

县级士官的待遇
A county-level warden's salary

文：莫久愚

居延遗址中有一座边长 23 米的正方形鄣城，外接一个边长约 46 米的屯兵院落。这里曾出土 12000 多枚汉简，被誉为汉简宝库。这里的最高长官甲渠塞侯是中下级军官，相当于县级待遇，月俸 1200 钱。据汉简中记录的当时物价折算，他的月工资可以买 100 公斤的肉或 680 公斤未去壳的小米。

At the remains of the Juyan Fortress there is a square fortification, 23 metres each the side. Outside of it, there is an approximately 46-metre long compound in which troops were stationed. Here, more than 12,000 precious Han Dynasty inscribed bamboo slips were unearthed, an amazing find. Here the highest-ranking official was a lower-level military officer, who was paid a county-level salary: 1,200 coins a month. According to the information contained in the bamboo slips, this was calculated to be enough to buy 100 kilograms of meat or 680 kilograms of unshelled millet each month.

微观内蒙古
INNER MONGOLIA: COLOURFUL AND MAGNIFICENT

黄河沿岸的昭君墓
Wang Zhaojun's Graves upon the Yellow River

文：莫久愚

内蒙古有多座昭君墓。历史学家翦伯赞说："王昭君究竟埋葬在哪里，这件事并不重要，重要的是为什么会出现这样多的昭君墓。"这些"墓"都分布在黄河沿岸，都是农田与牧场交汇重叠的地方，也就是农夫和牧人接触最频繁、最密切的地方，王昭君是他们的共同话题，她象征着和平、和解、和睦……

There are many "Wang Zhaojun's Graves" in Inner Mongolia. Historian Jian Bozan says: "It's not really important where the actual grave of Wang Zhaojun is. What's important is why there are so many of these gravesites." These graves are all distributed upon the banks of the Yellow River, all at places where agricultural and pasturing areas intersect. These are the places where herders and farmers come into contact the most, and for them Wang Zhaojun is a common topic. To them, she symbolizes peace, reconciliation, and harmony...

"中国历史的后院"
The "backyard" of Chinese history

文：莫久愚

大兴安岭浓密的森林隐藏着诸多的历史秘密。史学家翦伯赞曾把这片广袤的山林誉为中国历史"幽静的后院"。建立过北魏、辽、元王朝的鲜卑人、契丹人、蒙古人，他们的祖先都曾在大兴安岭的密林和山地草原中生活过。他们一拨拨地走出山林，也一次次改变了中国历史的走向。

In the dense forests of the Greater Hinggan Range there are many hidden historical secrets. Historian Jian Bozan once called this area the "quiet backyard" of Chinese history. The founders of the Northern Wei, Liao, and Yuan Dynasties—the Xianbei, Khitan, and Mongolian people all have ancestors who lived in the dense forests or on the mountain grasslands of the Greater Hinggan Range. As they walked out of the mountains, they changed Chinese history each time.

北魏王朝的历史摇篮——嘎仙洞
Gaxian Cave—the cradle of the Northern Wei Dynasty

文：莫久愚

鄂伦春旗境内大兴安岭一个少见的天然洞穴，1800年前生活在这里的拓跋人开始了漫长的南下历程。他们越过阴山进入呼和浩特平原，卷入了"十六国"动荡的历史漩涡，但他们没有让自己成为又一个行色匆匆的历史过客，而是变作中国北方大地的主人。接着又是南下、南下，直至融入中原大地。

Gaxian Cave is a rare natural cave, situated in the Greater Hinggan Range within the borders of Oroqen Banner, that was inhabited 1,800 years ago by Xianbei people who would go on to travel south and found the Northern Wei Dynasty. When they crossed the Yinshan Mountains and entered the plains of Hohhot, they became embroiled in the conflicts of the "Sixteen Kingdoms", but they didn't let themselves become those who simply passed through the history, instead they became the rulers of Northern China. They then went further and further south, and gradually integrated into the community of the Central Plains of China.

历史·寻踪
History and Exploration

草原"第一都"
The "first capital" on the grasslands

文：莫久愚

尽管学者们对于"都城"的概念有着规范的定义，但呼和浩特和林格尔县人却执着地认为，本县的土城子遗址是历史上第一座草原都城。因为1600多年前，拓跋鲜卑人就是从这里开始统一北中国的，北魏王朝最早的立足点也是在这里。当地建有一座遗址博物馆——盛乐博物馆，述说着这段历史。

Although scholars may have a specific definition for what constitutes as "capital city", the people of Horinger County in Hohhot strongly believe that the remains of Tuchengzi in the county is the first capital on the grasslands in history. 1,600 years ago, when the Tuoba tribe of the Xianbei people began to unify the northern part of China, the earliest capital of the Northern Wei Dynasty was established here. There's a museum for the ruins here, Shengle Museum, which tells their history.

摄影：高雪峰

敕勒川，阴山下
Chile Plain, at the foot of Yinshan Mountains

文：莫久愚

北魏时代，阴山以南黄河内外的广袤土地从秦汉时期的农田又变成了牧场。北魏拓跋人把大批的敕勒部落迁到阴山南面放牧生活，《敕勒歌》所描述的正是那时的场景。今天的呼包二市交界处，有一个名曰"哈素海"的天然湖泊，地势平阔，泛舟湖上，北望阴山，南眺黄河，仍有几分"天苍苍，野茫茫"的感觉。

During the Northern Wei Dynasty, the vast and wide lands south of Yinshan Mountains and along the banks of Yellow River transitioned from farmland in Qin and Han Dynasties to pastures. The Tuoba people, rulers of the Northern Wei Dynasty, sent large numbers of people of Chile tribe to the south of Yinshan Mountains to live as herders. *The Chile Song* describes the scene at the time. In present day between Hohhot and Baotou, there is a natural lake called the "Hasu Sea", surrounded by flat land. When one goes boating upon it, one can see Yinshan Mountains to the north, and the Yellow River to the south. It's a sight of open skies and vast landscapes, just like what is described in the old song.

微观内蒙古
INNER MONGOLIA: COLOURFUL AND MAGNIFICENT

"帝王之乡"
"Home of emperors"

文：莫久愚

武川县得名于北魏时的武川军镇，出身于此的将领及其后代曾长期主导隋唐时期的政治格局。北周的开国皇帝宇文泰出生于武川，隋、唐两代开国皇帝和皇后的祖辈都出自武川。清代赵翼曾感慨："区区一偏僻弹丸之地，出三代帝王……岂非王气所聚？"所以当地人自称武川是"帝王之乡"，并为此自豪。

The name of Wuchuan County comes from the Wuchuan Fortress of the Northern Wei Dynasty. The generals born here and their descendants would later go on to direct the politics of the Sui and Tang Dynasties. The founding emperor of the Northern Zhou Dynasty, Yuwen Tai, was born in Wuchuan, and the ancestors of the emperors and empresses who founded the Sui and Tang Dynasties were born here too. Zhao Yi of the Qing Dynasty remarked: "Mustn't there be something special about this tiny out of the way area, to yield up emperors of three dynasties?" Thus, the locals call Wuchuan "home of emperors", and are proud of its history.

额济纳黑城遗址
The remains of Khara-Khoto in Ejin

文：莫久愚

西夏人建立了这座军城，蒙古人把它变成了丝绸之路上的闹市，却没有发现隐藏在该城地下的秘密。二十世纪初，俄国军官科兹洛夫的几次盗掘使大量的西夏手稿、书籍、卷轴、佛像面世，轰动国际学术界。100多年来，这个黄沙中的城市的影像，经常出现在国内外的探险杂志和地理刊物上。

Built as a fortified city by the Xixia Dynasty, the Mongolians transformed it into a busy market town on the Silk Road, but didn't know of the secrets beneath it. At the start of the 20th century, Russian explorer Kozloff robbed the ancient site a few times, unearthing large amounts of manuscripts, books, scrolls, and Buddhist statues of Xixia Dynasty, rocking the international archaeological community. For more than a hundred years, images of the city in the yellow sand has frequently appeared in exploration and geographic magazines both in China and abroad.

摄影：刘兆和

历史·寻踪
History and Exploration

辽大明塔
Daming Tower of Liao Dyansty

文：莫久愚

这座位于赤峰市辽中京遗址的八角密檐式实心砖塔，高 80.22 米，周长 112 米，是中国现存辽塔中保存最好、体积最大的。大约建于 1098 年。它与北京广安门外的天宁寺塔极为相似，除基座明显高大外，其他部位比例结构大致一样。天宁寺塔建于辽晚期，是北京现存建筑年代最早、体量较大的古建筑之一，但比起大明塔来，无论是体量还是年龄都是"小字辈"。

Daming Tower, situated in the remains of the Middle Capital of the Liao Dynasty, in present Chifeng City, is solid octagonal tower built of bricks, with 80.22 metres tall and 112 metres around. It's the best-preserved and largest tower from the Liao Dynasty in China, built around the year 1098. It's similar to the tower at Tianning Temple west of Guang'anmen in Beijing, and quite smiliar in construction, except that it's clearly larger at the base. The tower at Tianning Temple was built in the late Liao Dynasty, and is the earliest and one of the largest old buildings in Beijing, but compared with the Daming Tower, in terms of either age or size, it is still a "junior".

摄影：王正

白塔
White Tower

文：莫久愚

白塔，其实只是俗称，塔身的匾额写着"万部华严经塔"。仿佛是天外来物，孤零零地坐落在呼和浩特市区边上。原先它并不孤独，身边是辽代的丰州城。塔内可见元明时代人们随手题写刻画的文字，据说在砖缝里发现过元代香客留下的一张小面额元代纸币，是现在世界上存世最早的纸币实物。

"White Tower" is actually a folk name. Upon the tower there is a plaque that reads "Tower of the Myriad Huayan Buddhist Sutras". It looks like it's from another place, standing lonely there at the edge of Hohhot. It originally wasn't lonely at all, being surrounded by the Liao Dynasty city of Fengzhou. Within the tower one can see carvings from people of the Yuan and Ming Dynasties. It's said that within the cracks between the bricks a Yuan Dynasty pilgrim left a small-denomination note of paper money, which is the world's oldest extant paper currency preserved now.

摄影：孔群

11

微观内蒙古
INNER MONGOLIA: COLOURFUL AND MAGNIFICENT

庆州白塔
White Tower of Qingzhou

文：莫久愚

巴林右旗辽庆州城遗址绿草地上的白塔，建于辽兴宗重熙年间，是辽塔中的精品，洁白纤丽、高贵清秀。辽兴宗的生母章宣皇太后与她宠爱的小儿子一度挑战辽兴宗的皇权地位。母子和好后，辽兴宗在母亲当初被幽禁的地方敕令"特建"了这座佛塔，作为一种特殊的纪念，代母亲远远守望着先皇帝的陵寝。

Upon the green grass of the Qingzhou Ruins of Liao Dynasty within Bairin Right Banner stands the White Tower, built in the Chongxi period of the Liao Dynasty. It's an excellent example of Liao towers, pure white, tall, noble and elegant. When the Emperor Xingzong was on the throne, his mother with her beloved younger son fought with him over the control of the kingdom. After they reconciled, he issued an imperial ordinance to have the tower built upon the site at which she was held under house arrest formerly as a special memorial, to look over the resting place of the deceased emperor for her.

蒙古高原上一个永恒的名字
An eternal name on Mongolian Plateau

文：莫久愚

东亚大陆的北方草原上，匈奴、鲜卑、柔然、突厥、契丹等众多的民族如走马灯般轮番登场，各领风骚。当800多年前成吉思汗在斡难河畔竖起他那"九游白纛（dào）"后，历史变成了另外一个模样。草原上不同地方、不同语言、不同身份的部族、部落的人们，从此有了一个共同的名字——蒙古人，高原上不再有民族变迁和更迭。

On the northern grasslands of East Asian continent, people have appeared and disappeared, such as the people of Huns, Xianbei, Roen, ancient Turks, and Khitans, all leaving behind glorious deeds. When Genghis Khan raised his Sacred Banners on the banks of the Onon River eight hundred years ago, the history of the region changed. People at different places on the grasslands, with different languages, in different groups of different ethnicities now had a common name for themselves—Mongolians. No longer would the ethnic groups come and go.

摄影：张贵斌

历史·寻踪
History and Exploration

摄影：乌热尔图

呼伦贝尔草原上的"海"——呼伦湖
A "sea" on the Hulun Buir Grassland—Hulun Lake

文：莫久愚

当地人也称它为达赉湖，意为海一样的湖泊。弱步湖畔，微风鼓浪，湖水如潮，一遍遍地冲刷着沙滩；涛声阵阵，浪花堆雪，给人似在海边的错觉。湖水曾映照过许多英雄民族的身影。走出嘎仙洞的拓跋鲜卑人在这里由猎手变成了牧人，十三世纪的蒙古人曾在湖水西边的草原上汇聚起激荡欧亚大陆的历史狂涛。

The locals also call it Dalai Lake, which means "lake like a sea". As you walk along its banks with soft steps, gentle breeze stirs up small waves as if a tide is coming in. They break against the sand on the banks, and kick up spray that falls like small piles of snow, making one feel as if one is at the shore of the sea. The water of the lake has reflected over the years many brave peoples. The Tuoba tribe of the Xianbei people that came out of the Gaxian Cave transitioned from hunting to herding here, and in the thirteenth century the peoples of Mongolia converged on the grasslands west of the lake to make big waves in both European and Asian history.

绥远将军衙署
The General's Office in Suiyuan

文：莫久愚

呼市新华大街立交桥北一个古色古香的院落，在闹市的街面上无言地伫立。这是中国保存最好的清代将军衙署，前为公廨，后为内宅。自清乾隆二年至1918年，一直是内蒙古西部的政治中心，先后有74位将军在此。成建制的满洲八旗将士带着家眷驻在周围，形成了绥远新城，呼市的满族多是他们的后裔。

There's an ancient compound north of the Xinhua Avenue interchange in Hohhot which has stood there silently for a long time. This is the best-preserved Qing Dynasty general's office, and the front part of the compound served as a government office and the back as a living place. From the time of the second year of the Qianlong period of the Qing Dynasty to 1918 it was an administrative centre for western Inner Mongolia. 74 generals in total served there. Manchu generals and officers under the establishment of Eight Banners would bring their wives and children to live nearby, and a new city named Suiyuan was thus formed. Most of the Manchus in Hohhot are their descendants.

微观内蒙古
INNER MONGOLIA: COLOURFUL AND MAGNIFICENT

应昌路故城
Old city of Yingchang Prefecture

文：莫久愚

达里湖西南一座保存极好的古城，曾是产生过 18 位皇后、16 位驸马的蒙古弘吉剌部的王城。元王朝在这里走过了最后一程，先后逃离大都、上都的元顺帝在这里驾崩后，元朝就终结了。城内荒草中正殿、后宫、街道遗址依稀可见，还有儒学、孔庙遗址和碑刻。中原传统文化也曾浸润过这座草原小城。

There is a very-well preserved ancient city to the south-west of Dalai Nur lake which produced 18 empresses, and 16 sons-in-law of emperors, the kings' city of Khoningrad. It's the site where the Yuan Dynasty ended: After his escape from the Great Capital (modern-day Beijing) and Xanadu, the Emperor Shundi came and died here, then the Yuan Dynasty came to an end. Amidst the wild grasses one can faintly see the remains of the main palace hall, back palaces, and streets, as well as remains of the Confucian school, temple, and some tablet inscriptions. This is a place that was once soaked in the culture of the Central Plains of China.

美岱召
Meidai Monastery

文：莫久愚

位于呼、包之间的美岱召是目前保留最完好的城庙合一的建筑。寺中的壁画描绘了一件大事：1583 年西藏僧界派出的麦达力活佛主持蒙古地区宗教事务，从此，藏传佛教开始在蒙古草原铺展开来，叩敲着一个英雄民族柔软的内心。

Located between Hohhot and Baotou is the Meidai Monastery, a very-well preserved small city and monastery. A mural inside the monastery describes an important event: In 1583, the Tibetan buddhist circle sent a living Buddha to Inner Mongolia to spread the religion. From that time onwards, Tibetan Buddhism spread widely across Mongolia, into the soft hearts of the heroic people of the region.

摄影：高雪峰

历史·寻踪
History and Exploration

古代牧人的画廊
An art gallery of ancient herders

文：莫久愚

巴丹吉林沙漠南缘曼德拉山一片十几平方公里的山坳，有 6000 余幅岩画。几千年间，不同的古代民族都对这里的黑色玄武岩石产生了强烈的创作欲望，或写实或抽象，或细腻或粗犷，都表现出很高的艺术技法，几乎囊括了世界上岩画的所有表现形式。似乎有一种神秘的力量驱使着他们在这里留下自己的印痕。

At the south reaches of the Badain Jaran Desert there is a level ground of over ten square kilometres in the Mandela Mountains, that has more than 6,000 rock paintings. Thousands of years ago, various ancient tribes enjoyed carving their works into the black basalt faces; realistic or abstract, fine or rough, they all show a high degree of artistic ability, and showcase almost every kind of rock painting style in the world. It's as if some kind of mysterious energy drove them to leave their paintings here.

摄影：高雪峰

草原上的召庙
Temples on the grasslands

文：莫久愚

"召庙"是一个蒙、汉语同义复合词，"召"就是蒙古语"庙"的意思。大概是清朝的皇帝们觉得笃信佛教的蒙古人不会再成为令人生畏的力量，所以召庙的兴建受到清廷的特别鼓励，蒙古草原上召庙林立，到处飘荡着礼佛的香雾和喇嘛的诵经声。时至今日，召庙仍然是内蒙古存留最多的古建筑。

These temples are known as "zhaomiao", with "zhao" being the Mongolian and "miao" being the Chinese word for a temple. The Manchu emperors of the Qing Dyansty believed that keeping the people of Mongolia hooked on Buddhism would prevent them from rising up and becoming mighty again, so they specially encouraged the construction of temples across Mongolia. With a large number of temples sprung up, the fragrant smoke of incense and chanting of monks covered the Mongolian grasslands. In modern times, they're the most prevalent old buildings in Inner Mongolia.

微观内蒙古
INNER MONGOLIA: COLOURFUL AND MAGNIFICENT

玄石坡
Xuanshipo
文：莫久愚

苏尼特左旗草原有两块灰黑色巨石，上面分别刻有"玄石坡""立马峰"六个大字。那是明成祖朱棣率大军北征途中留下的。当时他策马登顶，见山桃花盛开，情绪很好，遂题写了石壁。石壁顶端有人工凿刻的马蹄印痕，应是永乐帝登临的纪念。这大概也是汉族帝王在北方草原深处留下的唯一历史印迹。

On the grasslands in the Sonid Left Banner there are two giant black stones, and upon each one there are three characters inscribed: Xuanshipo (dark rock slope) and Limafeng (horse-summited peak) respectively. These were left by the Emperor Yongle of the Ming Dynasty. When he passed by with his army, he spurred his horse to climb upon the peak, and when he saw the peach blossoms beneath his eyes, his mood was excellent, and he wrote those six characters on the stones. Upon the top of the rocks there were also engraved with a chisel some hoof prints to commemorate the Emperor Yongle's summiting the peak. These are probably the only traces of a Han Chinese emperor in the depths of the northern grasslands.

历史名城多伦
Duolun, a famous historical city
文：莫久愚

浑善达克沙地南缘多伦湖畔美丽的小城，曾经拥有18万人口，是今天的两倍，号称"漠南商埠"，上海、天津都有以"多伦"命名的街道。城内汇宗寺前广场上的"会盟碑"记载着清代历史上的一件大事——1691年，康熙皇帝召集漠南蒙古49旗和漠北蒙古三大部在此会盟，确立了清王朝在整个蒙古高原的统治。

At the south of the Onqin Daga Sand Land, on the banks of Duolun Lake, Duolun is a beautiful little city, which once had a population of 180,000, double that of its current population. It was called "Monan Shangbu", meaning "commercial port south of the Gobi Desert". Shanghai and Tianjin each has a street named "Duolun Street". In the plaza in front of the Huizong Temple there is a "Meeting Tablet" which commemorates an important event in the Qing Dynasty. In 1691, the Emperor Kangxi convened a meeting for the 49 banners south of the Gobi Desert and the three major leagues north of the Gobi Desert in Inner Mongolia, which established Qing Dynasty's rule over the entire Mongolian Plateau.

召庙与商业
Temples and business
文：邓九刚

据1900年统计，整个蒙古高原有1260座召庙。茶叶之路开通之后，宗教的网络与商业的网络迅速地重叠，商人巧妙地利用召庙的权威和影响在草原上开展业务。召庙的影响达到哪里，商业的触角就伸到那里。

According to 1900 statistics, on Mongolian Plateau there were 1,260 temples. After the Tea Road was opened, the religious network and business network quickly overlapped; merchants cleverly used the temples' power and influence to develop business on the grasslands. Wherever the influence of the temples extended, the reach of the merchants extended.

历史 · 寻踪
History and Exploration

乌兰布统草原
Ulanbutong Grassland

文：姜苇

这片草原的核心又叫"将军泡子"，几百年前康熙皇帝与噶尔丹部曾在这里有过一场恶战。听名字我似乎闻到了兵刃相接时摩擦出的金属味道，看到马蹄踏碎草原的残破景象……然而我看到的却是红山倒映，绿草萋萋，秀美旖旎，温柔宁静。莫非是岁月冲淡了往昔，沉淀了人本性中的柔情？

The centre of this grassland is also called "General's Pond", a site where a few centuries ago the Emperor Kangxi had a fierce battle with Galdan Boshugtu Khan. When I heard the name I felt like I would smell the metallic scent of blades clashing with each other, and see ground, trampled by the hooves of horses... But seeing it in person, it's full of luxuriant green grass, and red mountains are reflected in the water, and scenery that's charming, gentle, and calm. Could it be that the passing of time softened the years passed, and instilled a gentle nature in us?

摄影：陈嘉磊

内蒙古"王府"多
Numerous prince houses in Inner Mongolia

文：莫久愚

清朝皇帝认为，云合则能成雨，蒙古部落合则能成兵，为使分散的蒙古部落不能集中到一起，清朝在漠南蒙古设立了互不统属的6盟49旗。旗与旗之间以山河或敖包分界。旗的首领札萨克，俗称"王爷"。这些大大小小的"王爷"陆续兴建了自己的府邸。所以内蒙古留存的古建筑中，王府的数量仅次于召庙。

The Qing emperors believed that when clouds would join, they could form rain, and when scattered Mongolian tribes would join, they could form armies. In order to keep the Mongolian tribes separate, the Qing rulers established in the region south of the Gobi Desert 6 leagues and 49 banners. They were divided by mountains, rivers, or obos. They were originally ruled by "princes". All these princes built their own official residences. Thus of the ancient constructions in Inner Mongolia, these "prince houses" are second only to temples.

微观内蒙古
INNER MONGOLIA: COLOURFUL AND MAGNIFICENT

世界文化遗产——元上都

Xanadu—a world cultural heritage

文：莫久愚

忽必烈始建的元代都城，如同一个王朝的巨大躯体僵卧在草原上，残垣颓壁诉说着昔日芳华。元代每到夏秋时节，来自西亚、欧洲的蒙古宗王、使节、商人络绎不绝，发达的驿站交通把这里与欧亚大陆连接在一起。当时文明世界的每一个角落，都能感受到这个国际大都会传递出的信息。

The capital city of Yuan Dynasty was founded by Kublai Khan. If a dynasty could lie rigid on the grasslands, then we could say the ruins of crumbling walls recount this grassland capital's flourishing years. During the Yuan Dynasty, every year from summer to autumn, imperial princes, ambassadors and merchants would come from Europe and Western Asia, continuously and in large numbers. The well-developed post station system linked different areas in Eurasia, with the major cultures of the world at the time all receiving information from this world metropolis.

摄影：莫久愚

喀喇沁王府

Harqin Prince House

文：姜苯

这是内蒙古现存等级最高、规模最大的清代王府。喀喇沁末代亲王贡桑诺尔布曾在王府院内开办学堂、报馆、邮政所、电报局甚至工厂，王府书房是当时蒙古族文人的图书馆。近代蒙古族文豪尹湛纳希在这里用蒙文译出了《红楼梦》《中庸》等经典。

This is the highest-level and largest Qing-Dynasty prince house in Inner Mongolia. The Harqin Prince Günsennorob once opened here a school, a newspaper office, a post office, a telegraph office, and even a factory. The study here was a library for the Mongolian literati. The eminent Mongolian writer Injannaxi made his classic translations of *Dream of the Red Chamber* and *The Doctrine of Mean* here, among other works.

历史·寻踪
History and Exploration

公主府
Princess House

文：莫久愚

远嫁漠北蒙古王公的康熙皇帝四女儿恪靖公主，不耐漠北的苦寒，迷恋大青山下的风光，于是便有了这座"西出京城第一府"。这是我国目前保存最完整的清代公主府建筑群，现已辟为呼和浩特市博物馆，也是呼市居民早春时节踏春、观赏桃花的好去处。

When Princess Kejing, the fourth daughter of the Emperor Kangxi married a local prince in the north of the Gobi Desert, she couldn't stand the intense cold there, and fell in love with the scenery south of Mount Daqing. Thus, the princess house for her was built here, the "First House" to the west of the capital. It's now the best-preserved princess house complex of the Qing Dynasty in China, and the land was allocated to the Hohhot Museum, and now is a place for sightseeing which many locals come to observe the peach flowers in early spring.

摄影：燕凫

摄影：乌热尔图

诺门罕战场
Nomohan battleground

文：莫久愚

1939年夏秋之间，在新巴尔虎左旗哈拉哈河畔的诺门罕草原上进行过一次大规模的战争，是世界反法西斯战争的经典战例。战后，牧民们不愿惊动逝者的亡灵，从不捡拾扰动草原上的遗物，战场遗迹被完整地保留下来，坦克残骸、炮弹、枪械、油桶、钢盔、水壶……直到纪念馆落成。

In the summer and autumn of 1939, a large scale battle took place on the Nomohan Grassland near the the banks of the Halhiyn River, New Barag Left Banner. It's a classic example of the world's anti-Fascist wars. After the battle, the herders, unwilling to disturbed the souls of the deceased, left the battleground untouched, taking nothing away. The battleground is preserved completely intact, with the wreckage of tanks, artillery shells, firearms, fuel cans, helmets and water bottles still lying there today, where a memorial museum is set up.

微观内蒙古
INNER MONGOLIA: COLOURFUL AND MAGNIFICENT

乌兰浩特成吉思汗庙
Genghis Khan Temple in Ulanhot

文：莫久愚

二十世纪四十年代，传闻日本关东军要在罕山建造供奉日照大神的神庙，蒙古族民众集资抢先在此建造了成吉思汗庙，祭奠自己心中的神。这是蒙古族自己设计建造的近代建筑，大殿和偏殿是典型藏式风格，蓝琉璃瓦圆形穹顶和长方形匾额，让人想到北京天坛。错落有致的九个攒尖穹顶，又使人联想到草原上游牧聚落的毡帐。

In the 1940s, when it was heard that the Japanese Kwantung Army was preparing to build a temple to Amaterasu on Mount Hanshan, the Mongolian residents hurriedly put together money to build a temple to Genghis Khan so they could worship their own god. This is a structure built and designed by the Mongolians themselves: the main hall and side halls are built in a typical Tibetan style, with round domes covered in blue glass tiles, and square tablets for inscriptions, which makes one think of the Temple of Heaven in Beijing. There are nine sharply-pointed smaller domes, well-arranged, which make one think of the yurts of the nomadic herders.

达斡尔，一个古老而又年轻的民族
Daur, an old and new ethnic group

文：莫久愚

很多学者认为他们是辽代契丹人的后裔，更古老的历史似乎可以追溯至鲜卑、室韦。他们务农，还会经常捕鱼，定期进山狩猎、伐木放排，是嫩江上游土地最早的开拓者。几个世纪中，他们一直自称"达斡尔"，清代几百年间的内外战争中，都有他们勇敢的身影。二十世纪五十年代的民族识别，正式确认了他们独立的民族身份。

Many scholars believe that the Daur are the descendants of the Khitan people of the Liao Dynasty, and before that, their lineage can be traced back to Xianbei and Shiwei. They farm, and frequently fish, and take regular trips into the mountains to hunt. They participate in lumberjacking, and are the earliest cultivators of the upper reaches of the Nenjiang River. They have called themselves Daur for centries, and participated in internal and external wars during several hundred years in the Qing Dynasty, reflecting their bravery. They were recognised officially as an ethnic group in the 1950s, confirming their independent identity.

摄影：苏伟伟

历史 · 寻踪
History and Exploration

勇敢的鄂伦春
The brave Oroqen

文：莫久愚

鄂伦春是兴安岭山地中一个古老的民族，曾被人视作森林民族生活的"活化石"。鄂伦春人是天生的猎手，严酷的自然环境锻造了他们勇敢坚毅的民族性格。1951年，鄂伦春成立了中国第一个民族自治旗，一步跨入了现代社会。上世纪五十年代一首风靡大江南北的《鄂伦春小唱》，让中国人都认识了这个不足3000人的民族。

The Oroqen are an old ethnic group in Hinggan Range that have been called "living fossils" of those ancient people living in the forest. They're natural hunters, and the harsh environment has instilled brave and resolute character in them. In 1951, Oroqen became the first autonomous ethnic banner in China, and they stepped into the modern world from primitive society. *An Oroqen Diddy* was popularly sung nationwide in the 1950s, which introduced this ethnic group of only 3,000 people to other Chinese.

摄影：顾德清

额尔古纳的俄罗斯族
Russians of Ergun

文：莫久愚

蒙古族祖先曾居住的额尔古纳河畔，如今分布着许多俄罗斯风情的村镇，中国唯一的俄罗斯民族乡恩和就在这里。100多年前，闯关东淘金、采伐、修筑铁路的中国劳工曾过河与俄罗斯人交往、生活，也有许多白俄贵族逃亡到河这边，两个民族青年男女之间演绎了一段段爱情，繁衍出一个乐观豪爽、能歌善舞的族群。

Ancestors of Mongolians once lived on the banks of the Ergun River, where there are now a number of Russian-style villages and towns. China's only Russian nationality township, Enhe, is located here. More than a hundred years ago, many Chinese workers migrated into North-eastern China to pan for gold, harvest lumber, and build railways. They met and interacted with Russians, lived together with them, and when a number of white Russian nobilities came across the river to flee, the young men and women of the two cultures met, and romances occurred. This gave birth to a group of optimistic and straightforward people who excel at singing and know how to dance.

摄影：麻然信

微观内蒙古
INNER MONGOLIA: COLOURFUL AND MAGNIFICENT

三支鄂温克人
Three branches of Ewenki

文：莫久愚

敖鲁古雅鄂温克人饲养驯鹿广为人知，他们十八世纪初从贝加尔湖的苔原地区驱赶着驯鹿一路游猎，来到大兴安岭北端的密林中安身。更早的时候，嫩江流域的鄂温克人越过兴安岭进入呼伦贝尔草原，由猎人变成牧人。一百年前通古斯鄂温克人自额尔古纳河西岸迁居号称"草原第一曲水"的莫日格勒河上游草原。

The Olguyaa Ewenkis are known for raising reindeer. They came from the tundra area around Baykal Lake in the early 18th century, hunting as they drove their reindeer along. They settled when they arrived at the dense forests in the north of the Greater Hinggan Range. Earlier, the Ewenki of the Nenjiang River region crossed the Hinggan Range into Hulun Buir Grassland and turned from hunting to herding. A hundred years earlier, the Turgus Ewenkis came from the west bank of the Ergun River to live upon the grassland near the upper reaches of the Morigele River, which is called "the first curved river on the grasslands".

摄影：张林刚

布里亚特蒙古人
Buryat Mongolians

文：莫久愚

他们是一个古老的蒙古部族，主要居住在贝加尔湖沿岸，其中部分人二十世纪初进入呼伦贝尔锡尼河畔。他们聪颖、手巧、爱整洁，乐于接受新事物，牧业机械化水平曾长期领先于全国的牧区。他们的服饰轻盈合身，剪裁得体。束宽腰带，穿翘头毡靴。夏秋时节，男子戴尖顶呢帽、女子头系绸巾，冬季则都戴尖顶红缨帽。

The Buryat people are an old Mongolian group who live mostly on the lands bordering Baykal Lake. A portion of their population came to the banks of the Seney River in Hulun Buir in the early twentieth century. They are intelligent, handy, clean, and happy to accept new things. They used to be in the leading position in mechanization among the pastoral areas of China. Their clothing is light, well-cut and form-fitting. They wear wide belts, and felt boots with points that curve up. In the summer and autumn, men wear pointed felt hats, and women tie silk scarves around their heads. In the winter men and women all wear pointed caps with red tassels on the top.

摄影：乌热尔图

历史·寻踪
History and Exploration

科右前旗的满族
Manchu people in the Horqin Right Front Banner

文：莫久愚

乌兰毛都草原是一片山地疏林草原，一个个泉眼溢出一条条蜿蜒曲折的小溪，绿地如毡，号称"五花草塘"。草原西南有全国唯一的以牧业为主的满族乡，他们的祖先是随公主下嫁草原的京城正白旗人。1949年以前，这里的旗人子弟一直保留着尚武、骑射的传统，因此连土匪都不敢来这里劫掠。

Ulanmaodu Grassland has a sparse forest with small springs giving rise to small creeks all over. It's blanketed in thick grass, and is an interesting and varied meadow with different flowers. In the south-west of the area, there is the only Manchu township in China that participates in animal husbandry. The inhabitants are the descendants of those who followed a princess from the capital who married a husband beneath her on the grassland, people of Plain White Banner division. Before 1949, the people here maintained their military customs and traditions of archery and horseback riding, so raiders did not dare to attack their settlement.

摄影：高丽

乌兰浩特
Ulanhot

文：莫久愚

1947年4月底，兴安岭山地一个叫"王爷庙"的小镇上，一所旧军校的礼堂中，来自内蒙古各阶层、各团体的代表在这里聚会，选举出内蒙古自治政府，率先走上了民族区域自治之路。也使辽阔的内蒙古草原与"巩固的东北根据地"连在一起，有力地支援了人民解放战争。小镇就此改名"乌兰浩特"（红色的城）。

At the end of April in 1947, in the hall of an old military school of a small town called "Wangye Temple" in the Hinggan Range, representatives of groups from all levels of Inner Mongolia came together to elect the government of the Inner Mongolia Autonomous Region. Thus Inner Mongolia took the lead in selecting the route of regional autonomy of ethnic minorities. This linked together the vast area of Inner Mongolia's grasslands with the revolutionary base areas of Northeasten China, and confirmed their strong support of the War of Liberation. As a result, the name of the town was changed to "Ulanhot" (red city).

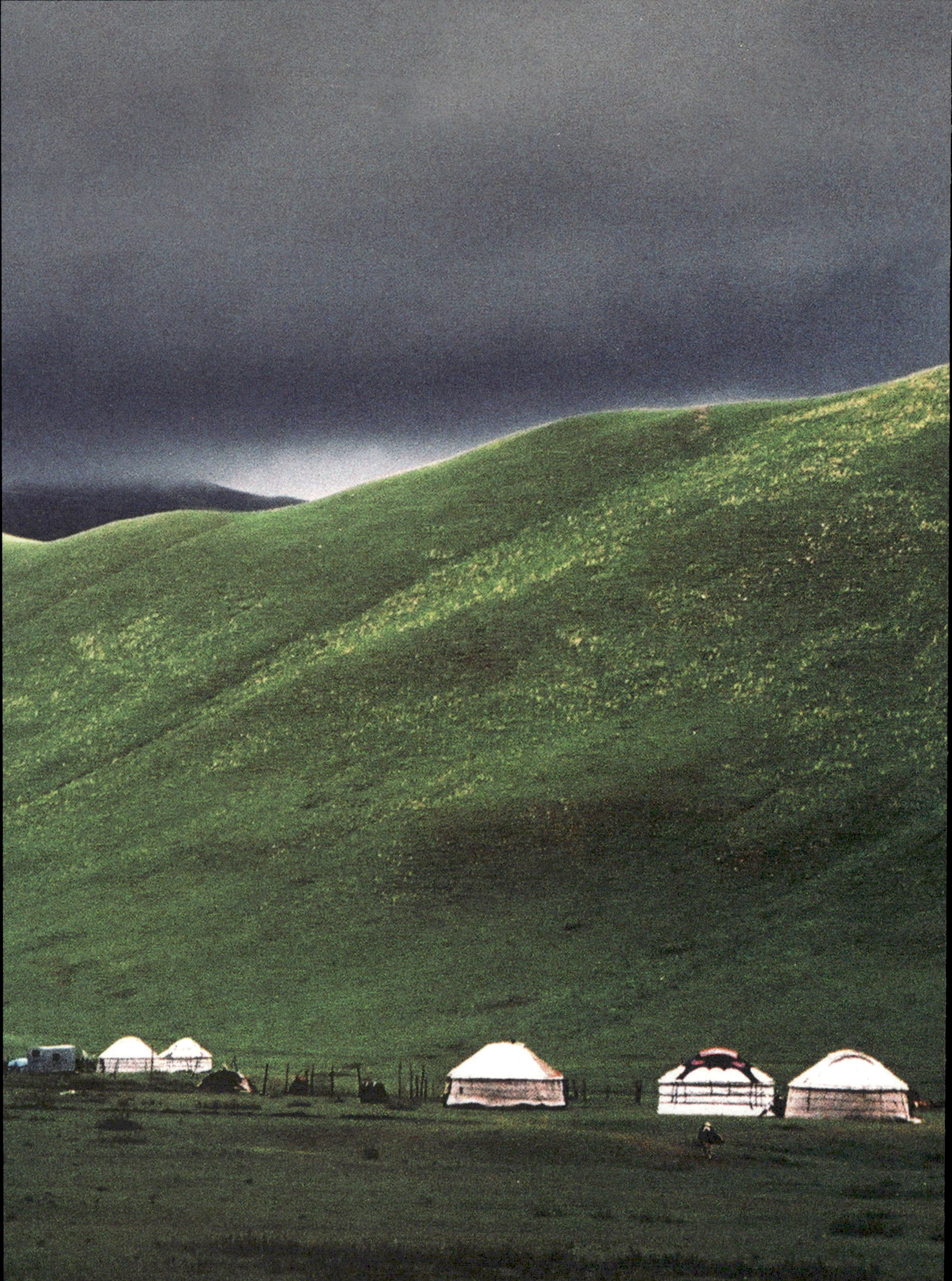

草原·印象

Impressions of the Grassland

微观内蒙古
INNER MONGOLIA: COLOURFUL AND MAGNIFICENT

草原印象

Impressions of the grassland

文：莫久愚

一位作家说，没有看过大海的人，可以凭借草原来想象大海；而没有到过草原的人，却无法根据大海去想象草原。相较而言，内蒙古近山草原多丘陵，像是充满浪涌的海，满眼是长调般悠长柔软的绿色曲线；远离山地的草原略显平旷，更像风平浪静的海，不断伸展的绿地，往往让人产生到天边探寻尽头的冲动。

An author said that people who haven't ever seen the sea can picture it via analogy with a grassland, but those who've never seen a grassland can't picture it via analogy with the sea. Grasslands near the mountains are usually covered in hills, like a surging ocean, with long, soft ridges of green as far as the eye can see. While those grasslands far away from mountains are mostly vast and flat, like a calm sea, green extending farther than you can look—gaze upon it and you'll be gripped by a desire to find where the rainbow ends.

象征"家"的草原

A grassland that symbolises "home"

文：莫久愚

四子王旗的杜尔伯特草原实际上是与锡林郭勒大草原连在一起的，只是更加平旷，四周没有树木、冈峦、现代设施。每当遥远的阿拉善戈壁传来飞船升空的消息时，这片草原就会出现许多忙碌的身影，神舟飞船的十几次回归都是降落这里，人们习惯了默默地期待、祝福。每个航天员都不会忘记这片象征"家"的草原。

The Dorbet Grassland on the Siziwang Banner is actually connected to Xilin Gol Grassland, except that it's flatter and vaster, and doesn't have any trees, hill ranges, or modern facilities. Every time when there's to be a launch at the far-off Alxa Gobi Desert, the grassland will become busy, as each of the Shenzhou missions has landed here upon returning. People have become used to quietly waiting and holding good wishes in their hearts. Each Taikonaut won't forget this grassland that symbolies "home".

摄影：张松云

草原·印象
Impressions of the Grassland

摄影：塔娜

金莲川草原
The Grassland of the Nasturtium River

文：莫久愿

元上都周边的金莲川草原，每值春夏季节，百花盈野，最多的是金莲花。远远望去，满目金黄，美艳夺目，渺无边际。这里曾经是辽、金、元三代帝王的避暑胜地。元代诗僧楚石说这里"赤日不知夏，清霜常似秋"；范玉壶的诗略显夸张："上都五月雪飞花，顷刻银妆十万家。说与江南人不信，只穿皮袄不穿纱。"

Around the ruins of Xanadu is the Grassland of the Nasturtium River. Every spring and summer, flowers bloom everywhere, the most numerous of which are the nasturtiums. As far as you look you'll see beautiful stretches of endless yellow. This is the place where the emperors of the Liao, Jin and Yuan Dynasties came to relax. Yuan Dynasty monk and poet Chu Shi wrote of this place: You'll forget it's summer here, even under the hot sun. It's always cool and fresh, as if it were autumn. Fan Yuhu's poem goes even further: In May the snow is still falling as flying flowers, turning myriad houses in silver. People of South China find it almost impossible to believe that people here wear fur-lined coats in the summer instead of thin clothing.

骑马去聊天
Take a horse ride to chat

文：张弓长

旧时草原上的蒙古包相距很远。蒙古包四周少有院墙，即使有也不装门，只插着两根木杆，那是防牲畜的。定居的牧人也很少扎堆居住，牧民们在空闲时，喜欢骑着马在茫茫草原上跑向他们看见的任何一个人或者蒙古包，没别的，只是为了找人聊聊天。

In old times the distance between yurts was quite large. Rarely, around the yurt there was a wall, but no door, just two wooden posts, to prevent livestock from coming in. The shepherds rarely lived in concentrated settlements, so when they had time they liked to ride their horses out over the grasslands to see if they could find another person or yurt—not for any particular reason, just to chat.

微观内蒙古
INNER MONGOLIA: COLOURFUL AND MAGNIFICENT

空中"牧羊犬"
"Sheepdog" in the air

文：莫久愚

30多年前，摩托车在城市中还是稀罕物件时，草原上年轻的牧人们就已经普遍驾摩托车甚至是吉普车放牧了。如今，阿巴嘎旗的一位牧民把一架航拍机改造成空中监视器替他照看1200多只羊，他年迈的母亲也能够熟练地操作它。他还琢磨着在航拍机上安装声响设备，能够命令羊群自己走到草场或由草场返回棚圈。

More than 30 years ago, when motorcycles were rare in Chinese cities, it was common to see herders with little crotch rockets or even jeeps. This trend of being ahead of the times continues today, where in Abag Banner a herder uses a drone to look after his more than 1,200 sheep. His very old mother is skilled at operating it too. He's also thinking of installing a speaker on the drone, so that he can tell the sheep to walk out to the field or return to the livestock shed.

摄影：燕亮

草原的丰收季节
Grassland harvest season

文：莫久愚

牧人的丰收是在春季。最忙碌的是那些女主人们，她们几乎要为每一只母羊接生，"劝导"羊妈妈给羊羔初乳，甚至像喂养初生婴儿那样给吃不到奶的新羔喂食奶水。看着一对一对的羊妈妈和小羊组成新的羊群，听着热热闹闹的咩咩声，老额吉会自言自语地嘟囔一声"都斯嘎啦"（累坏了），心里却是愉悦的。

The big harvests for the shepherds come in spring. The busiest are the women, who have to help almost every ewe give birth, and stimulate them to start lactating and nursing the young lambs. It's almost like caring for a human child who wants to nurse. When she sees the newly born lambs with their mothers, bleating as she mumbles to herself "I'm so tired" in Mongolian, the Mongolian mama is actually quite happy.

摄影：张先鸣

微观内蒙古
INNER MONGOLIA: COLOURFUL AND MAGNIFICENT

摄影：石玉平

把心放进一个嘎查
Put your heart in a Gacha

文：张阿泉

"嘎查"是蒙古语，意为"村庄"。它是内蒙古草原上最基层的行政单位，稀疏而谦卑地散落在大地上，生活节奏缓慢，完全保持着"野生"状态。如果你能有机会去草原深处的嘎查走一走，清清心，洗洗肺，那将是再幸福不过的事情。

"Gacha" is Mongolian for "village", which is the lowest-level administrative unit in Inner Mongolia. They are sparsely and humbly spread over the grasslands, and within them the pace of life is slow, where a fully "natural" lifestyle persists. If you have the opportunity, you should visit and walk around a Gacha, refreshing your heart, clean out your lungs, and have a great experience.

每一个毡房都是家
Every yurt is a home

文：班澜

在草原上赶路，前不着村，后不着店，到任何一个毡包都是回到了家。主人会热情地让你吃饱喝足，像家人一样安排你睡下。这时，外面就是狂风暴雨，你也可以舒舒坦坦地歇息困乏的双腿了。有时主人不在家，你也可以自己找些吃喝，自己休息。这是古老的民俗。蒙古族谚语云：谁也不会背着毡房走路。

On the road in the grasslands, when you can't find villages or hotels, coming to any yurt is like coming home. The owner will warmly invite you in to eat and drink your fill, and allow you to sleep there like family. At this time, it might be pouring outside, but you can comfortably rest your legs inside. Sometimes, if the owner isn't home, you can still help yourself to a bit of food and drink, and take a rest. These are the old customs. Mongolia has a saying: Nobody will walk with a yurt on his back.

草原上不可夸大人的作用
The role of men should not be overstated on the grassland

文：张弓长

蒙古族作家鲍尔吉·原野说：人在草原上只是大自然这条永恒链条上的一环而已。天对他们来说，是头顶的覆盖物，也是雨水的降临者。土地承接雨水长满青草，牛羊因此繁衍不息，蒙古人依赖这些生存。在草原上不可夸大人的作用，人与牛羊草木一样，谦卑地居于生存者的地位，天地雨水则属于创造者。

Mongolian author Borjigin Yuanye says: People on the grassland are just small links in the endless chain of nature. For them, the sky is a head covering, the bringer of rain. The earth is what catches this rain and covered with grass, and cows and sheep reproduce endlessly here, which is what the Mongolians rely upon to survive. Here, the role of men should not be overstated, because they, like the animals, are just humble residents, whereas the sky, the ground, and the rain are the true creators.

摄影：高雪峰

鲜花与牛粪
Flowers and manure

文：张阿泉

"鲜花插在牛粪上"，原本是"不配"的意思。可在草原，鲜花就是与牛粪相伴相生。草与鲜花茂盛地围绕一坨牛粪形成一个小生态圈。牛粪源于草又归于草，未被捡拾的牛粪慢慢变白、风化、分解，重新轮回，鲜花只是牛粪转世的一小部分，没有鲜花的草原略嫌寂寞，没有牛粪的草原会日渐荒芜。

The phrase "stick fresh flowers in the bull shit" in Chinese refers to things that don't go together. However, on the grassland, flowers and manure are connected. Grass and flowers are linked in a small ecosystem with manure. The manure originates from the grass cows eat, and the manure that's left behind turns white, dries out, splits apart and re-enters the cycle. Flowers are just a small part of the cycle. Without them, the landscape looks desolate, and without manure to fertilise it, grass disappears, leaving the land barren.

微观内蒙古
INNER MONGOLIA: COLOURFUL AND MAGNIFICENT

草原是这个时代的故乡
Home of modern era

文：张弓长

一年夏天，央视主持人白岩松带着朋友携家人来呼伦贝尔草原，大家都像是回到了少年。"当敬酒的长调响起时，一个孩子的妈妈瞬间泪流满面。这时，我知道，她落地了，心灵终于松弛下来，她已回家。每一个人心中，原来都有一个草原，这呼伦贝尔，分明是大家的故乡，甚至就是这个时代的故乡。"

One summer, CCTV anchorman Bai Yansong took his friends and family to the Hulun Buir Grassland, where everyone felt like they had returned to their childhood years. "When the cheers of raising our glasses rang out, a mother's face filled with tears. At this time, I knew that she had landed, and finally felt relaxation in her heart, as she was home. In everyone's heart there is a grassland, and Hulun Buir is in this way everyone's home; one could even say it's the home of our entire modern era."

梦境般的草原白云
Dreamworld of clouds over the grassland

文：张弓长

诗人席慕蓉这样描述过草原白云的飘移："……忽明忽暗，人好像走在梦里。一下子所有的青草都闪着金光，逆光处背后的丘陵像镶上了发亮的边线，身体被阳光照得暖烘烘的；然后忽然间所有的颜色都沉静了下来，在云影掠过之处，草色在泛白的灰绿和透明的青绿之间挪移，风也凉多了……"

Poet Xi Murong thus described the white clouds moving over the grassland: "...Sometimes light and then quickly dark, it feels like you're walking through a dream. One moment the green grass all glimmers with golden light, and backlighted hills shine with bright rims, your body is warmed by the sunlight. Then, suddenly all colours darken. Under the shadow of the clouds, the colour of the grass is changing gradually, shifting from pale grey to transparency green, and the wind becomes cooler..."

摄影：孙克威

草原·印象
Impressions of the Grassland

摄影：高雪峰

牧民为什么"总是搬家"？
Why are the shepherds always "moving house"?

文：黄薏

孩子问妈妈："我们蒙古人为什么总是搬家？"妈妈回答："孩子，我们要是固定在一个地方，大地母亲就会疼痛；我们只有不停地搬迁，如同血液流动，大地母亲才会舒服。"孩子说："我懂了，就像我给妈妈上下不停地捶背，妈妈就会觉得舒服；假如老是在一个地方捶，妈妈就会疼。"

A child asked her/his mother: "Why are us Mongolians always moving house?" The mother responded: "Dear, if we stay in the same place, the ground will feel painful. We have to keep moving, like the flow of blood, to keep the earth comfortable." The child said: "I get it, like if I rubbed you all over your back, you'd feel nice, but if I kept rubbing you in the same place it'd hurt."

草原"牲畜排行榜"
"Livestock ranking" on the grassland

文：黄薏

蒙古族传统的"牲畜排行榜"是这样的：马、牛、骆驼、绵羊、山羊最重要，被列为"五畜"；驴、骡为"其他牲畜"。五畜在蒙古族经济生活中"须臾不可或缺"，既是生产资料又是生活资料。猪、狗则不在蒙古族"家畜"之列。

The traditional ranking of livestock in Mongolia is as such: horses, cattle, camels, sheep, then goats. These are the "big five", whereas donkeys and mules are classed as "other livestock". The big five are indispensable to the Mongolian economy, and the products they produce are essential to life there. Pigs and dogs have not made themselves into the ranking at all.

微观内蒙古
INNER MONGOLIA: COLOURFUL AND MAGNIFICENT

蒙古族婴儿的"尿不湿"
Mongolian "diapers"

文：莫久愚

《民族画报》的编辑鹰鸽曾经感慨："蒙古族小孩睡在摇篮里，屁股底下垫的不是昂贵的尿不湿，而是故乡的沙子——是母亲或奶奶从河边背回家，又在锅里炒干消毒的沙子。婴儿娇嫩的皮肤在温暖、柔软的沙子上时刻感受着温馨，这样长大的人能不爱故乡草原吗！"

Ying Ge, editor of *Nationality Pictorial*, once reflected: "When Mongolian babies sleep in the cradle, instead of expensive diapers, they have sand from the land—the mother or grandmother collects sand from the riverside, and then disinfects it by frying it in a wok. The baby always feels warm with its tender skin on the soft sand—doesn't that kind of thing just make those grownups fall in love with the old grasslands?"

草原上的街市
Market on the grassland

文：莫久愚

在内蒙古草原上，每到那达慕大会时，举办盛会的地方都会变成一个街市。一个个认真搭建的蒙古包，风格各异，内部装饰就是一种竞争，也是特色的展示。在蒙古包组成的街市上，姑娘们身着靓丽的民族服装，宛如赶赴时装表演。参加比赛的搏克手（摔跤手）们不同的摔跤服似乎也在争奇斗艳……

On the Inner Mongolian grasslands, every year when the Nadam Festival comes around, the area where it's conducted becomes a market. Yurts of all kinds spring up, the interior decoration of which becomes a kind of competition, and an exhibition of local specialty. They form a kind of fair, and girls come out in beautiful ethnic clothing, showing off their styles. There's also the spectacle of traditional wrestling, and the wrestlers' costumes are really quite something to see.

摄影：高雪峰

草原·印象
Impressions of the Grassland

摄影：乌热尔图

清澈曲折的小河
Clear, winding little rivers

文：张弓长

席慕蓉描述：草原深处，有时会遇见一泓弯泉极尽曲折地流过。小河的流水清澈，河中长长的水草顺着水流忽左忽右轻轻摇荡，连几颗小石子的滚动也看得清清楚楚；薄暮时分，从山腰往下眺望，那样一条狭窄弯曲的河流映着天空的霞光在暗绿的旷野上蜿蜒伸展，不知道从何处起始，到何处终结。

Xi Murong thus described: When deep in the grassland, sometimes, you will discover a small, winding river originating from a spring. The flow of the river is clear, and long aquatic grasses bend in the direction of the river's flow, swaying left and right. You can even see a few little stones roll by at the bottom. At dusk, when you look down from a mountain to see a narrow winding little river reflecting the light of the red clouds, you know not where it starts nor ends.

牛粪的气息
The scent of manure

文：张阿泉

牛粪这个词，在蒙语中有"炊烟"的意思，欧洲人有时称蒙古人是"烧牛粪的民族"。牛粪作为烧茶、做饭、熬制奶豆腐的燃料，有着古老的历史。牛粪在蒙语中没有任何"脏"的含义，牧民把它当成宝贝。牧人对牛粪燃烧后所发散出的清新烟味有着特殊感情，因为它给人一种家的温暖气息。

The word "manure" in Mongolian has the meaning of "cooking smoke", and the Europeans sometimes refer to Mongolians as "those that burn manure". Manure is the fuel used to boil tea, cook, and make dried milk cakes, and has a long history in Mongolia. The word doesn't have any dirty connotations in Mongolian, rather the material is treasured. The fresh smoke emitted when burning the material has a special meaning for the Mongolian people, as it gives them a feeling of the warmth of home.

微观内蒙古
INNER MONGOLIA: COLOURFUL AND MAGNIFICENT

摄影：高雪峰

牧人与牲畜
Herders and their livestock

文：莫久愚

长期生活在草原上牧群中的学者刘书润认为，牧民对牲畜像对家里的成员一样，从来不打骂。牧民最难受的时候就是出售牲畜的时候。有个牧民卖了一批骆驼，因为骆驼说什么也不离开家，买的人只好硬把骆驼拉上车，这牧民看见后疯了一样去追车，又把骆驼拦下来领回家。草原上这样暖心有趣的故事很多。

Scholar Liu Shurun, who has lived on the grasslands for a long time, discovered that the livestock are like family members to their herders—they never hit or scold them. What's hardest for them is when they have to sell them. There was one time a herder sold a camel, and because it was unwilling to leave his home, the buyer had no choice but to forcefully pull it onto the truck. The herder changed his mind, ran after the truck like a crazy person, and blocked the camel from leaving and took it home. There are many stories like this on the grasslands.

草原・印象
Impressions of the Grassland

摄影：乌热尔图

花中"野兽"
"Beasts" among the flowers

文：莫久愚

在呼伦贝尔的近山草原，每年 6 月中下旬的十几天里，草地里几乎没有别的花，唯有野芍药花独霸草原风光。牧民说，野芍药性格厉害，它开花，别的花不敢开。鲍尔吉·原野说："野芍药花在我们眼里是花，在别的花眼里，它们是野兽。"

On the grasslands near the mountains of Hulun Buir, less than twenty days each year to July, there are no other flowers, only peonies. The nomads say that the peonies have a tough character, so that when they bloom the other flowers dare not. Borjigin Yuanye said: "The peonies to us are flowers, but to the other flowers, they are horrible beasts."

风吹牛肉干子哗哗响
The sound of beef jerky in the wind

文：张阿泉

在草原，牧民住房的窗前或院子里，经常悬挂着成排的条状牛肉干，晾晒过程一般要持续四五个月。风一吹，发出哗哗的声响，别有一番北地萧瑟。

On the grasslands, in front of windows or in yards, shepherds frequently put long strips of beef out to dry, a process which takes four to five months. When the wind blows, they make a rattling noise, a distinct kind of rustling in the north land.

微观内蒙古
INNER MONGOLIA: COLOURFUL AND MAGNIFICENT

剪马鬃、打马印

Trimming manes and branding

文：莫久愚

每年春夏之交给马剪鬃、打马印是牧民的盛会。通常是众骑手围住马群，争相套马；马群东突西奔，蹄声雷动，烟尘滚滚。驯马人手持烧热的印模，待马被套牢后在它左胯上烙下印记。也有的立地双手揪住马尾，徒手将马摔倒在地，再剪鬃打印。这种时候往往是小伙子在姑娘面前显露自己驯马技能的好机会。

Every year between spring and summer, the time to cut the manes of horses and brand them comes. Riders encircle and attempt to lasso the horses. The horses run around wildly, hooves beat, and dust flies everywhere. Horse tamers take a hot brand and make their mark on the horse's left hip. Sometimes, they grab the horses by the tails and wrestle them to the ground with their bare hands before trimming the manes and branding them. This is a good opportunity for young men to show their prowess with horses to the onlooking girls.

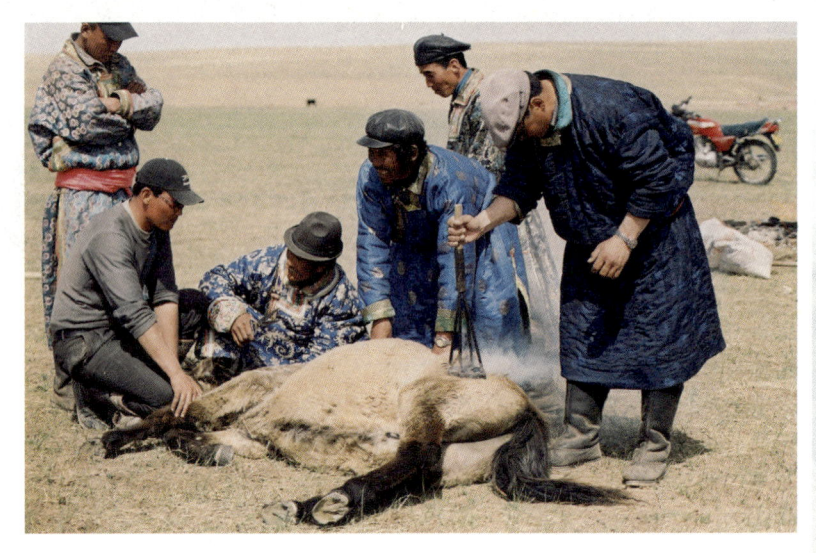

摄影：高雪峰

上天开设的中草药铺

A Chinese pharmacy from heaven

文：张阿泉

上天创造了草原，顺便也把为人治病的中草药赐给大地。人类在伴草而生的同时，也依靠智慧，从草中提纯出了药品。阿鲁科尔沁旗草原上生长着蕨类、裸子、被子等800多种药用植物，是上天开设的一间超大规模的中草药铺。

When the grasslands were created, a traditional Chinese pharmacy came with the package. People who live on the grasslands have the knowledge of how to extract medicines from the environment. On the grasslands of the Ar Horqin Banner all kinds of ferns, seeds, and other components of more than 800 plants grow, from which medicines can be derived—the resources of this large pharmacy are all around.

草原·印象
Impressions of the Grassland

摄影：乌热尔图

苏尼特草原遇雨
The rain on the Sonid Grassland

文：姜苿

乌云像是嫉妒了天的湛蓝、草的新绿，瞬间覆盖了全部，没有一丝缝隙。我，仿佛就是世界的中心。四周都是模糊的地平线，都是闪电。雨，笼罩了世界，灰雾弥漫，没有缠绵，没有风情，狂怒、凶猛……不多时，雨渐渐平息了，雨丝柔顺了，调皮了，敲击着小草的身体，一下一下，一束阳光穿透云层，天边挂起一弯彩虹。

The dark clouds are jealous of the sky's blue, the ground's green, and almost completely cover the sky in a second, without a beam of light leaked from it. I am almost the centre of the world. All around me is a hazy horizon, lightning everywhere. Rain covers the earth, mist extends everywhere. There is nothing continuous, angry, wild... The rain gradually deserts its angry fires, as strands softly float down, capricious as they strike at the bodies of the grass. Then, a beam of sunlight breaks through the clouds and a rainbow appears.

蒙古马安然于天地间
Mongolian horses between heaven and earth

文：张弓长

有人说，不管怎么柔弱的男人，只要一骑上蒙古马立刻就显得英武雄壮了。作家鲍尔吉·原野则说：蒙古马"安然于天地之间，灵慧而和蔼。与蒙古人一样，它也有性格的另一面，暴躁与拼挣。骑兵部队的战马，受伤卧下，一听到冲锋号便站立疾驰。对流血的主人，它会痛心疾首地围转，甚至悲鸣不已"。

Some people say no matter how much a gomer a man might be, put him on a horse and you'll see a sharp-looking, upright fellow. Author Borjigin Yuanye said: "Mongolian horses look great in this setting both sharp and kind. Just like the Mongolian people, the other side of their personality is irascible and fighty. The horses of warriors will lie down when wounded, but still stand up and charge when the order is given. When an injured rider lies bleeding on the ground, they'll run circles around them, painfully calling out."

摄影：石玉平

草原·印象
Impressions of the Grassland

醉人的歌
Intoxicating songs

文：王芳

从踏上草原那一刻起，我们便被淹没在歌的海洋，沉浸在舞的世界，更醉倒在这多情的草原上。草原朋友高举酒杯，一遍遍躬身邀请："远方的朋友，一路辛苦，请你喝一杯下马酒……献上洁白的哈达，献上一片草原的深情。" 在这优美的歌声中，我们早已忘了东南西北，忘了自己不胜酒力，怎能不醉呢？

When we step onto the grassland, we feel as if we're bathed in a sea of songs, surrounded by a world of dance, intoxicated by the feelings of the landscape. When friends on the grassland raise their glasses, they bow as they sing: "Friends from far away, you must be tired, have a glass of liquor to refresh youself from long riding, let me present you with a white khatag, and present the grasslands with my deep feelings." Hearing this song, I forgot my surroundings, and also that my tolerance for alcohol isn't anything to brag about—how could I not be overtaken with intoxication at a time like this?

摄影：高雪峰

苍穹之上的目光
Eyes in the sky

文：张弓长

鲍尔吉·原野说："来到草原，我感到苍穹之上有成吉思汗隐隐的注视。这是一种神的注视，我感觉他一直在看我！其实他看着每一个人。只有神才有这样的目力……每个人都有这样的感觉。"

Borjigin Yuanye says: "On the grasslands, I feel that Genghis Khan is looking down over us from the sky. I feel like I'm always under his watchful eyes. Actually, he watches over everyone. Only with the existence of a god can there be this kind of power; I think everyone believes so."

微观内蒙古
INNER MONGOLIA: COLOURFUL AND MAGNIFICENT

牧人的绿色情感
The green feelings of the shepherds

文：莫久愚

学者陈岗龙讲过一个故事：有一个蒙古族大学生放假回家的时候给牧民父亲买了一双硬底皮鞋。父亲接过皮鞋之后，很生气地对儿子说："这么硬的鞋底，不是把草都踩烂了吗？"草原是脆弱的，草原上的牧人无法容忍对草原的任何伤害。正是他们千百年来的细心呵护，才留下北疆这片宝贵的绿色。

Scholar Chen Ganglong told a story: A Mongolian university student returned from his studies, and brought his father a pair of hard-soled leather shoes. His father angrily scolded him upon seeing them, saying: "What do you think will happen to the grass with soles this hard?" The grass is weak, and the nomads that live upon it can't bear to harm it. It's because of their continued care over centuries that the precious green resource of the north remains intact.

朋友圈找羊
Looking for lambs on WeChat

文：白江宏

城里人朋友圈里找孩子的帖子多，牧民的朋友圈里却常常在找羊："我家的羊丢了，谁看见了？""在我的场子里呢，快来认领啊，晚些就吃了。"

In the city on social media you might see posts where people are looking for lost children, whereas among the nomads it's frequent to see "missing lamb" posts. "I lost a lamb, has anyone seen it?" "I have it here, man. Come get it or it's gonna be dinner."

摄影：高雪峰

草原·印象
Impressions of the Grassland

牧人朋友
A herder friend

文：姜苇

牧人朋友领我们游草原，途中有人随手将烟蒂扔出车窗，牧人朋友赶紧喊停车。车还没有停好，他已跳下车，四下寻找，找到那个仍在燃烧的烟蒂，拾起来，一丝不苟地拧息，直到确认没有一点火星，才回到车上。

A herder friend of mine brought us out into the grasslands, and on the way someone threw a cigarette butt out of the window of the car. The herder immediately called for the car to stop, and before it had done so all the way he jumped out, found the offending item, stomped it out so that he could be sure it was completely extinguished, and then got back in the car.

急车慢牛
Fast cars halted by slow cows

文：张弓长

牛，总是悠然地游逛在辽阔的草原上，即便走到了柏油路中间挡住了疾驰而来的汽车，它依然是那副慢悠悠的姿态。如果这个时候司机鸣笛催促，它还会扭过头来瞪你几眼，那神情仿佛在说："这是我的地盘儿，你牛什么牛？"于是，在草原上，开车的人们学会了耐心地给牛让路。

Cows are always slowly wandering over the grasslands. On the asphalt road, when a cow blocks the path of the fast cars, it's just taking its time. At a time like this if you honk your horn, the cow will just slowly turn its head and look at you, as if to say: "This is my turf, what's wrong with you?" Thus, if you want to drive on the roads of the grasslands, you need to learn to be patient and let the cows go first.

摄影：苏伟伟

43

微观内蒙古
INNER MONGOLIA: COLOURFUL AND MAGNIFICENT

摄影：赵如意

马背上
On horseback

文：莫久愚

初到草原的人，都希望骑在高高的马背上，像蒙古人那样傲视草原。当我真的上了马背，又不禁产生奔驰的冲动，马跑了一阵变成悠闲地漫步，马头高扬，步履舒缓，夕阳让我和马的身影变得异常高大，远处的羊群，像是蓝天抖落的白云……望着这无际的绿色原野，我的心胸似乎突然间疏朗开阔了。

First-time comers to the grasslands all want to ride on horseback, and look down over the grasslands like the Mongolian riders. When I first got on a horse for real, I was gripped by a desire to take off running. The horse galloped for a bit and then slowed down to a canter, head raised high, steps slowed and measured, as the setting sun cast a very long shadow of us. In the distance, a flock of sheep looked like a group of clouds dropped from the blue sky… Looking over at this boundless expanse of green grass, all of a sudden I felt a surge of emotion in my chest, and my heart is open.

爱护在细节
Love is in the details

文：莫久愚

蒙古人对于草原的爱护，往往体现在一些细节上。迁徙时要把搭建蒙古包的地方清理干净，深埋垃圾。北京学者定宜庄回忆在阿巴嘎草原插队生活时说："每次搬迁，拔下拴马桩后，牧民都要用牛粪把留下的洞口糊上。"

Mongolians have love for the grasslands in all its details. When moving they clean up the sites where their yurts were, and bury rubbish deep in the ground. Ding Yizhuang, a scholar from Beijing, remembers his time as an educated youth working in a production team on the Abag Grassland: "When they move, they even fill in with manure the holes where the sticks they post to tie up the horses."

草原·印象
Impressions of the Grassland

摄影：高雪峰

土地的呼唤
Call of the earth

文：张弓长

在席慕蓉的回忆中，第一次踏上父亲的草原，感觉就像走在自己的梦里。游牧族群祖祖辈辈几千几万年的高原记忆，在踏上草原的一瞬间全部醒过来，就像回到梦里，重临旧地。这就是所谓"土地的呼唤"——乡愁不是软弱无用的情绪，它是生命的驱动力。

In Xi Murong's memories, the first time she stepped onto her father's grassland she felt like she was walking in a dream. The memories of generations of nomadic ancestors about the plateau over the millennia all were awakened in an instant, as if in the dream she was returning to these places of old. This is the so-called "call of the earth". Longing for home isn't a weak, useless emotion, but rather the driving force of our lives.

歌与草原
Songs and the grassland

文：张弓长

白岩松说："呼伦贝尔大草原，是一片大自然的绿色，而《呼伦贝尔大草原》是一首歌。到了呼伦贝尔，总会有人在唱，你会不止一次地听到，然后觉得，没有比这再好听的旋律，于是，这歌与这草原就再也分不开。"

Bai Yansong says: "The Great Grassland of Hulun Buir is a huge stretch of green, and *The Great Grassland of Hulun Buir* is also the title of a song. When you go there, there will always be someone singing the song, again and again, and you'll feel you've never heard such a great melody before. Therefore, the song and this grassland are inseparable."

45

微观内蒙古
INNER MONGOLIA: COLOURFUL AND MAGNIFICENT

书桥河
Book Bridge River

文：莫久愚

达里湖畔的贡格尔草原坦荡壮阔。夏日里碧草连天、百花盈野。草原上长17公里的"耗来河"，如同一条袖珍型草原曲水。多数河段只有几十厘米宽，最窄处只有十几厘米，放置一本书就可当桥，当地人又称"书桥河"。它河道稳定，具备草原天然河流的一切特征，千曲百折，缓缓前行，恋恋不舍。

The Gongger Grassland of Dalai Nur lake are broad and magnificent. In the summer, all manner of flowers bloom on the verdant grassland under the bright blue sky. There is also a 17-kilometre long river, "Haolai River", that winds over this landscape. Most reaches of the river are only about several decimetres wide, the narrowest point is only over one decimetre wide, enough to be bridged with a book, a fact that has given rise to the name "Book Bridge River". Its flow is stable and has all the characteristics of a natural grassland river, with its many twists and turns, slow flow, and romantic feel.

摄影：黄蕾

草原·印象
Impressions of the Grassland

蒙古人的"什一律"
Mongolian's "1/10th" principle

文：张弓长

蒙古人的游牧法则是不等水枯草败，便拔营起帐到别处去了。也许你会觉得蒙古人浪费：这么好的草，还没吃完就离开了？按照现代环境学的"什一律"，自然界在消耗不超过十分之一的情况下才可能自行恢复，持续再生。而蒙古人千百年来就一直遵守这一定律，善待自己的生存环境。

The nomadic herders of the Mongolian grasslands don't wait until all the grass is used up or dried out to pick up their yurts and move on. You might think this is wasteful: Why leave a pasture that still has perfectly good grass? Their conduct is actually in line with the principles of environmental science which state that only with a consumption of less than 1/10th of the resources in an area can it easily recover naturally. The Mongolians have understood this for many centuries, always protecting their environment.

雪原月夜
Moonlit nights of the snow land

文：莫久黑

一位来自江南的朋友兴奋地对我说，他喜欢呼伦贝尔草原冬季的落日，更喜欢雪原的月夜。白茫茫的大地托举起蓝得透明的夜空，夜空中缀满钻石般的星星，一轮新月总是悬挂在距南方地平线不高的地方。这让习惯了"举头望明月"的他们感到新奇。空气又是那么纯净，每一口呼吸，仿佛都是在洗涤内脏，净化血液。

A friend from the south excitedly told me how he likes the sunset on the Hulun Buir Grassland in the winter, and likes even more the moonlit nights of the snow land. As the white snow contrasts with the clear blue night sky, with so many bright diamond-like stars inlaid, one can see a new moon hanging low above the horizon in the south. The moon on the grassland is so novel for them, since they have been acustomed to look at a moon high in the sky. The air is pure, so pure that you feel your lungs are cleansed and your blood is purified with each breath.

摄影：石玉平

微观内蒙古
INNER MONGOLIA: COLOURFUL AND MAGNIFICENT

摄影：高雪峰

草原的风
Wind on the grassland

文：姜苇

在一望无际的苍穹下，领略没有遮挡的风。心门被风吹开，吹落一地愁绪，心境如草原般浩瀚。风吹近了天地间的距离，似乎举手便可触碰天边的云——可你刚要伸手，云却又被风吹散了。

Under an endless sky, one appreciates the lack of obstructions to the wind. The blowing of the wind opens your heart, and carries all worries away; your feelings overflow with the vastness of the landscape. The wind blows away the distance between the sky and the earth, and you feel as if you could reach out and touch the clouds. You stick out your hand, however, and the wind blows them away.

草原在退化
The degeneration of the grassland

文：莫久愚

记者丁铭在乌珠穆沁草原听到过这样的事：上世纪六十年代，当地牧民自豪地说，我们的羊只吃草尖，不吃其他，否则品种退化；七十年代，牧民退了一步说，我们的羊只吃草梗，不吃别的；八十年代牧民则说，我们的羊只吃站着草，不吃躺下草（指干草）；九十年代牧民又说，我们的羊，只吃草，不吃料；现在……

Reporter Ding Ming heard this story on the Ujimqin Grassland: In the 1960s, local herders would proudly say: "Our sheep only eat the tips of the grass, nothing else, otherwise the species would disappear." In the 1970s, they took a step back, saying "our sheep only eat the stems of the grass, nothing else". In the 1980s, they would say: "Our sheep only eat grass that stands up, and not dry grass." In the 1990s, they said: "Our sheep only eat grass, not feed." Nowadays...

草原·印象
Impressions of the Grassland

草原上衡量的尺度
Measurements on the grassland

文：张弓长

都市人总是局促于也悲喜于形形色色的尺度考量。作家鲍尔吉·原野说："草原只有几种浑然的大尺度，天地为之一，父母为之一，牛羊为之一，如此而已。"

City residents are always obsessing over the dimensions and forms of various objects. Author Borjigin Yuanye says: "There are only a few rough concepts of units of measurement on the grassland: the size of the landscape, the size of one's parents, the size of a cow, or sheep. Things like that."

躺在草原上看星星
Lying on the grassland to look at stars

文：张弓长

名叫柳暗花明的网友写道："草原的夜晚宁静安详，天地都溶入一片墨色，和着草叶与花朵的清香，慢慢地在空中飘散。躺在草原上仰望漫无边际的星空……星星们一闪一闪好像灯光下的钻石。在城市的车水马龙中间，我常常会感到孤独。我坐在空旷寂静的草原夜色里，心灵却是那么的温暖祥和。"

An internet user named "Dark Willows and Bright Flowers" wrote: "The grasslands are peaceful and quite at night, where the sky and earth both dissolve into a plane of blackness. The clear fragrances of the grass and flower waft slowly through air. Lying on the grass I see the endless starry sky… So many points of light sparkle like diamonds. Among the crowds and clamour of the city, I frequently feel lonely, but when I sit on the wide, calm grassland under the night sky, I feel comforted and warm."

摄影：高磊

微观内蒙古
INNER MONGOLIA: COLOURFUL AND MAGNIFICENT

摄影：乌热尔图

雨后的草原
Grassland after the rain
文／张弓长

在雨后的草原上行走，脚下软绵绵的，发出"悉踏，悉踏"的声响，鞋面上不时沾上一片片黄色、白色的花瓣，湿漉漉的青草将它洗净，又不时换上另一种颜色。新鲜的空气令你沉醉，令你痴狂。在草原，任何一种颜色，都那么纯净的清新。什么都会悄悄变得洁净美丽，不论是你的眼睛你的神情还是你的心⋯⋯

When walking upon the grassland after the rain, you'll feel the ground under your feet is soft and emits squishy sounds as the surfaces of your shoes becomes covered with little white and yellow petals which the wet grass then wipes away, sometimes painting them with a different colour. The fresh air intoxicates you, makes you crazy. On the grassland, all the colours are pure and bright. Everything quietly becomes clean and beautiful, be it the sights, your emotions, or your heart…

草原和云
Grassland and clouds
文／姜苹

夏日的草原，一览无余的空旷，只有浮云遮挡才会有些许阴凉。但是浮云调皮，停停走走，蹦蹦跳跳，时而浓郁涌动，时而浅淡绵延，像是在戏弄追不上她的草原。而草原像一个沉默的大哥哥任由她戏耍，用一成不变托举她的百态千姿。

During the summer on the wide-open grassland, only clouds can provide you with a bit of relief from the heat. However, the clouds are capricious, stopping and going, jumping back and forth, sometimes appearing thick and in clusters, sometimes as long, thin strips. It's just like a naughty girl teasing her silent elder brother. He can not keep her pace, instead, he is willing to serve as the background of her changing forms.

草原·印象
Impressions of the Grassland

摄影：乌热尔图

草原上的"包豪斯"
"Bauhaus" on the grasslands

文：张阿泉

蒙古包是游牧生活土壤中绽放出的民居奇葩，仅由套脑（圆顶天窗）、乌尼（套脑上伞骨辐射下来的细木椽）、哈纳（网格状支架）三段体组成，可拆卸组装，极其符合"忠实于原材料""形式服从于功用""少就是多"的包豪斯建筑法则，是草原上的"包豪斯"。

The yurt, originated from the nomadic life of herders, is an interesting apparatus for living on the grassland. It's constructed of three things: the "skylight", the "umbrella frame", and the "netting fence". It's easy to disassemble, and adheres to "faithfulness to the material", "function preceding form", and "less is more"—three of the principles of the Bauhaus architectural movement. It's actually the "Bauhaus" on the grasslands.

"可调温"的蒙古包
A yurt with a "thermostat"

文：张弓长

蒙古包通过更换和加减材料，就可以从容应对天气的冷暖。冬天冷，就加毡，一层不行加两层，还不行，就把薄的换成厚的。夏天热了，就翻卷起围毡让风进来，或索性撤掉围毡变成凉亭。

One can control the temperature of a yurt by adding or removing material in accordance with the changes in the outside temperature. In the cold winter, if one layer of felt isn't enough, you can add two, and if that's still not enough, you can switch light felt for thick. In the summer, you can remove layers, or even take away the wrapping entirely to let in some cool air and chill your pad out.

51

微观内蒙古
INNER MONGOLIA: COLOURFUL AND MAGNIFICENT

爱护水源
Protecting water resources

文：莫迪

蒙古草原古代的各种法令中，都有"流水不为肮脏不洁之物所玷污"的条款，禁止夏秋季节下水洗浴或在水中洗手。时至今日，在牧人的生活规范中，仍然禁止在河中便溺，禁止向河中投掷秽物，不得污染水源……

Among the many rules of the grassland in ancient times, there is that of "don't dirty running water with unclean things", which forbids one from bathing or washing hands in a body of running water during summer and autumn. Even today, people don't urinate in or throw filthy objects into streams as to keep them clean…

草原上的名字
Names on the grassland

文：莫久愚

蒙古人为家乡或人取名多涉及植物。学者刘书润说："女孩的名字也多和植物有关，只要你喊几声其其格（花儿）、巴德玛（荷花）、那日苏（松树）这些花草名字，就会有姑娘从蒙古包出来向你微笑。"

Mongolians like name their homes and children with the words for plants. Scholar Liu Shurun says: "Girls names often come from plants. Step into a village and say aloud Qiqig (flower), Badma (lotus) or Narz (pine tree) and you'll likely see a girl come out of a yurt and smile at you."

摄影：和平

草原·印象
Impressions of the Grassland

这个世界好得不得了
This world is amazing

文：张弓长

诗人席慕蓉的父母故乡在内蒙古。她说蒙古文化就像她生命中的火种燃烧着，从第一次踏上蒙古高原开始，足足燃烧了25年："虽然蒙古高原是我的原乡，但其实它对我来说是全新的世界，诱惑很大。那里文化的诱惑、大自然的诱惑、人心里美德的诱惑，对我来讲，这个世界好得不得了。"

Poet Xi Murong's family hails from Inner Mongolia. She says that Mongolian culture is like an ever-burning flame in her life which has burned since she first set foot on the Mongolian Plateau twenty-five years ago: "Although the Mongolian Plateau is my ancestral homeland, to me it's like an entirely new world, full of allure. The culture, nature, and people all have a great allure which to me is quite amazing."

《牧歌》诞生的草原
The grassland gave birth to *The Nomad's Song*

文：莫久愚

巴尔虎草原上有过一个凄婉的爱情故事。故事里的小伙子面对草原和草原上的蓝天，不断哭诉着在一场草原大火中遇难的恋人。哭诉化成了一段震颤心灵的旋律，被记录下来，这就是《牧歌》。即便没来过草原的人，也能从这悠远的旋律中，看到草原深邃的天空，低垂的白云，甚至能嗅到牧草的芳香。

There is a sad love story of the Barag Grassland. In the story, a young man faces the grassland and blue sky and cries over his love who died in a great fire upon the steppe. The sound of his sobs was transformed into a song and recorded as *The Nomad's Song*. Even for people who haven't visited the grassland, they can feel the profundity of the sky, the low hanging clouds, and even the fragrance of the grass when they hear the long and distant melody.

摄影：高雪峰

摄影 任海鑫

城市·风情
Flavour of the City

微观内蒙古
INNER MONGOLIA: COLOURFUL AND MAGNIFICENT

呼和浩特博物馆
Hohhot Museum

文：莫久愚

这座二十世纪五十年代的建筑，在借鉴俄式建筑的基础上，吸收了内蒙古西部地区召庙的建筑风格，奶白色外墙及蒙古族特色装饰和屋顶飞腾的骏马雕塑浑然一体，轻盈、精致、典雅、高贵。竣工后便成为呼和浩特市的标志性建筑，在这里留影不会被误解你到了其他的城市。

This museum, built in the 1950s, has an architectural style based on that of Russia, with a few touches reminiscent of the temples in western Inner Mongolia. The milk white walls, Mongolian decorations and sculpture of a handsome horse on the roof are in perfect harmony, which is refined and elegant. The museum became a landmark in Hohhot after its construction. It's a unique place to take photos, and you can nerver find a similar one anywhere else.

摄影：马日平

"云"的城市
"Cloud" city

文：莫久愚

呼和浩特地区古称"云中"。近几年国内的"云"产业正快速向这里聚集。亚洲最大的火力发电基地提供的稳定电力，令几大电信运营商情有独钟，一批国内外知名的大数据企业积极跟进。这座草原都市正在创造未来互联网的新生活，成为国内规模最大的云计算数据基地——"云中"的名号成了现实。

Hohhot's old name was Yunzhong (literally "among the clouds"). In recent years, the "cloud" industry has come here. With the largest thermoelectric power generation base in Asia providing stable power, it's enticing to large telecommunications operators. A number of well-known big data players have set up operations in the city. This grassland city has been transformed by the arrival of futuristic internet technology and has become one of the largest-scale cloud computing centre in the country. Thus, the name Yunzhong has regained relevance.

城市·风情
Flavour of the City

城市的基因
Genes of the city

文：邓九刚

400多年的商业历史让呼和浩特积淀了太多的商业因素、商业经验和商业智慧。以大盛魁为代表的晋商曾经在这里创造了惊天动地的商界伟业。旧商人和商业字号不见了，但是商业智慧和商业冲动没有泯灭，它们作为一种城市基因保留在这座城市的某个地方。一旦时机成熟，它们就会发挥作用，显示力量。

More than 400 years of history of commerce have given a commercial character to Hohhot, adding up to a lot of experience and wisdom in trade and business for the city. Merchants from Shanxi Province achieved brilliant business feats here, such as those done by the business house named Dashengkui, and while the old businessmen dispeared with their shops, the business knowledge and drive of the city haven't been eroded, but handed down and been existing as the city's genes until today. When the opportunity to carry out a transaction, the prowess of the city's residents becomes apparent.

摄影：李克

塞上老街
Old Street beyond the Great Wall

文：姜苇

这里保留着呼和浩特古老的记忆。古朴的青色铺面，悬挂着老字号牌匾。在这里穿行，仿佛化身布衣长衫的古人，时而把玩古董器件儿，时而品尝旧时风味儿。一条老街，隔离了五光十色的都市光景，一个拐弯，就拐进了尘封已久的慢悠悠的从前。

Here, you can see the face of old Hohhot, with plain black storefronts hanging signboards of time-honored brands. Walking through here, it's almost as everyone's in period dress, with antiques everywhere, and the character of a previous era permeating the atmosphere. The old street separates itself from the gleaming modern city. Stepping into this place is like blowing the dust off a long-stored object to reveal what lies beneath.

摄影：高雪峰

57

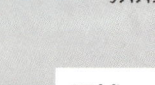

微观内蒙古
INNER MONGOLIA: COLOURFUL AND MAGNIFICENT

旧城
Old Town

文：姜茉

呼和浩特人将市区西部的老城区称为"旧城"，包括玉泉区和回民区。通道街至大南街构成一条贯通南北的文化大道，把两个区连接起来。街边坐落着秀丽的清真寺、百年天主教堂、雄伟的大召和席力图召。在这里流连，看着来来往往的信众、游客出入寺、召，或沿街闲逛选购喜欢的小吃，心里平静而又温暖。

The people of Hohhot refer to the older area in the west of the city as "Old Town", which includes Yuquan and Huimin Districts, and a cultural corridor that extends from Tongdao Avenue to Danan Avenue, connecting the two districts. On either side of the street there are magnificent mosques, and even a century-old catholic church, in addition to the Grand Temple and Xilitu Temple. Walking around here, looking at the adherents coming and going, and tourists entering and exiting the temples, or just kicking about it, shopping and snacking, you'll feel relaxed and warm.

摄影：额博

城市·风情
Flavour of the City

摄影：马日平

摄影：张阿泉

烧卖一条街
Shaomai Street

文：黄蔷

许多呼和浩特人的早晨是从一笼热腾腾的烧卖开始的。玉泉区的"烧卖一条街"，东头连接着五塔寺、西头连着席力图召、大召，都是著名景点。不同品牌的十几家烧卖馆不仅讲究馅儿料、面皮，佐餐的黑茶也讲究产地。老食客不仅能品出各家烧卖口味的细微差别，还能喝出茶叶的来路。

A basket of steaming shaomai is a typical breakfast for many in Hohhot. In the Yuquan District, there is "Shaomai Street", which extends from the Five Tower Temple in the east to the Xilitu Temple and Grand Temple in the west, all of which are scenic spots. There are over ten shaomai shops in the street. These shops not only have great shaomai in terms of filling and wrapping, they also have great black tea to go with it. The origin places of the food materials are given particular attention. Frequent customers can distinguish between the distinct flavours of the shaomai as well as the tea.

一碗面煮沸一座城
A bowl of noodles draws the attention of a whole city

文：苏怀亮

鄂尔多斯东胜区一个两岁的孩子患了急性白血病，孩子的爸爸开着一家面馆，希望更多人去吃一碗面，挣些医药费。消息在网上传开，第二天一大早，面馆就挤满了顾客。有人吃一碗面付了一两百元，还有人进面馆留下钱就走。两天时间，面馆收到爱心款近40万元。

In Dongsheng District of Ordos, the father of a two-year-old child suffering from leukaemia opened a noodle shop with the hope of earning more money to pay for his child's treatment. The news went viral on the internet, and the next morning it was packed with customers. Some people paid one or two hundred yuan for a bowl of noodles, others just came in, put down money, and left. In two days, he was given almost 400,000 yuan for his child's treatment.

微观内蒙古
INNER MONGOLIA: COLOURFUL AND MAGNIFICENT

摄影：任海鑫

神奇的鄂尔多斯
Mysterious Ordos

文：莫久愚

有人这样描述鄂尔多斯：它是中国第一煤炭城市却几乎看不到煤，煤是封闭开采的；是工业大市却几乎看不到工厂，厂房都在产业园；是畜牧业大市却几乎看不到羊，羊都在圈养。这里号称"国家级"的能源和新型化工基地，天是蓝的，水是清的；领跑内蒙古经济，城区却不喧闹，人们都很悠闲……

Some people thus describe Ordos: It's China's coal capital, but you hardly see coal anywhere, as it's extracted in a sealed setting. It's a huge industrial centre but you don't see any factories, as they're all grouped together in the industrial park. It's a centre for livestock, but you don't see any sheep as they're all fenced away. This "National Level" energy resource centre and new chemical industry base has blue skies, clean water... It leads Inner Mongolia in economy, but it's not noisy, and the people are chilling out...

逛市场的尴尬
Awkward shopping

文：苏怀亮

鄂尔多斯男人很少去农贸市场或早市摊点买东西。男人们说，逛市场最怕遇见摊主是老乡或熟人，本想去捧场添点儿生意，但摊主不论男女，要么就多给，要么干脆不收钱，还总是说："啊呀，拿上拿上，几斤瓜菜么，给甚钱了！"这会让他们很不好意思。

Men in Ordos rarely go to farmers' markets or morning markets, because they're afraid of running into old friends or people from their hometowns —they go with the intention of contributing a bit of business, but be the salesperson male or female, more ofen than not give extra pieces or won't take their money, making remarks such as "come on, just take it, it's a few pounds of vegetables, I don't need your money". It makes them uncomfortable.

城市·风情
Flavour of the City

鄂尔多斯"风暴"

The Ordos "storm"

文：莫久愚

进入新世纪后，鄂尔多斯刮起了一场"经济风暴"。曾经最贫穷的地区成了自治区最富庶的地方。若以常住人口计算，这里的人均 GDP，2007 年就超过了北京，2010 年开始人均 GDP 位居全国地级市之首。尽管眼下正在经历产业转型的阵痛，仍然是自治区经济体量最大的市。在康巴什新区的广场上可以体验到鄂尔多斯高速发展的气势。

After entering into the new century, Ordos has experienced an economic "storm". Formerly the poorest area in Inner Mongolia, it is now the richest. Looking at its permanent population, the per-capita GDP exceeded that of Beijing in 2007, and in 2010 it became the first among China's prefectural cities. Even though it's going through some pains at the moment in economic transition, it's still the leader in Inner Mongolia as to the economic volume. You can get a feel for the rapid pace of development by visiting the plazas in the Kangbashi New District.

摄影：白雪峰

有鹿的城市

A city with deer

文：莫久愚

"包头"，蒙古语意为"有鹿的地方"。城市标志就是三只腾飞的鹿。但是自包头得名二百多年来，鹿，似乎只是一个古老的记忆。而如今，在城市中心绿地上真的能够见到驯养的鹿群在安闲地游荡。作家许淇自豪地说："别处的孩子在广场上喂鸽子，我们的孩子可以和亲爱的小鹿相依相拥。"

"Baotou" in Mongolian means "place with deer". The insignia of the city is three jumping deer. However, after 200 years of having the name, deer are mostly an old memory. Still, though, in the green of the city centre you can see tamed deer roaming. Author Xu Qi says proudly: "In other places children feed doves, but here we have deer to keep us company."

摄影：王书墉

61

微观内蒙古
INNER MONGOLIA: COLOURFUL AND MAGNIFICENT

草原钢城
Steel City on the Grassland

文／姜苿

这是包头的昵称。60年前，昆都仑河畔崛起的大型钢铁企业——包头钢铁厂，结束了内蒙古"手无寸铁"的历史。可这座城市并不像它的名号那样坚硬，随处可见的广场和绿地，还有包头人的热情，如同铁血中的柔情，能熔化钢铁。

This is a nickname for Baotou. Sixty years ago, a large steel mill, Baogang, was constructed on the bank of the Hondolon River, which ended Inner Mongolia's history of being an "iron free" region. However, with greens and plazas everywhere, the city isn't as hard as its name would imply. The people are also friendly—the warmth of their blood could even be said to melt steel.

绿地环绕的城市
A city surrounded by greens

文／姜苿

包头是一个不拥挤的城市。现代建筑被大片大片奢侈的绿地环绕，给人一种滨海城市的视觉印象。那扑面而来的绿啊，是从草原流淌过来的吗？

Baotou isn't a crowded city. The modern construction is surrounded by a large amount of green space which makes it appear like a coastal city. One wonders, did the green here flow in from the surrounding grasslands?

阿尔丁植物园
Arding Botanical Garden

文／姜苿

包头的阿尔丁植物园很大，很难步量，然而你却总想漫步其中，伴着满园馨香。紧张的城市生活中，你需要一个空间让心休息。多幸运！这样的所在就在近前，无须跋山涉水，无须远走他方。

Baotou's Arding Botanical Garden is quite large, to the extent that it would be quite a task to walk the entire grounds. On top of that, it has the kind of landscape that makes you want to slow down your pace as you walk through it. In the busy city, one needs a place to unwind and relax. How nice! It's close by, so you don't even have to take a trip far away to get your downtime.

摄影：刘长杰

城市·风情
Flavour of the City

包头的大
Bigness of Baotou

文：莫久愚

包头是一座充满阳刚之气的"大城市"，格局大、企业大、产品大、矿山大……出身江南的作家许淇说："这里的居民的气派和胃口都大，每年岁末，扛回家半扇半扇猪、整只整只羊，贮存在过冬的凉房里。此举会使京津沪那些只买一小包肉丝放在菜篮里的主妇咋舌。"

Baotou is a big, beefy city, with large layout, large enterprises, large products, and large mines. Xu Qi, an author from the south says: "The people here have big flair and big appetites. At the end of the year, you'll see them take half a huge pig, an entire lamb home, and store it in their chiller. Housewives from Beijing, Tianjin or Shanghai that just buy a little bag of shredded meat at the market would have their eyes pop out of their heads to see such a scene."

包头的广场
Baotou's plazas

文：姜苹

包头有很多的广场，广场是包头妩媚而多情的眼睛。鲜花簇拥，生机盎然，一个个大小不等的喷泉，鲜活而灵动。点缀着包头的刚毅，竟有那么多柔情。

Baotou has many plazas, all of which are lovely places to behold. Crowded with flowers, teeming with life, decorated with fountains large and small, they're cute embellishments to the serious face of the city.

摄影：刘长杰

舒展通透的包头
Vast and convenient Baotou

文：庞月莲

"有一种舒展和通达叫包头。"内地大都市的人来包头，感觉呼吸都随着道路畅快了。六车道、八车道的路，纵横交织，四通八达。作为中国的新兴工业城市，大格局的城市设计为发展预留了充分的空间。60年来，包头的掌门人坚持一张蓝图绘到底，才有了今天靓丽、大气的面貌。

"There's a vast place that's easy to get around called Baotou." When people come from other places to Baotou, they feel that it's easy to breathe, and easy to travel around the city. There are roads six and eight lanes wide that run all over the city. As a new burgeoning industrial city in China, the city was designed to have a lot of space reserved for furture development. Over the past 60 years, in line with a clear blueprint that takes everything into consideration, a beautiful, grand city has developed.

微观内蒙古
INNER MONGOLIA: COLOURFUL AND MAGNIFICENT

告别老屋
Farewell to old homes

文：庞月莲

包头老城区的北梁曾是全国面积最大的棚户区。北梁居民形容自己的居住环境："长巷巷短巷巷里面尽是黑浪浪（很窄的小胡同），土房房泥墙墙旁边盖个炭仓仓，没厨房没书房推门看见一盘炕……"只三年工夫，北梁居民就告别了老屋，全部迁入新区的高楼。包头因此被授予全国唯一的"棚户区改造示范城市"称号。

Beiliang in the old area of Baotou used to be the country's largest favela. Former residents described their previous living condition: "Among long and short alleyways are narrow alleyways. Besides adobe houses and walls are adobe coal storerooms. Nobody had a kitchen or study, just earthen beds on the ground…" In just three years all the residents said farewell to their old homes as they were moved into modern high-rises. For this, Baotou is lauded as the country's sole exemplar for de-favelication.

城中草原
Urban Grassland

文：庞月莲

干旱少雨的重工业城市包头，市区有1万平方米以上的广场绿地39个，最大的是赛汗塔拉生态园，"赛汗塔拉"蒙语意为"美丽的草原"，它是一个难得的原始草原湿地生态系统，占有8000多亩的草场和森林，号称"城中草原"，位于市区的要道上。一边高楼林立，一边绿草幽幽，一边繁华喧嚣，一边宁静安和。

In the dry heavy industry city of Baotou, there are thirty-nine 10,000-square-metre grassy plazas, the largest of which is the Tara Khan Ecological Garden (Tara Khan, Mongolian for "beautiful grassland") a primitive grassland wetland, 5.3 square kilometres in area. It's known as the "Urban Grassland", and is located on a major road in the city. On one side are tall buildings, and on the other, lush grassland—clamour and noise over here, relaxation over there.

摄影：王立文

城市·风情
Flavour of the City

北方兵器工业城
Northern China Weapons City

文：姜苇

包头青山区的北方兵器工业城其实是一个兵器主题广场，像一个严阵以待的战场，诠释着这个城市的硬朗。这座城市生产的大炮、坦克等军工装备，就是锻造着国家的尊严与安宁。

Baotou's Qingshan District has a Northern China Weapons City, which is actually a weapon theme-park. It looks like a battlefield ready to take action, which shows the hardness of the city. The artillery and tanks produced here guard the dignity and safety of the country.

百里绿道
One-hundred-li green road

文：庞月莲

在包头，沿黄河徒步成了一种时尚。九原区的"城市绿道"全部由彩色透水混凝土铺装，脚踩上去很舒适，水落上去不会淤积。绿道沿途的公园、绿地，让行人感受着"路在林中，人在画中"的惬意。

In Baotou, walking along the Yellow River has become a kind of fashion, where the "Green City Road" in Jiuyuan District is covered with colourful permeable concrete. The road is comfortable to step on, with no water left on it. As you walk on the road crossing the parks, gardens and woods, you will feel you are a character in a painting.

摄影：娄元艺

温柔的钢铁大街
Soft Steel Street

文：姜苇

包头市昆都仑区的主街叫"钢铁大街"。听到这个名字你会觉得这条街硬朗得能发出金属的光泽，但当你走在街上，看到街边满眼迎人的花草，妩媚，温柔，你无论如何也不会联想到那个铿锵的名字。

The main thoroughfare of Kundulun District in Baotou is known as "Steel Street". When you hear this name you might think of a sterile, metallic area, but when you walk the street you'll see it's flanked by flowers and grasses, lovely, charming and warm. You might think the name doesn't fit.

微观内蒙古
INNER MONGOLIA: COLOURFUL AND MAGNIFICENT

摄影：白立新

白云鄂博的奉献
Bayan Obo's contribution

文：莫久鹏

草原上曾经的山峰，如今成了两个深达几百米的矿坑，像是两枚巨大的指纹，印证着草原的奉献；又如两幅硕大的年轮，记录着包头的成长。学者邢晨声形容它："已经随着包钢的火红锤炼，注入祖国躯体的各处，在我们的身边或者手中，都可能有白云鄂博无声的影子。它用自己的凹陷筑起国家的崛起。"

Where there was originally a mountain on the grassland, now there are two mining pits hundreds of metres deep, like a pair of giant fingerprints on the landscape, a testament to the grassland's contribution. Like two huge annual rings, they show the growth of Baotou. Scholar Xing Chensheng describes them: "They're key components of the development of mining and steelmaking in the Baotou area and their traces can be found in every corner of the country. The shadow of Bayan Obo is probably hidden in our hands or around us. They deepened as China rose."

城市 · 风情
Flavour of the City

玄武岩上的花园城市
Basalt-based garden city

文：莫久棵

乌兰察布地下是坚固的玄武岩，市区的白泉山几乎就是裸露的砂岩，当地人硬是在石头山上铺了一米多厚的土层，让草木落地生根，又疏浚了淤滞多年的霸王河，为城市引进灵气，一座园林城市已经初见模样。作家张抗抗形容市区说："直而宽的街道，坦坦荡荡铺陈开去，像是为正在起飞的西部内陆预备的一条条跑道。"

Ulan Qab City is built upon a foundation of basalt, with Baiquan Mountain in the city being made almost entirely of naked basalt. The local people, however, weren't satisfied with this and thus went through the effort of covering the entire mountain with a layer of soil more than one metre thick so that plants could grow upon it. They have also dredged and deepened the Bawang River, which previously was clogged up with many years of silt, to make a nicer landscape to live in, and a garden city thus born. Author Zhang Kangkang thus describes the city: "The streets are straight, wide and flat, like a series of runways for the western inland, which is taking off."

中国"冷极"
China's coldest point

文：莫久黑

最近几十年，中国大陆冬季的极端气温都是在根河市记录到的，零下40℃很寻常，因而被称之为中国最冷的地方。在外地人无法想象的气温里，小城的生活依旧。街面上照例有摊贩的叫卖声，市民往往拖着简易的"雪爬犁"盛放物品。喜欢刺激的南方游客，越来越多地来这里体验滴水成冰的寒冷。

In recent decades, all of the extreme low temperatures in China have been recorded in Gegen Gol City, where temperatures of 40 below zero are perfectly normal. For this, it's been called China's "cold capital". In temperatures that people from other places can hardly comprehend, life goes on as normal, with people buying and selling things on the street, carrying their goods around on little simple snow sleds. People from more southerly areas looking for a chill thrill are starting to come here in increasing numbers to experience the extreme cold.

摄影：金红霞

微观内蒙古
INNER MONGOLIA: COLOURFUL AND MAGNIFICENT

边境线上的"二连"
"Eren" on the border
文 / 莫久愚

"二连"不是军事建制，它是二连浩特的简称，属于中国最小的市，却是中蒙之间最大的陆路口岸，地处大漠戈壁上。市郊的额仁淖尔盐池经常出现海市蜃楼的迷幻景象，被牧民称作"额仁"（幻景），这里的"额仁驿站"，先是被清朝人读作"伊林驿站"，又被后来人讹读为"二连"。

"Eren" (literally "the second company" in Chinese) isn't a military division, but rather a short name for the city of Erenhot, China's smallest prefectural city. It is also, however, the largest land port between China and Mongolia, located upon the Gobi desert. The Erennur Salt Lake frequently displays mirages, which are called "eren" (illusion in Mongolian) by the nomadic shepherds. The "Eren Station" here was originally "Yilin Station" in the Qing Dynasty, but this was later mistaken as "Eren".

通辽的盘子
Tongliao's plates
文 / 莫久愚

通辽的餐馆，不论豪华简陋，都不约而同地用大盘子，菜量也比别处多出一倍。外地口音的食客点菜时，服务员常会善意地提醒："俺们家的菜量大，够吃了。"

In any restaurant in Tongliao, be it simple or fancy, the plates are quite large, and the portions are double what they would be elsewhere. If you show up at a restaurant and don't sound like a local, the waitstaff will friendlily remind you: "Our portions are big, I think what you have ordered already will be enough."

"黄牛之乡"
"Home of Yellow Cattle"
文 / 姜苹

通辽市号称"黄牛之乡"，科尔沁牛、西门塔尔牛以肉质鲜嫩、微量元素丰富、蛋白质含量多著称。"科尔沁肥牛"是知名品牌，每年向香港供应活牛万头以上。这里的牛肉干，味道独特，清爽香滑。在科尔沁区，循着烤牛肉的香味一路走去，就会找到著名的"牛肉干一条街"。

Tongliao City is also known as "Home of Yellow Cattle". The Horqin and Simmental cattle that are raised here have excellent meat that is rich in trace elements, and contains lots of high-quality protein. The "Horqin Cattle" is a well-known brand, and each year more than ten-thousand live heads are sold to Hong Kong. The beef jerky here is also famous for its unique flavour and excellent taste. In the Horqin District, the smell of barbecued beef permeates the air, due to the existence of the famous "Beef Jerky Street".

城市·风情
Flavour of the City

摄影：汤军

有历史的赤峰
Historical Chifeng

文：莫久愚

赤峰号称"中国有色金属之乡"，当地人爱对外来人讲的却不是金属，而是历史：新石器时代最具代表性的"红山文化"得名于市区北面红色山峰；辽王朝的核心地带在这里；各个旗县都可以看到象征最早的玉质礼器的"中华第一龙"造型和象征契丹民族起源的青牛、白马雕饰……赤峰，确是一个有历史的地方。

Chifeng is known as "the home of non-ferrous metals" in China, but what the locals like to introduce to visitors isn't the metals, but rather the slightly more interesting topic of history. In the Neolithic age, the "Hongshan Culture" (Hongshan: "red mountain") existed, and is so named for the red mountain peak in the north of the city. The core of the Liao Dynasty was here, and one can see remnants of the earliest jade culture in all the counties and banners, including "China's First Dragon" sculpture and carvings of black cows and white horses—the symbols of the origins of the Khitan people. All of which show the city's rich history.

习惯早起的赤峰人
Early risers in Chifeng

文：张弓长

赤峰人多有早起的习惯。天刚蒙蒙亮，大多数赤峰人就起床开始劳作了。他们以为生活在其他地方的人们也都起得早。所以要是赤峰人在早晨六点给你打电话，不是他不懂礼貌，只是他不知道你那会儿睡得正香。

Most people in Chifeng wake up early. When the sun has just risen, most people in the city are already up and working. They also think that this is what it's like everywhere, so if someone from Chifeng is blowing up your phone at 6 am, they're not disrespecting you, they just don't realise that you're probably still sleeping sweetly at that time.

微观内蒙古
INNER MONGOLIA: COLOURFUL AND MAGNIFICENT

摄影：高雪峰

贝子庙
Beizi Temple

文：莫久愚

为便于牧人礼佛，草原上的召庙大都建在交通便利的地方，也是往来客商云集的地方。草原上最早的城镇，往往是在召庙周边形成的居民聚落。锡林浩特市原名"贝子庙"，贝子庙就是今天市区北面敖包山下那座著名的召庙，它为这座城市保留着古老的文化基因，仿佛用苍老的目光俯瞰着这座熙熙攘攘的草原边城。

For the convenience of nomadic shepherds, temples are located at convenient junctions on the grasslands, and are places where people gather. The earliest cities on the grassland arose from gatherings around these temples. The original name of Xilinhot was "Beizi Temple"—the famous temple still stands at the foot of Obo Mountain, a preservation of the old genes of the city, in present day still looking down over it under the clear blue sky.

海拉尔印象
Impressions of Hailar

文：莫久愚

海拉尔，呼伦贝尔的心脏。发源于大兴安岭的伊敏河滋养着小城的人。城市在快速发展，克制的建筑却让城市敞亮，没有压抑感，依然是草原城市的秉性。清晨推开窗，所见的颜色都是干净透明的，湛蓝的天，洁白的云，碧绿的地，整洁的街区。呼吸到的空气也都是纯净清新的。入夜，哈萨尔斜拉桥下，繁星落满河中……

Hailar is the heart of Hulun Buir, and the Imin River originated in the Greater Hinggan Range nourishes the people here. The city is developing rapidly, but the construction progresses at a checked pace, so the building-up doesn't feel oppressive, and the character of the grassland still persists. When morning opens your window, you see a palette of clean colours, a deep blue sky, pure white clouds, a green landscape, and clean street. The air you breathe here is clean, and at night, the stars come out under the Hasar Bridge...

城市·风情
Flavour of the City

草原城市的味道
Grassland city flavour

文：姜苹

草原上的城市几乎都以蒙餐为主，来自其他地方的餐饮也不得不适应当地人的口味。炒米、奶茶、手把肉，那醇香的味道飘满小城的每一个角落。当你面对大致雷同的水泥建筑，不知自己身在何处时，闭上眼睛，仔细闻闻这个城市的味道，就会知道，此刻你正身处草原。

The restaurants in the cities on the grassland almost all serve Mongolian food, and cuisines from other place are adapted to local tastes. Fried millet, milk tea, and mutton all contribute to the scent of the air in every corner of the city. Looking at all the duplicate cookie-cutter buildings in the cities, you might have trouble placing where you are, but if you close your eyes and take a deep breath, you'll know you are on the grassland.

中国最大的门
China's largest door

文：莫久愚

中国陆地边境上最大的国门是满洲里国门。国门横跨 105 米，高 43.7 米。实际上是一个面积近 6000 平方米的大楼。门下有 2 条宽轨和 1 条标轨与俄罗斯铁路接轨。每年几千万吨的货物进出大门，国内许多城市发往欧洲的货运专列由此出关。门下还预留了建造复线的位置，隐喻着对这条亚欧大通道未来的期待和信心。

The largest "door" in China is that of the border gate at Manzhouli. 105 metres wide and 43.7 metres high, this gate is in fact a 6,000 square metre building. Under the gate are two wide rails and one standard rail that connect train traffic with Russia. Every year, tens of millions of tonnes of freight come into and out of China through this gate, and much of the rail cargo traffic bound for Europe from China passes through this gate. There is even space for new rails under the gate, which points to a plan and hope for increased Eurasian traffic.

摄影：莫久愚

微观内蒙古
INNER MONGOLIA: COLOURFUL AND MAGNIFICENT

满洲里书城
Manzhouli book city

文：莫迪

冬日的满洲里如同一个童话的世界，是一个容易让人找回童真的地方。广场上一座俄式建筑前，风雪中矗立着几座雕像：屠格涅夫、莱蒙托夫、托尔斯泰、果戈理……深沉地注视着过往的行人。那么多人冒着严寒前来买书、读书，这让我对这座边塞小城顿生敬意。

During the winter Manzhouli is like a fairy land, where all the memories of your childhood come back to you. On the plaza, there is a Russian style architecture, in front of which erected several statues of famous authors—Turgelev, Lermontov, Tolstoy, and Gogol, etc.—looking deeply at you in the snow as you walk past. So many people come there buying and reading books in spite of the bitter cold weather, from which you'll have respect for the place.

满洲里风情
Regional aroma of Manzhouli

文：莫久愚

这座中俄蒙三国交界处的小城是中国最大的陆路口岸。满街都是行色匆匆的俄罗斯面孔和用俄、汉两种文字标注的招牌，餐厅飘出俄罗斯歌曲，耳边不时听到俄语的问候和讨价还价，比比皆是的俄式建筑，使人有如身临异域。到满洲里购物、度假、吃中餐，已经是俄罗斯远东居民的消费时尚。

This city, at the intersection of China, Mongolia and Russia, is China's largest land port. The streets are full of busy Russian faces, and signs are written in both Russian and Chinese. The restaurants play Russian music, and you can hear people haggling in Russian in the streets, where stand many Russian style buildings. It seems the city is an alien place. Coming to Manzhouli to shop, vacation, and eat Chinese food has already become a trendy thing for residents of far-eastern Russia.

摄影：莫久愚

城市·风情
Flavour of the City

摄影：刘秉忠

警察的敬礼
Police's salutations

文：莫久愚

一位常年跑运输的卡车司机说，他每年夏末秋初在巴彦淖尔运送瓜果时都会有交通警察向他敬礼。河套号称"瓜果之乡"，每年8月，八百里河套到处飘荡着蜜瓜的浓香，地头垛满刚刚采摘的西瓜。这时候瓜农最着急的是尽快把大批成熟的瓜果销往内地，交警也会向外运瓜果的车辆表达河套人的敬意。

A lorry driver that has runs freight for years says that every year at the end of summer and start of autumn when he visits Bayannur, the traffic police would salute him. Hetao district is known as "the home of fruits", and every year at the end of August the thick fragrance of melons is all about, with piles of watermelons all over the ground. At this time the farmers rush to have their crop transported to the hinterland of China, and thus the police salute the drivers transporting these fruits.

阿里河
Alihe Town

文：姜苪

鄂伦春旗政府所在地阿里河是一个小城，不招摇，不喧闹，像一朵普通的野花，独自芬芳美丽。在这静谧的兴安岭深处，与驯鹿为伴的小城就这样守候着一个民族的传承，默默地，像是怕惊扰了遥远的记忆。

The government of the Oroqen Autonomous Banner is in the small Alihe Town. It's not ostentatious or noisy, resembling a plain wildflower with unique fragrance and beauty. Embedded in the tranquil forest of Hinggan Range, the small city safeguards the local enthic culture. Reindeer roam about the city quietly, as if for fear of disturbing its distant memory.

73

微观内蒙古
INNER MONGOLIA: COLOURFUL AND MAGNIFICENT

奶茶馆意味着"蒙餐"
The milk tea house offers Mongolian food

文：莫久愚

不仅是蒙古族人，很多在内蒙古长期生活的其他民族的人也都习惯了奶茶和蒙餐。所以这些年城镇中各种名号的奶茶馆多起来了，他们大都雇用来自牧区的务工人员，都能提供地道的奶茶和蒙餐。就像成都的茶馆可以供应小吃，广东人喝茶意味着早餐一样，在内蒙古走进奶茶馆，也意味着品尝地道的蒙餐。

Not just native Mongolians, but also people who have lived for a long time in Inner Mongolia are accustomed to drinking milk tea and eat Mongolian food for dinner. For this reason, in the cities there are many milk-tea houses which employ workers from the pasturing areas, and make the most authentic milk tea and Mongolian food. Just as teahouses in Chengdu provide snacks, and Cantonese people say "drinking tea" to mean having breakfast, milk tea house with Mongolian food is a real staple here.

冰雪阿尔山
Arxan, a city of ice and snow

文：莫久愚

这是一座没有城乡接合部的小城，步出街口就是茫茫林海、皑皑雪原，雾凇千里，悬珠缀玉。城在林中，城在雪中，既是城市，又是山野，无污染的雪令人神清气爽，空气都带着丝丝甜意。白天，大人拉着小雪爬犁出行购物，孩子带着自制的雪车爬滚戏闹；入夜后，冰灯点点，又成了晶莹剔透的世界……

In this small city, there is no rural and urban linking areas, taking a slight detour off the street will land you in the forest, in fields of snow and expanses of mist where dew drips off the trees and becomes pearls of ice. The city exists amidst forest and snow. It's both a city and wilderness, a place free of pollution where your spirit will be cleansed, and the air is sweet. During the day, adults drag sleighs about upon which they carry their shopping, and children play on homemade sleds. At night, the ice lanterns are lit, and the world becomes a sea of bright and sparkling gems...

摄影：高丽

城市·风情
Flavour of the City

乌海市书法家协会　供稿

乌海的味道
Taste of Wuhai

文：莫久愚

这是一座黄河穿城而过的小城，因煤而兴，却见不到煤，似都化作浓墨，全城瀚墨飘香，号称"中国书法城"：全城50万人口，书法爱好者近万人；市中心公园叫"青山瀚墨园"；当地报纸有书画专版；两所小学被命名为"兰亭小学"。此外城市周边的沙地遍布葡萄庄园，当地酒庄产的中高档葡萄酒又给乌海的墨香添了另一种香甜。

This city on the Yellow River is based on coal, but you won't see coal there. It's as if been transformed to ink which has been used to paint the entire city, earning it the nickname of "China's Calligraphy City". With a population of only 500,000, there are more than 10,000 calligraphy enthusiasts. The central park is known as the "Qingshan Ink Garden", the local newspaper has a calligraphed page, and two of the elementary schools are named "Lanting Schools" (Lanting is the place where the famous calligrapher Wang Xizhi wrote his masterpiece). Additionally, there are vineyards outside of the city, and the locally-produced quality wine brings a hint of sweet to the inky landscape.

摄影：薛晓先

摄影：赵如意

传统·习俗

Traditions and Customs

微观内蒙古
INNER MONGOLIA: COLOURFUL AND MAGNIFICENT

摄影：张松云

牧人的待客之道
Shepherd's hospitality

文：莫久愚

草原地广路遥，旧时若有客来访，牧人定会款待留宿，若是谁家在日落后还放客人走，是会被乡邻看不起的。如今道路通达，住的也不再是草原毡帐了，可牧人纯朴、豪爽、好客的民风依旧。客人进门，不论相识与否，来者是客，定会躬身相迎，奶茶伺候，席间一定有酒有肉。

Distances on the grassland are vast, and in old times when a guest came to visit he would definitely be offered to stay the night over, as neighbors would look down upon someone who turned a guest out after sundown. Today the roads on the grassland lead to all directions, which make it convenient for people to travel around, and there are far few people living in yurts, however, the plain and hospitable customs remain. When you enter someone's house, whether or not you two are familiar, you will be met with a bow, some tea, and the offer of some meat and liquor.

迎娶新娘自报祖籍
Telling the family history to the bride

文：莫久愚

内蒙古乌拉特部落婚礼的程序是先聘后娶。娶亲一般在天亮时。聘娶双方祝颂人要有一番问答。女方人提问"祖籍为何地……什么缘故，前来此地"，男方通报自己祖籍起源时吟诵"故地呼伦贝尔，远祖布尔海……现居穆那汗山阳"，几经周折后，接下来便是女方的盛大宴会。

The Urad people of Inner Mongolia have a defined system for engagement before marriage. They are normally conducted at daybreak, and involve a question and response format. The girl's family will ask: "Where are your ancestors from?" And the young man's family will repeat story of their origins: "My ancestral home is known as Hulun Buir, before that there was Burkhai… Now we live at the south of Mount Munahan". After a few rounds of such talk, the girl's family will put on a big celebration.

传统·习俗
Traditions and Customs

喝茶的讲究
Tea culture

文：邓九刚

新熬的茶喝前先要向天地泼洒，以敬山水土地和神灵。倒茶时右手持壶或勺，壶嘴或勺头向北向里，不能向南（朝门）向外；茶不可倒得太满，也不可只倒半碗；手指不能蘸进茶里，也不能洒溢。敬茶按长幼之序，给老人或贵客添茶要接过茶碗。客人茶喝到半碗就得添，喝完后长者端碗说唱《茶的祝词》。

Before drinking the new tea one first throws a little into the air, to show respect for the heavens, the earth and the spirits. When pouring tea out, one uses the right hand to hold the pot or ladle, and makes sure the head of the spoon or spout of the pot faces north, and not south or towards the door. The cup can't be filled too much, but it also can't be half-filled. One mustn't dip a finger in the tea, and must take care to make sure it does not overflow. The elders are respected and drink first. The elders or honored guests' tea cups should be taken over in hand to refill. When the guest's cup is half-empty, it must be refilled, and a song is sung by the eldest after the drinking of tea is finished.

蒙古族赛马
Mongolian horse racing

文：莫久愚

蒙古族赛马通常在平坦的草场上举行，赛程30—50公里。既不分组，也不计时，骑手不分男女老幼，马不分雌雄岁口。获奖者不是骑手，而是马匹和它的主人。每年在西乌珠穆沁草原上都会举行世界上规模最大的赛马活动。几百匹马同时出发，如惊涛滚滚，雷霆阵阵，排山倒海，遮云蔽日，场面令人震撼。

Horse races are frequently conducted on the vast open grassland, with lengths between 30 and 50 kilometres. The races aren't divided in groups or timed, with old and young, male and female riders, and horses of all ages and genders. The prize-winners aren't the riders, but rather the horses and their owners. Every year on the West Ujimqin Grassland, the largest-scale horse race in the world is conducted. Hundreds of horses take off at the same time, hooves pounding as they kick up a huge cloud of dust—it's an awesome sight.

摄影：石玉平

微观内蒙古
INNER MONGOLIA: COLOURFUL AND MAGNIFICENT

鄂温克人育婴
Ewenki infant care
文：莫久愚

鄂温克人的摇篮叫"额莫贺"，用山丁树或红柳树制成。背面挂上野鸡腿骨、鹰爪或野猪獠牙等串起来的饰物。婴儿出生几天就开始睡在摇篮里，一直到两岁多。母亲唱给婴儿的歌谣男女不同。男孩唱"……走高山能打到马鹿，穿峡谷能打到驼鹿"，女孩唱"……出大门能吃到山丁果，出远门能吃到红莓果"。

The cradle used by the Ewenki people is known as the "emohe", made from the wood of the Siberian crab apple or red willow. Pheasant bones, eagle talons, the tusks of wild boars, and other such items are hung upon its back. The child will sleep in this cradle from a few days after its birth until it is a bit more than two years old. The mother sings different songs for boys and girls. Boys' songs contain themes like "...you can hunt red deer in the mountains, and moose in the valleys" whereas the themes for girls' songs are things like "near home you can pick crab apples, far from home you can pick red berries".

天箭
Arrows of the sky
文：莫久愚

学者孟松林发现，巴尔虎草原许多蒙古包的天窗旁挂着锈迹斑斑的箭头，主人告诉他那是"腾格里速穆"（天箭）。这里夏日雨天经常打雷，有时会击中蒙古包起火。每次雨水冲刷地面后会露出一些古战场遗留下来的箭头。老人说，这是从天上来的箭，挂在蒙古包里能避邪，雷就击不着了。这是从祖辈传下来的习俗。

Scholar Meng Songlin discovered that on the Barag Grassland, many Mongolian yurts have rusted arrowheads hung beside the top window as decoration. An owner of such a yurt told him they are "arrows of the sky". Here, in the summer there is frequently lightning, which sometimes strikes yurts and sets them on fire. After the rain, the disturbed ground will contain ancient arrowheads. The old folk say, these arrowheads come down from the sky, and hanging them upon one's yurt can ward off evil, and protect the yurt from lightning. This is an ancient tradition.

最早的自然保护区
The earliest nature reserves
文：莫久愚

内蒙古各旗大多有自己的"罕山"或"敖包山"，是当地蒙古人心目中的神山，是祭天的地方。上面的一草一木、一石一土都不许动，世代相传。有人认为这可以算是"最早的自然保护区"。事实上，有"罕山"的地方，大多真的成了今天的自然保护区。

In most Mongolian banners there is a "Rare Mountain" or "Obo Mountain" which is considered to be sacred, and a site for sacrifices. Nobody is allowed to disturb any of the grasses, trees, rocks or soil upon it, a tradition which has lasted for generations. Some people think that these can be considered the earliest "nature reserves". In fact, many of these places that have "Rare Mountain" are now modern-day nature reserves.

传统·习俗
Traditions and Customs

摄影：苏伟伟

冬钓
Winter angling

文：莫久愿

宋朝有人出使契丹时看到，人们在冬季的河湖冰面上搭建毡庐，凿开冰洞后"举火照之"，等冰下的鱼迎着光聚过来，然后垂钓。达斡尔人至今延续着这个传统，每年年末，都会在嫩江的冰面上举办"冬钓节"，展示这种悠久的渔猎习俗。

The envoys of the Song Dynasty to the Khitan state noticed that in the winter the Khitan people would set up their yurts on the ice of the lake, and they would chisel a hole in the ice and illuminate it with a torch. When the fish gathered around, they would catch them with hooks. The Daur people continue this tradition into the present day, and at the end of every year they have "Winter Angling Festival" on the Nenjiang River, where they show off their ancient fishing customs.

牧民不赌钱
Shepherds don't gamble

文：张弓长

草原上有各种或简或繁的棋类游戏，但从不拿来赌钱。胜者可获得一些牧民自制的点心和奶食品，负者则要用嘴咬着棋盘向胜者行礼问安，或按所输棋子个数"赏喝"几碗凉水。

In all manner of chess games on the grassland, simple or complex, one doesn't bet money. Winners might be given some snacks or milk products, and losers can bite the chessboard and salute the winner, or drink a few "penalty" bowl of cold water for each piece yielded.

蒙古人天生爱唱歌
Mongolians are born with a love for singing

文：黄蕾

蒙古人天生爱唱歌，不管欢乐还是悲伤，逢节必唱，有酒必歌。歌声伴随蒙古人的生活，让他们获得心灵的自由。

Mongolians are born with a love for singing; be they happy or sad songs they must be sung at every festival, and accompanied by liquor. Songs are the constant companions of the Mongolian people which allow their souls to feel free.

微观内蒙古
INNER MONGOLIA: COLOURFUL AND MAGNIFICENT

第三个"妈妈"
The "third mother"

文：莫久愚

土默特蒙古族婚礼保留着一些传统的迎娶习惯。婚礼开始前，要为新娘行梳头礼，请一位家境体面的成年妇女为新娘改换发型，象征姑娘从此变成媳妇，而为她梳头的妇女就此把新娘当成自己的女儿一样关怀照顾，终生来往，成为新娘除生母、婆婆以外的第三个"妈妈"。

The Tumd people of Mongolia have preserved some traditional wedding customs. Before the wedding starts, a woman from a respected household is selected to perform the hair brushing ceremony for the bride, doing her hairstyle to mark her transition to married life. The woman who does this assumes a role in which she cares for the bride as if she were her own daughter, and from then on is considered her godmother, the "third mother" after her own mother and mother-in-law.

郭雨桥　供稿

鄂伦春男人
Oroqen men

文：莫久愚

鄂伦春作家敖长福、敖荣凤说，每一个民族都有许多或悲壮或缠绵的故事。"鄂伦春男人并非全是粗犷、剽悍，他们也温柔敦厚。放下猎枪后的鄂伦春男人，腼腆起来却像是一个姑娘。他们机灵、精悍、能干，而且善于忍耐。"

Oroqen authors Ao Changfu and Ao Rongfeng say that every ethnicity has its own story, be it solemn and stirring, or lingering and lasting. "The Oroqen men aren't completely rough and doughty. They're also honest and sincere. After they lay down their shotguns, some of them become timid and shy as girls. They are clever, capable, vigorous, and patient."

传统·习俗
Traditions and Customs

摄影：苏伟伟

鄂伦春女子
Oroqen women

文：莫久愚

作家雪枝子认为，鄂伦春女子个个有本事，能制作各种桦皮工艺品。随着社会变化，"鄂家女子深入到了每一个行业，且多有建树。政界、商界、科研、艺术界，在哪里都像练过武功一般身手齐全，要风得风，要雨得雨，到处闪光……鄂族女人敢于与剽悍的鄂族男人争高低"。

Author Xue Zhizi believes that all Oroqen women are quite capable, and fashion all manner of works out of birch bark. As society changes, "the Oroqen women have penetrated all fields of social life deeply. In government, business, science, and art, one will find many skilled and successful Oroqen women, capable of all kinds of things. They're definitely a match for the agile and brave Oroqen men".

83

微观内蒙古
INNER MONGOLIA: COLOURFUL AND MAGNIFICENT

爱分享的鄂伦春人
Sharing among the Oroqen people
文：莫久愚

旧时鄂伦春猎人有与人分享猎物的习惯，自己的食物过多时也要分给别人。作家敖长福感慨，这种传统"致使一部分鄂伦春人今天还没学会积累"。

The Oroqen people have a tradition of sharing after a hunt, giving whatever excess they have to others. Author Ao Changfu remarks with emotion, this tradition means that "there are some Oroqen people even today that don't have a concept of stockpiling".

针线好呀不好？
Sewing skills
文：郭雨桥

过去蒙古族人说媒，要问："针线好呀不好？"针线营生是蒙古族姑娘成婚的重要条件。她们见面时会打量对方的衣服，看看有没有好的图案花纹可以"替回去"，出嫁前要亲手缝制自己的婚礼礼服，还要给曾一起玩耍的小姐妹们每人做一个绣花鼻烟壶袋、荷包或针插子，作为纪念。

When matchmaking occured in past Inner Mongolia, sewing skills would be asked about. Skill at sewing is an important factor for deciding matches. When the girls meet each other, they will evaluate the quality of the stitching and patterns on the clothing, and see if there's something they can learn from. Before a girl marries, she must make her own wedding dress, and make snuff bottle bags, pouches, or pincushions for her playmates as presents to remember the occasion by.

摄影：郭雨桥

传统·习俗
Traditions and Customs

口耳相传的家谱
Orally taught family history

文：莫久愚

呼伦贝尔巴尔虎蒙古族的许多家庭，男孩子每天早晚要像背诵歌谣一样，稚声稚气地背诵自家父系祖先十几代以来的名讳和顺序。这是一种辨别父系血缘的古老习俗。《魏书》序纪中关于拓跋鲜卑人的早期世系，《蒙古秘史》中黄金家族祖先的记载，就是依赖这种口耳相传的家族记忆传承下来的。

There are many families among the Barag Mongolians of Hulun Buir in which the sons each morning and night recite the names of their ancestors like rehearsing a song. With their young voices, they chant the names of more than ten generations of ancestors and their titles. This is an ancient tradition for keeping track of one's paternal lineage. *The Book of Wei*'s description about the early history of the Tuoba tribe of the Xianbei people, and *The Secret History of Mongolia*'s records on the Golden Family's ancestors are all told in this way from fathers to sons.

达斡尔人的摇篮
Daur cradles

文：莫久愚

达斡尔人制作"达日德（摇篮）"非常讲究：要请心地善良、正派、手巧的工匠，最好是兄弟姐妹多或儿女多的人。要从茂密的林子里精心挑选稠李子树，树干得是向太阳方向弯斜的，不选独木，被雷击、被风刮倒的也不能入选。他们相信这样的摇篮里长大的孩子才会身心健康，才会多兄弟姐妹，能互相照应。

The cradles that the Daur people produce are quite well-crafted. One must hire a virtuous, upright and skilled worker, preferably those with many siblings or children. A good plum tree growing in the thick wood with branches curving in the direction of the sun must be used, with trees growing alone, having been struck by lightning, or felled by wind not being eligible for selection. They believe that only with this kind of material for a cradle will the child who sleeps in it grow up healthily, with many siblings that will get on nicely.

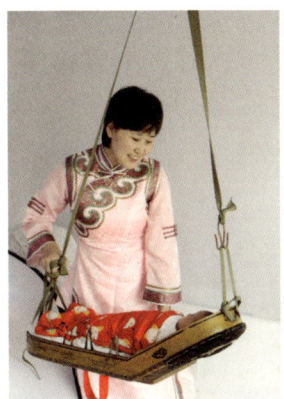

摄影：苏伟伟　　　　内蒙古达斡尔学会　供稿

微观内蒙古
INNER MONGOLIA: COLOURFUL AND MAGNIFICENT

达斡尔人的思乡菜

Daur nostalgic vegetables

文：莫久燕

柳蒿就是内地的蒌蒿，是达斡尔人最喜欢食用的时令野蔬。达斡尔人几乎都是吃着柳蒿长大的。他们喜欢在近水台地上居住，伴水而生的柳蒿成了他们生活的一部分，即使移居城市，也会在五月里寻找城外的河滩水淖，看看是不是有柳蒿生长其间，每年一度的采摘成了他们对自己家乡的定期礼拜。

The common mugwort is the favourite vegetable of the Daur people. The Daur grow up eating it and, as they like to live next to bodies of water, thus they traditionally had easy access to the water vegetable which has become part of their lives. Now that many of them live in the city, in May they'll go to the outskirts and look around to see if the mugwort is growing—thus, they worship their ancestral homelands at this time every year.

摄影：苏伟伟

达斡尔妈妈的顶针

Daur thimbles

文：达子

达斡尔妈妈缝衣服的时候戴的顶针跟汉族妈妈的不一样。汉族的顶针戴在中指，像戒指一样；达斡尔的顶针戴食指上，是锥形，戴上不露指尖，这样的形状不容易顶着指尖。达斡尔妈妈缝衣服的时候，针尖朝着自己的身体，不会扎到别人。一个小小的顶针透露了人性的温暖。

When Daur mothers sew clothing, they use a different kind of thimble from the Han Chinese. Han thimbles are worn on the middle finger and resemble a ring in form; Daur thimbles are worn on the index finger and are conical in shape, covering the fingertip, in which case the fingertip will not be hurt by the needle. When Daur mothers sew, they point the tip of the needle towards their own bodies, as to avoid poking others. A small detail like this shows their loving care.

传统·习俗
Traditions and Customs

蒙古包的功用
The functions of the yurt

文：张弓长

许多定居的蒙古人家庭仍然储备着蒙古包。它搭盖方便，两个人拆卸一座蒙古包不会超过10分钟。千百年来，蒙古人搬迁时，对每个部件的功用早已烂熟于心，闭着眼也不会装错。更令人叹服的是，蒙古人在搬迁时还要把蒙古包的围毡做成驮屉，把乌尼（细木椽）做成驮架，把哈纳（网格状支架）变成铺车板，把覆盖的毛毡或布用来裹包袱。

Many people who live in fixed homes in Inner Mongolia still keep a yurt around. It's easy to set up, and two people can disassemble it in less than 10 minutes. For centuries, when Mongolians moved the yurt, it was a process they knew by heart, something they could do with their eyes closed. What's even more impressive is that they could use the wooden poles to make a horseback cargo rack with the felt as a container on it, and use the grid-shaped supports to make the floor of a cart, and the other cloth coverings to wrap objects into bundles.

达斡尔族"其卡密"
Qikami boots of the Daur

文：达子

"其卡密"是达斡尔人特有的一种皮制的靴子。用狍子的下腿皮毛朝外拼缝成靴靿，用生牛皮做底。把牛皮用水泡软后跟靴帮缝合，牛皮干后会变得异常坚硬耐磨。然后在脚背上镶嵌一些漂亮的具有民族特色的牙边，一双漂亮的"其卡密"就可以穿在脚上了。

"Qikami" are the special leather boots worn by the Daur people. The skin from the lower legs of a roe deer is used to make the body of the boot, and cow rawhide is used to make the sole. The rawhide is soaked in water until it's soft and then sewn onto the body of the boot. After it dries, it becomes especially hard and durable. On the back of the foot some ethnic tooth-patterns are inlaid, and then the boot is ready to wear.

摄影：孔群

微观内蒙古
INNER MONGOLIA: COLOURFUL AND MAGNIFICENT

草原人尊崇母亲

Respect for mothers on the grasslands

文：张弓长

在蒙语中，母亲叫作"额吉"。鲍尔吉·原野说："草原上的人们极端尊崇母亲。在蒙古民歌中，对母亲的思念挚情，超过对爱情的咏诵。母亲是创造者。在牧人眼里，天地之后居于第三位的，不是君主，而是母亲。"

The Mongolian word for mother is "eji". Borjigin Yuanye says: "People on the grasslands have great respect for their mothers. In Mongolian folk songs, there are more songs about thinking of one's mother than there are simple love songs. The mother is the creator. In the eyes of the nomads, on the third place just behind Heaven and earth, is their mothers, rather than the reigning monarch."

"移动的家"

"Mobile home"

文：张弓长

民俗学者郭雨桥说，汉族把住宅叫"家园"，因为家后面总跟着个"园"子。蒙古族家庭主人的后面往往跟着一溜"勒勒车"。"勒勒"据说是牧民吆喝牲口的声音。赶着牛马，载着一家老小，车一走，家就跟着走了。

Folklorist Guo Yuqiao says that the traditional Han Chinese concept of a "home" includes a garden or yard, whereas that of the Mongolians includes a string of "Lele carts". "Lele" is said to be the word used by herders urging the animals. When the carts move, the home moves.

摄影：贾文廷

传统·习俗
Traditions and Customs

摄影：高雷峰

餐桌上识别蒙古人
Mongolians at the table

文：莫久愚

在吃过手把肉的餐桌上，你见谁面前的骨头洁白干净不见一丝肉，就知道他一定是蒙古人。虽然草原不乏肉食，在草原生活过的蒙古人，无论贫富高下，都会用刀将骨头缝隙的肉刮得干干净净。许多在内蒙古牧区下过乡的北京知青，也保留着这种习惯。

When eating boiled meat, if you see people eat the bones so clean that no meat or cartilage remains, you'll know they're Mongolians. Food isn't scarce on the grasslands, but people who've lived there, regardless of economic standing, will use a knife to dig out all the meat from every crevasse in the bone, leaving it completely clean. A number of educated youth from the capital who've lived in Inner Mongolia have picked up this habit.

临时决定的婚礼
Shotgun wedding

文：莫迪

蒙古族传统婚礼，犹如一场悠长的歌舞表演。1987 年秋，在乌兰察布旅游的美国青年肯特·马丁和琳达·斯文森被草原美景和民俗打动，临时决定就地举行婚礼。牧民为他们操办了一场蒙古式的婚礼，一些老人自愿扮演双方的"家人"，"聘娶"时仍有虚拟的问答、诙谐的对歌及热情的祝颂辞，浪漫而热烈。

Mongolian traditional wedding ceremonies are like a long song and dance performance. In the autumn of 1987, an American couple Kent Martin and Linda Swanson travelling on the grasslands of Ulan Qab were quite moved by the sights and local customs, and decided to have a local-style wedding there. The locals organised a real Mongolian wedding for them, where a number of old people played the part of their respective "families". For the more traditional question-and-answer, humorous antiphonal singing and congratulatory speech, the locals filled in with songs and poetry to make a great atmosphere full of romance and energy.

89

微观内蒙古
INNER MONGOLIA: COLOURFUL AND MAGNIFICENT

阿爸
Daddy

文：娜仁托娅

妈妈说，阿爸在我刚出生没多久就带着朋友来家里看他的女儿，这在鄂温克人家是禁忌。阿爸全然不顾家门上挂着的红布条，迫不及待地炫耀女儿。童年时，阿爸经常带我去森林里捡木头，采野果，让我趴在地上喝河水，扶我骑马，让我养狗，带我打鱼……教我野外生存的本领，他以为，我会在那里生活一辈子。

Mummy said that right after I was born, daddy brought his friends around to see his new-born daughter, which is a taboo in Ewenki culture. Daddy ignored the red strip of cloth hung around the door, as he couldn't resist showing off his child. When I was young, daddy would frequently bring me into the forest to collect wood and pick wild fruits, let me lie on the ground to drink from streams, help me ride horses, show me how to raise dogs, take me fishing, etc. He thus taught me the principles of survival in nature. He believed I'd live there my entire life.

包子塔人家
People of Baozita

文：苏怀亮

准格尔旗黄河岸边包子塔梁峁上，有一个不足 20 户人家的村寨，村子房屋除了门窗，完全用石头建造；家家户户都是工匠，木匠、石匠、铁匠、泥瓦匠都有。20 户人家的小村里竟有大小 19 座庙宇，其中一座还供奉着人根。真是一个神秘的村落。

On the Baozita Ridge beside the Yellow River, Jungar Banner, there is a village of less than 20 families where all the structures, except for the windows and doors, are constructed entirely of stone. Everyone there is a craftsman—carpenter, mason, smith, or plasterer. In addition to the 20 or so homes, there are also 19 temples large and small in the village, and in one of which there is a man's penis being enshrined and worshiped. It's truly a mysterious place.

摄影：莫久愚

传统·习俗
Traditions and Customs

女人有钱戴在头上，男人有钱拴在马上
Women's money is on their heads, while men's on their horses

文：郭雨桥

蒙古牧民不像汉族农民那样有点儿小钱就攒起来，也没有多少坛坛罐罐。妇女喜欢往头上打扮，除了玲珑精美的头戴外，还有许多附属佩饰。男人则把自己的马鞍镶银、雕花、烧蓝，华美多彩。王公贵族的鼻烟壶，一个就能换一群马。王爷的蒙古刀，刀鞘上往往镶满珊瑚和松石，极尽奢华之能事，是身份和地位的象征。

Unlike the farmers of Han nationality, the herders of Mongolia don't save up small amounts of money, and don't have moneyboxes, either. Women like to decorate their heads with all kind of precious adornments and accessories. Men decorate their horses' saddles with silver inlay, carving, and enamel, which look gorgeous. A single snuff bottle of the nobilities is worth as much as a herd of horses. The special knife carried by the princes is inlaid with all manner of coral and turquoise in a very luxurious manner, as it is a symbol of status.

摄影：高晋峰

微观内蒙古
INNER MONGOLIA: COLOURFUL AND MAGNIFICENT

禄马风旗
Lumafeng Banner

文：张弓长

鄂尔多斯多数牧人家房前，都可以看到两杆长矛状的旗杆，旗杆之间由一根长绳或衡木连接起来，上面拴挂着迎风飘舞的五色彩旗，中间地面上往往垒砌有一座可以燃火焚香的祭台。这是鄂尔多斯蒙古人特有的标志——象征吉祥、兴旺的禄马风旗。除夕夜，要换上新旗；婴儿降生、子女结婚，要重新升旗；有老人去世，要降下旗来。

In front of the houses of many Ordos herders one can see two lance-shaped flagpoles with a rope or horizontal wooden pole connecting them, hung with pennants in five colours. There is an altar on the ground between the poles, burning with incense. These decorations are unique to the Ordos Mongolians—Lumafeng Banner, a symbol of luckiness and prosperity. On new year's eve, new pennants are put up. When a child is born or there is a marriage, the pennants are raised up. When an elder dies, the pennants are lowered.

摄影：戴东辉

传统·习俗
Traditions and Customs

摄影：希龙道尔吉

对旗帜的祭奠
Banner worship ceremonies

文：莫久愚

哈日苏勒德（黑纛 dào）是一面神圣的旗帜，蒙古人把它作为民族精神和意志的象征，尊奉了八百年，时至今日，成吉思汗陵仍将此旗作为神灵祭祀。在鄂尔多斯，象征祖先功业的旗帜都被当作神来供奉、祭祀。查干苏勒德（白纛）和阿拉格苏勒德（花纛），也都有说不完的故事。牧人们虔诚的祭礼让人感到心灵的震撼。

The Black Banner is a sacred flag and a symbol of the spirit and will of the Mongolian people. It's been respected for 800 years, and still flies at the gravesite of Genghis Khan. In Ordos, it flies as a testament to the achievements of the ancestors. There are also the White Banner and the Patterned Banner, which have long stories of their own. The pious rituals of the shepherds are a moving sight to see.

砖茶情结
The love for tea bricks

文：莫久愚

蒙古族多食肉、奶，少蔬菜，故须喝茶来消食解腻。蒙古族民谚说："宁可三日无粮，不可一日无茶。"旧时到朋友家中做客或参加喜庆活动，带去砖茶做见面礼会很有面子。土默特蒙古族婚嫁时会把砖茶当作最重要的彩礼。今天蒙古族的重大祭礼上，砖茶仍是必备祭品。

Drinking tea helps the Mongolians to digest the meat and milk which account for a high proportion in their daily meals. A Mongolian saying goes: "It's better to go three days without food than a day without tea." In ancient times when people would visit a friend's home or participate in a celebration, bringing a tea brick as a gift was considered a very good move. The Tumd people of Mongolia consider a tea brick to be an important gift at weddings, and at large-scale sacrificial ceremonies even today, a tea brick is an essential item.

摄影：石玉平

地理·物产

Geography and Products

微观内蒙古
INNER MONGOLIA: COLOURFUL AND MAGNIFICENT

大地的色彩
Colours of the landscape

文：莫久愚

内蒙古的大地，犹如一位粗心的画家，笔蘸绿色漫不经心地涂抹了一笔。起始的东北部色重饱满，那里有兴安岭浓密的森林和亚洲最好的草场；到了中部色彩逐渐变淡甚至开始枯涩，那是由典型草原向荒漠化草原过渡；再向西部，笔枯墨竭，色彩逐渐消失，那是荒漠草原最后没入戈壁、黄沙中了。

The landscape of Inner Mongolia looks like that it is painted by a careless painter, with broad green brush strokes. The northeast is where one finds the most saturated colours, and in the Hinggan Range areas, one sees the dense forests and Asia's best pastures. By the time it comes for the "painter" to paint the middle region, the ink runs thin and colours transit from pale to wilted, as this is where we see the transition from grassland to desert. Further west, the ink runs out, and almost all of the green colour is gone—this is where the landscape of the Gobi desert appears, all sand, all yellow.

温柔的兴安岭
The gentle Hinggan Range

文：莫久愚

在内蒙古东部，南北绵延 1400 公里的大兴安岭并不高耸，绝少陡峭突兀的山峰。老舍先生形容："每条岭都是那么温柔……谁也不孤峰突起，盛气凌人。"世代居住在森林中的鄂伦春人、鄂温克人，也如这山岭般内敛、沉默、善良、宽厚，不急躁不计较，严酷的生存环境锻造了他们超凡的耐力，也给了他们包容的温柔。

In the east part of Inner Mongolia, the Greater Hinggan Range stretchs for 1,400 kilometres, peaks mostly humble in height, neither steep nor towering. Writer Lao She thus described them: "Each peak has such a gentle feel... none will experience that feeling of oppression one does when looking upon a giant mountain." The Oroqens and Ewenkis that live in the forests in these areas for generations are the same: calm, reserved, kind, generous and welcoming. Living in the harsh environment has given them patience, as well as compassion and warmth.

摄影：石玉平

地理·物产
GEOGRAPHY AND Products

摄影：闫钟鹏

大地的脊梁
"Backbone" of the land

文：莫久愚

内蒙古东西狭长，横跨东北、华北、西北，很多朋友喜欢把内蒙古地图喻作一匹腾飞的骏马。大兴安岭、阴山、贺兰山这个弧形的隆起就好似它的脊梁。又好似群山协力，托举着北方草原。

Inner Mongolia extends quite far from west to east, lying in the Northwestern, North, and North-eastern China regions. Some people liken its shape on the map to a galloping horse. The Greater Hinggan Range, Yinshan Mountains, and the Helan Mountains form a long arc known as the "backbone" of Inner Mongolia. It's as if this giant geological structure lifts and supports China's northern grasslands.

贺兰山
Helan Mountains

文：莫久愚

内蒙古弧形山系最西端的贺兰山，是内蒙古最像"山"的山体。高耸伟岸的身躯阻挡着北方的寒冷和风沙，分隔出泾渭分明的两个世界。山前是良畴千里的银川平原，号称北国江南；背后是一望无垠的黄沙戈壁，那是骆驼的乐土。山脚下长城上那三道关口，曾是明王朝西北方向的重要门户，如今是银川通往阿拉善盟的必经之路。

The west most section of the arc-shaped mountain ranges in Inner Mongolia are Helan Mountains, which are most typical in shape among many others in this region. The coldness and dust brought by the north wind cannot get over the high mountains; therefore two totally different worlds are created. To the south spreads the fertile Yinchuan Plain, which looks like an area south of the Yangtze River. To the north are the endless Gobi deserts, which are happy homes for camels. A section of the Great Wall lies at the foot of Helan Mountains, on top of which there are three passes—formerly the northwestern gateways vital to the Ming Dynasty, and now the must-pass routes between Yinchuan and Alxa League.

微观内蒙古
INNER MONGOLIA: COLOURFUL AND MAGNIFICENT

摄影：石玉平

不冻河
Unfreezing river

文：莫久愚

神奇的阿尔山，既有夏日不融的冰沟，也有入冬不冻的河流。由于附近有大量地热，哈拉哈河一段长约20公里的河道，在大雪封山的时候，在零下40℃以下的气温里仍不封冻。隆冬季节，两岸白雪皑皑，玉树琼枝，而近水草木，仍然青翠不凋；河中清流汩汩，碧草摇曳；河面烟雾蒙蒙，云蒸霞蔚。

Mount Arxan has some ice ditches that stay frozen in the summer, as well as some rivers that don't freeze in the winter. As there is a large amount of geothermal energy here, the Halhiyn River has a stretch of about 20 kilometres that doesn't freeze even when there's heavy snow around, and the temperature reaches 40 ℃ below freezing. In the depth of winter, the banks are covered with snow, and the branches on trees hang heavy with ice, but the trees and grasses near the river are still green. The river flows vigorously, with green grasses wavering in it as mists rise from the surface.

黄河至北点
Northernmost point of the Yellow River

文：张铁良

黄河从青藏高原走来，一路奔腾，百折千回，在阴山脚下，让本该是沙地的河套成为八百里沃野，灌渠密布，麦浪滚滚。河水肆意奔流，在五原县境内，黄河龙身一摆，向北甩来，差一点就和阴山接吻。这里就是万里黄河流经的最北点，坐标东经107°53′55″，北纬40°52′24″。

The Yellow River originates on the Qinghai-Tibet Plateau and flows rapidly for a great distance through many twists and turns. At the foot of Yinshan Mountains is the vast and fertile Hetao Plain, which should be a barren sand land if not for the Yellow River. The Yellow River rolls and bubbles freely, and is the source of many irrigation canals in Hetao Plain, which provide plenty water for the wheat fields. In Wuyuan County, the river takes a turn northward, and "kisses" the Yinshan Mountains. This is the northernmost point of the river, at 107°53′55″E, 40°52′24″N.

地理·物产
GEOGRAPHY AND PRODUCTS

农牧交界地带
Ecotone between pasture and farmland

文：莫久愚

北起大兴安岭东麓经辽河上游至阴山南麓平原，向西南到鄂尔多斯高原，东西几千公里，是世界四大农牧交错带之一，可耕可牧。随着历史上气候的变化，有过多次牧场和农田的转换，一些大规模的民族冲突和深层次的民族融合也在这里开始，让农夫同牧人们接触不断，把草原和中原紧密联系在一起。

Travelling upon the Liaohe River from the eastern feet of the Greater Hinggan Range south to the plains at the southern feet of the Yinshan Mountains, and then southwest to the Ordos Plateau is a journey of a few thousand kilometres, one of the world's four largest ecotones between pasture and farmland. Both herding and cultivating crops are possible here. As climates have changed over history, there have been many instances of pasture turning into farmland and vice versa. Large-scale ethnic conflicts and long-term ethnic blending have also taken place here, putting farmers and herders into contact, forming a tight relation between the two groups, and drawing nearer the northern area to the Central Plains.

"一面山"
"The mountain with only one face"

文：莫久愚

如果是晴日，在往来于呼和浩特和巴彦淖尔的航班上透过舷窗俯瞰阴山，会看到它南面陡峭，河套平原和土默川大地如同从阴山山前塌落下来；北坡平缓，化作一系列低山丘陵没入高原。若是从地面跨越阴山，汽车会沿着山路盘旋至高耸的山脊，然后便不知不觉地进入了草原，并无下山的感觉。

On a clear day, if you take a flight between Hohhot and Bayannur, you'll see Yinshan Mountains beneath you, with a steep south face. The Hetao Plain and Tumd Plain seem to have toppled down from the mountain. The northern face of the mountain are gentle slopes, blending smoothly in the grassland below. If you cross the mountain from the ground, driving down a twisting route up to and down from the peak you'll suddenly discover you're in the grassland, without feeling you have descended a mountain.

可以输出的阳光
Solar power output

文：莫久愚

从清晨的第一缕阳光投射到内蒙古东部，太阳需要两小时才能照亮整个内蒙古。内蒙古大部地区年降雨量不足300毫米，一年四季阳光明媚，太阳能总辐射仅次于西藏。加之拥有丰富的优质硅矿资源，光伏制造产业不断向内蒙古集中。2015年，太阳能发电装机规模达到2600兆瓦，内蒙古正在成为"阳光能源"输出基地。

It needs as long as two hours after the first ray of sunlight reaches the easternmost portion of Inner Mongolia for the entire autonomous region be illuminated. Since annual rainfall in most regions is less than 300 mm, sun shines all year long, with the solar flux over the surface second only to that of Tibet. Combined with plentiful silicon resources, photovoltaic device production has continuously been concentrated in the region. In 2015, capacity reached 2.6 GW, making Inner Mongolia a huge outputter of solar energy.

微观内蒙古
INNER MONGOLIA: COLOURFUL AND MAGNIFICENT

黑与白
Black and white

文：莫久愚

鄂尔多斯地下蕴藏着丰富的煤炭，一座城市，每年提供全国六分之一的用煤。这里的优质高岭土探明储量占全国的半数以上。高岭土往往与煤炭共生，白的细腻，黑的纯净，相伴而生，却又黑白分明，仿佛是大自然的某种昭示。

There are extensive coal resources under the ground in Ordos—the city yields one-sixth of China's annual coal output. The high-quality kaolin porcelain clay here coexists with the coal, and the clay's reserves are also more than half of China's total. Fine white and pure black clay come together here, a sharp contrast that seems almost to be a kind of sign from nature.

阿尔山·柴河火山群
Arxan-Chaihe volcanic cluster

文：莫久愚

在大兴安岭中段的林业开发中，一个火山地貌景观被揭开了神秘面纱。面积超过欧洲最大的火山地质公园奥弗涅火山群数倍，世界最大的功能型矿泉群、亚洲最大的火山熔岩地貌都在这里。高山火山口湖、平地火山口湖、火山熔岩堰塞湖、火山锥、熔岩丘、熔岩断裂峡谷……如同一部火山地质教科书。

In the middle of the Greater Hinggan Range where forestry development is taking place, an impressive volcanic landscape has been revealed. With an area a number of times larger than Europe's largest volcanic park, the Auvergne region, the cluster also has the world's largest functional group of springs, and the largest landscape composed of volcanic rock in Asia. With crater lakes both at the tops of high mountains and on the flat ground, volcanically-formed barrier lakes, volcanic cones, lava domes, and lava canyons… the place is like a geological encyclopaedia.

摄影：高雪峰

地理·物产
GEOGRAPHY AND PRODUCTS

摄影：张松云

草原上的"空中三峡"
A "Three Gorges" power plant on the grassland

文：莫久愚

戈壁草原的风，亘古不变地向南吹，送来的不只是寒流，还是一种可以转换为光和热的力量。内蒙古可开发风能资源1.5亿千瓦，居中国首位。如今在戈壁中、草原上、农田旁，到处矗立着风力发电机，2015年全区风电装机容量达到2256万千瓦，超过了"三峡大坝"的装机容量。

The wind on the Gobi grasslands blows continually towards the south, but what it brings isn't cold, but rather the potential to be converted into warmth and light. The wind here could generate 150 GW of energy, the most in China. In the Gobi deserts, on the grasslands, in the fields, everywhere one sees wind turbines, and in 2015 the power generation in Inner Mongolia reached 22.56 GW, exceeding the Three Gorges Dam in power generation capacity.

稀土之都
Rare earth capital

文：莫久愚

包头的白云鄂博是一座宝山，稀土储量占全世界探明储量的近50%。众多的稀土企业和科研院所是包头的特色。稀土是铁的共生矿，包钢选出铁矿粉后，富含稀土的"尾矿"被排入尾矿坝中。一位看护尾矿坝的工人说："别小看这些像淤泥一样的矿浆，现在的高新材料都离不开它，全世界可都盯着这儿呢。"

Bayan Obo in Baotou is a resource-rich mountain which contains nearly 50% of the world's rare earth element resources, and for this reason there are a number of rare earth companies and research institutes in Baotou. These elements occur in ores with iron, and after the Baotou Steel Group extracts the iron, the tailings are added to a reserve, from where the rare earth elements can be extracted. One of the watchmen at the reserve said: "Don't think of the slurry as waste, there are some important things within it—things which the whole world wants."

微观内蒙古
INNER MONGOLIA: COLOURFUL AND MAGNIFICENT

摄影：黄美荣

中国最长的省际大通道
Longest interprovincial road in China

文：莫久愚

从鄂尔多斯高原的蒙陕边界直通呼伦贝尔的阿荣旗，纵贯大半个内蒙古，全长约 2512 公里。双向四车道，道路平，路况好，车辆少，视野开阔。一路扑面而来的是沙漠、荒漠草原、沙地疏林、一望无际的农田，先后跨越阴山丘陵、兴安岭山地。景色粗犷，民风豪放，是一条认识内蒙古地貌的景观长廊。

From Ordos Plateau on the border with Shaanxi Province to Arun Banner in Hulun Buir, this road extends through a large portion of Inner Mongolia and has a total length of 2,512 kilometres. With two lanes in each direction, the road is flat, in good condition, sparsely used, and enjoys a great view in all directions. One can see desert, arid grasslands, sandy savannah, endless fields, and the Yinshan Mountains and Hinggan Range. The views are vibrant, and full of ethnic feeling. It's as if the road is a corridor in a museum of natural Inner Mongolian beauty.

乳都
Milk capital

文：莫久愚

呼和浩特是目前中国牛奶产量最大的乳业生产基地，奶牛存栏、鲜奶产量和人均鲜奶占有量均在全中国大中城市居第一位。中国两大著名乳品企业伊利集团和蒙牛集团总部都在这里。2005 年 8 月，呼和浩特市被中国乳制品工业协会命名为"中国乳业之都"。那座 8 米见方的花岗岩巨鼎雕塑就是呼和浩特乳业兴盛的标志。

Hohhot is currently China's largest production base for milk. It's first in terms of livestock on hand, milk produced, and milk consumption per capita in all of China. It is also the site of the headquarters of both Yili and Mengniu, China's two largest milk producers. In August of 2005, Hohhot was designated by the Chinese Dairy Industry Association as the "Capital of Chinese Milk". There is even a giant, 8-metre-tall granite statue here which marks its significance as the centre of milk production in China.

地理·物产
Geography and Products

内蒙古的煤炭
Coal in Inner Mongolia

文：莫久愚

内蒙古大地经历了多次海陆变迁，把曾经繁茂的陆地植物和海洋生物反复地埋在地下，转化为丰富的煤炭、天然气。它们地质构造简单，埋藏浅，煤层厚，有的厚达四五百米。中国五大露天煤矿，正在运营的四座都在内蒙古。一座煤矿的产量动辄几千万吨，让一些来自贫煤省份的客人咋舌。

Over the eons, Inner Mongolia has undergone a number of land-sea changes, with formerly dense land plant and aquatic life buried underground over and over again, which have been tranformed into a large amount of coal and natural gas reserves. The geologic construction is simple, and the resources are not buried deep underground, with thick layers of coal, some four or five hundred metres thick. Four of the five largest open pit coal mines in China are in operation, all of which are in Inner Mongolia. A coal mine here can easily produce tens of millions of tonnes coal, evoking jealousy in people who come from provinces lacking the resource.

胡杨
Poplars in Inner Mongolia

文：莫久愚

为抵御干旱，胡杨体内贮存了很多水分。划破树皮，它会流"泪"，锯断树干，它会喷溅出三尺高的"血水"。即便枯死，它也会倔强地挺直身躯，迎风挥舞着枯萎的臂膀，仿佛在召唤绿色，挽留时光。

The poplars in Inner Mongolia have large internal water reserves to protect against the dangers of dry spells. If the bark is cut, "tears" will come out, and if the tree is chopped down, a metre-high "fountain" of water will erupt. Even when the trees die, they stand firmly, withered branches dancing in the winds, almost as if beckoning the green to return, to turn back time.

摄影：石玉平

微观内蒙古
INNER MONGOLIA: COLOURFUL AND MAGNIFICENT

摄影：达楞

阿尔巴斯绒山羊
Alpas white cashmere goats

文：莫久愚

全球 2／3 的山羊绒来自中国，其中近一半出自内蒙古。世界上最好的白绒山羊，是鄂尔多斯阿尔巴斯羊。周岁羊产绒 350 克以上，细度达 13 微米（国际标准是 15.3 微米以下）。当地的自然环境很适合绒山羊生长，羊绒的光泽、白度、手感、抗拉强度都堪称世界之最，有"白如雪、轻如云、细如丝"的美誉。

Two thirds of the cashmere in the world comes from China, and of that portion almost half comes from Inner Mongolia. The best white cashmere comes from the Alpas white cashmere goats of Ordos. The yearling yields wool that exceeds 350 grams in weight, and is thinner than 13 micrometres (the international standard requires the strands to be less than 15.3 micrometres in width). The natural environment there quite suits the growth of cashmere goats, and the wool that's yielded is of excellent quality in terms of lustre, whiteness, feeling, and tensile strength, earning it the distinction of the best wool in the world—"white as snow, light as a cloud, thin as silk".

"苏里格"
"Sulige"

文：莫久愚

在鄂尔多斯，"苏里格"是一个敖包的名字，当地人坚信，成吉思汗征讨西夏时曾在此地驻扎；它也是寺庙的名字，敖包脚下的苏里格庙是鄂尔多斯最大的寺庙；它还是我国最大的整装大气田的名字，苏里格气田探明储量近 30000 亿立方米。年产天然气 290 亿立方米，占全国天然气产量的 21.5%。

In Ordos, "Sulige" is the name of an obo, which people believe it is the place where Genghis Khan stationed his army on his expedition against the Xixia Dynasty. It's also the name of a temple, the Sulige Temple, which is the largest in Ordos. It's also the name of the country's largest natural gas field, the Sulige Gas Field, which has proven reserves of more than 3 trillion cubic metres. Each year it yields more than 29 billion cubic metres of gas, 21.5% of the country's total output.

地理·物产
Geography and Products

中国"薯都"
China's potato capital

文：莫久愚

在乌兰察布市乡间，到处可见马铃薯喷灌大田。全市马铃薯种植面积超过 400 万亩，占自治区的 1/2 以上，总产量达 50 亿公斤，在全国地级市中位居第一。这里的马铃薯原种基地可满足全国 70% 以上的马铃薯田的需求。当地马铃薯块形好，含淀粉高。这里有亚洲最大的马铃薯全粉生产线。

In the countryside of Ulan Qab, you can see irrigated potato fields everywhere. The area has more than 2,600 square kilometres of land dedicated to potato cultivation, more than half of the total for the entire autonomous region. Yearly production amounts to 5 billion kilograms, making Ulan Qab the top-producing city for potatoes in China. The potato seedling base here can satisfy 70% of the country's total demand. Potatos produced here have a nice shape, and are high in starch. Asia's largest production line of potato flour is situated here.

红干椒之都
The capital of dried red peppers

文：莫久愚

最喜欢吃辣的是四川人、湖南人，而辣椒产量最大的县却在内蒙古。每年秋收时节，通辽市开鲁县的田间地头成了红色的世界，空气中弥漫着辣椒的气息。种植面积超过 40 万亩，年产 1 亿公斤以上，号称"中国红干椒之都"。当地的红干椒，品质好、无污染、有独特的清香。

While those most enamoured with spicy tastes are people from Sichuan and Hunan Provinces, the biggest producer of spicy red peppers is in Inner Mongolia. At the end of each autumn, Kailu County in Tongliao City becomes a world of red, with the thick smell of red peppers permeating the atmosphere. More than 260 square kilometres are planted with red peppers, and more than 100 million kilograms are produced every year, giving the place the name "the capital of dried red peppers". The peppers produced here are of high quality, without any pollution, and have a unique flavour and fragrance.

摄影：王金

微观内蒙古
INNER MONGOLIA: COLOURFUL AND MAGNIFICENT

巴林石
Bairin stone

文：莫久愚

巴林右旗特尼格尔图山的石头，与福建、浙江的寿山石、青田石、昌化石并称为"中国四大印石"，上品可与黄金同价甚至超过黄金。这里的田黄石、鸡血石、冻石，质地细腻，色彩丰富，艳丽温润。2001年上海亚太经合组织会议上，与会各国及地区领导人都收到了一枚金黄色石料印章，它们都出自同一块巴林石。

The stones of Mount Tenegel in the Bairin Right Banner, along with the Shoushan, Qingtian, and Changhua stones of Fujian and Zhejiang Provinces, are called "Four Great Seal Stones of China", sometimes worth their weight or even more in gold. Here, the "field-yellow stones", "chicken-blood stones", and "agalmatolite" are of high quality, and exhibit beautiful bright colours. At the APEC meeting in 2001, each of the leaders was given a golden-coloured stone seal, which were all made from the same piece of Bairin stone.

荞麦之乡——库伦旗
Home of buckwheat—Hure Banner

文：莫久愚

白居易诗云："独出门前望野田，月明荞麦花如雪。"这是唐代大面积种植荞麦的景象，如今大概只在内蒙古通辽市的库伦旗才能看到了。这里荞麦种植面积超过40万亩，年产4000万公斤以上，占全中国的1/3。荞麦以单产高、色白、味香著称，已获国家原产地商标认证，日本和韩国客商是这里荞麦的老主顾。

Poet Bai Juyi said in a poem: "When you walk out of the door and look upon the vast wild fields, you'll see an expanse of buckwheat flowers, like a snowy landscape." This poem described the scene of large scale cultivation of buckwheat in Tang Dynasty, and now it is most likely only available to the modern viewer in the Hure Banner of Tongliao City in Inner Mongolia. There are more than 260 square kilometres of buckwheat under cultivation here, with more than 40 million kilograms produced each year, one third of all of Chinese production. Each area produces high-growing crops of white, fragrant grain that have been recognised as a local honored brand, and are in high demand by Japanese and South Korean customers.

摄影：王金

地理·物产
Geography and Products

摄影：石玉平

笤帚之乡
The centre of brooms

文：莫久愚

金秋时节，巴林左旗乌力吉木伦河两岸大片大片的红色笤帚苗随风摇曳，车辆满载着笤帚苗和加工好的笤帚来来往往。这里的笤帚苗是制作笤帚、炊具及各种特色工艺品的上好原料，很受内地客户的欢迎。全旗年加工销售笤帚3300万把，是全国最大的笤帚苗种植基地、加工基地和产品交易中心。

Against the backdrop of golden autumn colours, along the banks of the Uligi Murun River in Bairin Left Banner, large patches of red Kochia scoparia, wave in the wind, and trucks full of these plants and brooms made from them come and go. The plants here are used to make brooms, cooking utensils and all manner of other special crafts, and these products are widely sought after elsewhere in China. Every year more than 33 million of these brooms are sold, making this place the foremost producer of this kind of plant in China, as well as a production and trade centre.

中华麦饭石
Chinese maifanite

文：莫久愚

麦饭石是一种次火山岩斑状岩石，外观与大麦饭相似，故名。据说奈曼旗平顶山下有一个缺医少药的贫困村屯，人均寿命却比全国平均寿命高15岁，且很少有人患传染病和癌症，连家禽家畜也不染瘟疫。有人认为这得益于当地随处可见的麦饭石。由它浸泡的水相当于优质矿泉，可以吸附各种对人体有害的物质和菌群。

Chinese maifanite is a porphyritic rock that has the appearance of cooked grains ("maifan" in Chinese). It's said there is a poor village in the Naiman Banner where the people live about 15 years longer than the national average, rarely suffer from infectious diseases or cancers, and even have healthier livestock. People believe that this is due to the prevalence of the mineral maifanite in the area. Water that seeps through it is of excellent quality, as the material can absorb all kinds of toxic compounds and microorganisms.

微观内蒙古
INNER MONGOLIA: COLOURFUL AND MAGNIFICENT

黑骏马
Black fine horses

文：莫久愚

锡林郭勒草原流传的长调《黑骏马》歌唱一个骑着黑骏马的小伙子追寻恋人，歌中唱到的那匹骏马，纯黑发亮。阿巴嘎旗的特产"僧僧黑马"就是一种通体纯黑的蒙古马。在那达慕大会上，阿巴嘎旗的黑马队入场，犹如飘进一团黑雾；马队奔跑起来，乌云翻滚、遮云蔽日，又如黑色的风暴。

There is a Mongolian Long Song from Xilin Gol titled *Black Fine Horse*, which tells the tale of a young man riding a black horse pursuing his love. The horse is described in the song as being pure, deep black. Abag Banner's specialty are these black horses, a particular breed of Mongolian horses. During the Nadam Festival, the black horses of Abag come on the scene, like a cloud of black smoke. When they run together on the ground, kicking up the dust and blocking out the sun, it's like a dark windstorm.

蒙古马
Mongolian horses

文：莫久愚

蒙古马体型不够舒展，粗壮、矮小，但终年在草原上大群野放，是古代最理想的战马。比起当时在马厩中由专人精心饲喂的欧洲骑士马，它们忍耐力强，能适应最严酷的气候，持久力好，可以长距离奔跑、持续作战。有人认为，十三世纪征服欧洲的蒙古人，主要是依赖这种个头矮小、不知喘息的马。

The Mongolian horses are stout and short, but they were ideal warrior horses in ancient times for their breeding freely on the grasslands in large groups all over the year. Compare to horses of the European knights taken care of meticulously in barns, they have remarkable stamina and sustainbility, are suited to harsh climates. They can also gallop for a long distance without a stop. Somebody says that the Mongolians who conquered the Europe in 13th century should attribute their achievements to their little tireless horses.

摄影：石玉平

地理·物产
GEOGRAPHY AND PRODUCTS

摄影：高丽

绰尔河畔的稻田
Paddies on the banks of Chaor River

文：莫久愚

金秋9月，吃过手把肉，耳边飘着悠扬的草原乐曲，眼前却是金灿灿的稻田，一望无垠，沉甸甸的稻穗泛着诱人的光泽，田中沟塘中不断有鱼跃出水面，空气中弥漫着稻香。这是在大兴安岭下绰尔河畔的体验。这里的绿色有机水稻连续获得国际农产品交易会和世界农业博览会金奖。每公斤价格七八十元，却供不应求。

In September of golden autumn, eating hand-ripped mutton and listening to lilting melodies flow across the grassland, you'll see the brilliant rice paddies, bright gold themselves, ears of rice shining with an enticing bright light, fish jumping in the water of the irrigation channels as the fragrance of grain permeates the air. This is what it feels like at the foot of the Greater Hinggan Range, on the banks of the Chaor River. The organic rice grown here has won golden medals at both the International Agricultural Trade Fair and the World Agricultural Exposition. The price of the rice is high at 70-80 yuan a kilogram, however, the supply never meets demand.

"羊煤土气"
Wool, coal, clay and gas

文：苏怀亮

鄂尔多斯经济四大资源——羊（羊绒）、煤（煤炭）、土（高岭土）、气（天然气）——驰名中外。有人说，"羊煤土气"不仅是物质的，也可以用来比喻鄂尔多斯人的精神特质：性格像羊一样温顺随和，感情像煤炭一样蕴藏热情，品格像土地一样厚道承重，志气像天然气一样光焰万丈。

Ordos' four major economic areas are known as "yang mei tu qi" (there is a Chinese idiom with the same pronunciation means proundness or satisfaction about something): "Yang" is wool, "mei" is coal, "tu" is china clay, and "qi" is natural gas, all well-known in China and abroad. Some people say that these resources aren't just of economic significance, but also form a part of the soul of people living in Ordos. Their character is as soft as the wool, warm like the heat coal provides, kind like the land and soil that grows all living beings, and brilliant like a gas flame.

微观内蒙古
INNER MONGOLIA: COLOURFUL AND MAGNIFICENT

草原上古老的植物
Relic plants on the grassland

文：苏怀亮

西鄂尔多斯的荒漠草原，生长着一些古老的植物。半日花，名曰"半日"，却已开了三千万年；四合木是地质时期古地中海的残遗植物，被誉为植物中的"大熊猫"……植物学家说，这里是地球上第三纪残遗植物在亚洲大陆的避难所。

On the desert steppe of Ordos, there grow a number of relic plants. The "rock rose" is a species that is more than 30,000,000 years old. Tetraenamongolica is another species that is a relic of the Tethys in the geological time that is likened to the giant panda in terms of rarity. Botanists say that this area serves as a kind of refuge for these plants from the Tertiary Period.

摄影：戴东辉

河套的"红"
Hetao red

文：莫久愚

夏秋时节，河套平原到处是满载番茄的各种车辆，经常会排成红色的长龙。巴彦淖尔是全国番茄种植加工第一大市。所产番茄固形物和红色素含量高，酸甜适度。番茄酱、番茄汁、脱水番茄、番茄沙司等行销37个国家和地区，约占西欧市场20%的份额、日韩市场的30%、非洲市场的40%。

During the summer and autumn, the Hetao Plain is covered with all kinds of carts full of tomatoes, forming "red dragons" with their trains. Bayannur is the number one producer of tomatoes in China. The tomatos there contain a large amount of solid content and red pigments, and a good balance between sourness and sweetness. Ketchup, tomato juice, dehydrated tomatoes and tomato sauce from this area are sold to 37 countries and regions, and the supply from here constitutes 20% of the European market, 30% of the markets in Japan and South Korea, and 40% of the African market.

摄影：张铁良

地理·物产
Geography and Products

摄影：张铁良

河套的"黄"
Hetao yellow

文：莫久愿

夏秋之交的河套大地，几百万亩的麦田、葵花，让八百里河套成了金黄色的世界。巴彦淖尔市的五原县号称"中国第一葵花大县"，当地葵花种植面积 100 万亩，年产 1.5 亿公斤以上，占全国总产量的 1/10。县城的葵花广场上，一座高达 16 米的"葵花神韵"雕塑随着太阳的起落徐徐转动，像每一朵向日葵追随着阳光。

During the change of season between summer and autumn on the Hetao Plain, thousands of square kilometres are covered in fields of wheat and sunflowers which turn the landscape into a world of gold. Wuyuan County of Bayannur City is known as "the capital of sunflowers" in China, with more than 60,000 hectares dedicated to sunflower cultivation, and an annual output of more than 150 million kilograms, a tenth of the total domestic output in China. A 16-metre-tall heliotropic sunflower-like statue has even been erected here, which rotates slowly and turns its face towards the sun every day.

沙漠中的财富
Wealth of the desert

文：莫久愿

内蒙古西部沙区的梭梭林越来越多了，往往是几万、十几万亩乃至几百万亩连片成林。梭梭林下寄生的苁蓉给人们带来了财富。额济纳旗东风镇牧民图门·巴依尔兴奋地告诉记者："过去靠放羊，一年收入也就是七八千元，去年我光是种苁蓉就收获了两吨多，卖了十万块钱，不仅买了车，还能给孩子们贴补。"

Large stretches, many hundreds of square kilometres of the deserts in the western portion of Inner Mongolia grow with the Saxaul. The desert cistanche, which parasitizes this plant, growing underneath it, has brought fortune to many people living there. In Dongfeng Town of the Ejin Banner, resident Tumen Bair tells reporters excitedly: "In the past, we relied on raising sheep, and made maybe seven or eight thousand yuan a year. Last year I just picked 2 tonnes of cistanche, and earned more than 100,000 yuan. I managed to buy a car and give my children some money, too!"

微观内蒙古
INNER MONGOLIA: COLOURFUL AND MAGNIFICENT

扎蒙花
Wild onion flowers
文：苏怀尧

鄂尔多斯山梁地生长着一种植物，一丛丛的，叶顶开花结籽，当地人叫"扎蒙"，学名叫细叶葱或细叶韭。初夏第一场雨后，粉红的扎蒙花漫山遍野，妇女孩子提篮采摘，加盐捣碎，捏成饼状，晾干备用，是炝菜炝汤的上好佐料。胡油烧至七八成热，掐一撮揉碎放入油中，欻啦一声，满屋飘香！

There is a kind of wild onion that grows in dense clusters in Ordos upon the mountains, which yields blooms and seeds at the top. The plant is called "zhameng" by the locals. At the start of summer after the first rain, these pink blossoms cover the landscape. Children and women go out to pick these flowers, grind them up with salt, pound them into cakes, and set them out to dry. The finished product is an excellent addition to season dishes and soups. When fried in nearly boiled cooking oil, they will send out a glamorous fragrance around the kitchen.

美女与黄米
Beauties and millet
文：刘秉忠

河套农村有一首酒曲儿："一条扁担软溜溜，担上黄米到苏州，苏州爱我的好黄米，我爱苏州的好闺女。"把黄米和苏州美女相提并论，足见河套人对黄米的偏爱。从此曲还能看出，苏州人也爱吃黄米，河套人与苏州人有过黄米和美女的"交易"。

There's a song to accompany drinking in the villages of Hetao: "I carry the millet upon a shoulder-pole to Suzhou, where they love my product, and I love their beautiful girls." The people of Hetao even put millet up against the beauties of Suzhou—an evidence of their love for millet. The song also reflects the fact that the people of Suzhou like to eat millet; there has in the past been a flow of millet in one direction, and pretty girls in the other.

沙地柏
Savin Juniper
文：莫久愚

一种原产于乌审旗的灌木，树形美观，四季常青，散发着一种能驱除蚊蝇的香味。它耐旱节水，根系发达，蘖生很快，头年植一株，来年就是一片。国内外许多城市把它当作美化环境的观赏树种，身价日高。当地牧民说"沙地柏枝子贵得很"，常常有人盗剪、盗挖，乌审旗现在像保护野生动物一样保护它。

A type of shrub that grows in the Uxin Banner, the Savin Juniper is an evergreen with a pleasing shape that emits a scent that repels mosquitoes and flies. It's drought-tolerant and has a wide root system, can grow back quickly after being cut down. Planting one will yield a whole thicket the next year. A number of cities both in China and abroad use the shrub for landscape decoration, thus it is considered a valuable plant. The nomads say it's a valuable plant, and a number of people "poach" it, cutting off branches, or simply digging up plants from the ground. There are now protection efforts for the plant, just like protecting rare wild animals, in the Uxin Banner.

地理・物产
Geography and Products

"煤电铝"循环产业
A cycle: coal, electricity and aluminium

文：莫久愚

内蒙古每年向内地输送1396亿千瓦时的电力，大量的煤灰留在了当地。人们发现，内蒙古西部的煤炭中氧化铝含量达10%，发电后产生的高铝粉煤灰，氧化铝和硅铝合金含量达48%，是能够替代铝土矿的可利用再生资源。目前，呼包等地从粉煤灰中提取铝硅钛合金技术已打通全部工艺流程，实现了循环利用。

Inner Mongolia transmits almost 139.6 billion kWh of electricity to the rest of China every year, with most of the coal ash remaining. People have discovered that the alumina content of the coal is almost 10%, and after use in power generation a large amount of ash with high aluminium content remains, with alumina and silumin content reaching 48% after complete use—this represents a large amount of minerals that can be extracted instead of mining of bauxite deposit. Currently, in Hohhot, Baotou and other areas, a large amount of aluminium, silicon, and titanium compounds are regularly extracted from what would otherwise be waste, representing a huge savings in resource extraction.

空气罐头
Canned air

文：莫久愚

呼伦贝尔25万平方公里的绿色净土，天蓝，草绿，90%以上的河流、湖泊保持着天然优良水质。全市年空气质量良好以上天数超过350天，空气中负氧离子含量，是世界卫生组织规定标准的6倍。呼伦贝尔一家公司推出"负离子缓冲便携式空气罐头"，想让身陷雾霾的人们"品尝"到大草原醉人的气息。

Hulun Buir is an area of 250,000 square kilometres of clean earth, green grass, and blue skies where more than 90% of the rivers and lakes are still in their naturally clean state, full of clear water. The air in the city is very clean at least 350 days each year, and the amount of negative oxygen ions in the air is more than six times the WHO standard. There is a company in Hulun Buir making "portable ionised air cans" to give people who live in areas with polluted air the opportunity to "taste" the intoxicating air of the grasslands.

摄影：苏伟伟

微观内蒙古
INNER MONGOLIA: COLOURFUL AND MAGNIFICENT

摄影：任志堂

马兰花海
Iris sea
文：莫久愚

在西鄂尔多斯和阿拉善高原，五月里盛开的马兰花一望无际，如青紫色的"火"燃遍了大地，是西部奇特的美景。同行的植物学家告诉我，马兰花是草原退化的标志，在荒漠化草原，只有耐干旱、耐盐碱的马兰花才能形成连片的花海。我沉默了，马兰花，你是草原美艳的挽歌，还是荒漠顽强生命的象征？

In western Ordos and on the Alxa highlands, you will see a veritable sea of irises in May, as if a green and purple fire is burning over the entire landscape, one of the beautiful sights of the western region. My travel companion, a botanist told me, these irises are a sign of grassland degeneration. On the desertifying grasslands, they manage to dominate and form a "sea" as they are some of the few flowers that can stand such dry conditions and alkaline soil. I became silent. Are these beautiful irises a kind of elegy for the grassland, or a testament to the tenacity of life?

草原白蘑
Grassland white mushrooms
文：莫久愚

草原上的白蘑往往和优质牧草伴生。雨后的草原蘑菇是一圈一圈地萌发出来的。找到一个"蘑菇圈"，往往能捡拾一大包。几天后又会长出来。白蘑是上好的菌类食材，味道鲜美，还有药用功能。过去锡林郭勒草原上的白蘑大都经由张家口销往内地，故有"口蘑"之称。

Alongside the excellent grass that grows on the grasslands, the white mushrooms often grow as their companions, with rings of mushrooms known as "fairy rings" springing up all around after a rain. When one finds a fairy ring, it's easy to collect a large amount of mushrooms in a short time, enough to fill a big bag. These white mushrooms are excellent to eat, having a nice flavour, and can also be used for medicine. Most of these mushrooms from Xilin Gol are sold via Zhangjiakou, giving them the name "Zhangjiakou Mushrooms" throughout China.

地理・物产
Geography and Products

"甜根子"的价值
The value of sweet roots

文：苏怀亮

一位鄂尔多斯老乡说："我们这地方，甜根子（甘草）到处都是，野生加种植，总有几百万亩，绝对全国第一。你想想那是个甚光景？瞭不见边沿啊！这苗子本身有甜味，开花的时候，十几里外就能闻见。这玩意儿能防风固沙，绿化美化，还有经济效益。我们这儿的人，过去掏根子送命了，如今掏根子挣命了。"

A native of Ordos says: "We've got sweet roots (liquorice root) everywhere here, both wild and cultivated, about several thousand square kilometres worth. We're definitely number one in China, more liquorice than you can imagine, and the liquorice fields extend as far as your eyes can see, man! The roots are really sweet, and when the plants bloom, you can smell the fragrance of the flowers from a far distance. They act as a barrier against sand, add green to the landscape, and are good for economy. In the past we toiled to death in planting and harvesting sweet roots, but now we have a better life because of them."

科尔沁沙地中的五角枫
Horqin's five-point maples

文：莫久愚

枫树叶片多为三裂，科尔沁沙地中的枫叶却为五裂，故称"五角枫"。深秋时节，6万多公顷的稀树疏林，在金黄色的裸沙映衬下，色彩斑驳。由于老枝新梢有别，叶片颜色也有深红、大红、浅红、橘红、橙色、鹅黄以至嫩绿的变化。早晚时分，雾霭漫漫，霜叶重重，更显宁静和辽远。

Most maples are trifoliate, but the maples of the Horqin Sand Land are pentafoliate, and have thus been called "five-point maples". In the late autumn, more than 60,000 hectares of a sparse forest turn golden against a background of the yellow sand land, flecked with colour everywhere. As the leaves on branches of different ages have different colours, one sees a whole spectrum of reds, both deep and bright, combined with oranges, yellows, and greens. Every day when the sun rises and sets, a dense mist flows throughout the landscape, making the quiet landscape even more peaceful.

摄影：张启民

微观内蒙古
INNER MONGOLIA: COLOURFUL AND MAGNIFICENT

摄影：王顺

草原上最大的鸟——大鸨
Big bustard—the largest bird on the grassland

文：莫久愚

它身躯肥大，身高可达60—90厘米，两翅短圆，不能高飞。但有一双长而强健的腿爪，善于奔跑。它的喉管已退化，几乎无法发声。每当百灵、云雀欢歌鸣唱，它们就会伸长脖子伫立聆听，似忠实听众。由于大鸨肉嫩味鲜，羽毛片可用作帽子插饰，曾被滥捕滥杀，兴安盟的几个保护区正在试图恢复它的种群数量。

With a big, fat body, reaching heights from 60 to 90 cm, the bustard has two small, round wings and can't fly high. However, it has powerful talons, and excels at running. Its throat has devolved so that it can hardly make a sound. Every year when the Mongolian skylarks and Eurasian skylarks are singing, they stand there listening, forming a respectful audience. As the meat of the bird is tender and delicious, and its feathers can be used as decorations for hats, they had been poached heavily, and protection organisations have established preserves in Hinggan League for them in the effort to maintain their numbers.

"世界黍粟之乡"
The world's millet capital

文：莫久愚

"敖汉小米"的品质远近闻名，近百万亩的种植面积和近亿公斤的年产量均居全国旗县之首。敖汉旗兴隆沟出土的8000年前的黍和粟，被认为是最早的人工栽培谷物标本，专家推论中国旱作农业起源于敖汉，这里是小米的故乡。联合国粮农组织认定敖汉旗为全球重要农业文化遗产保护地暨"世界旱作农业发源地"。

"Aohan millet" is a famous product throughout China, with almost 666 square kilometres dedicated to its cultivation and an annual production capacity of close to 100 million kilograms here, the first in the nation. At Xinglonggou, Aohan Banner, grains from 8,000 years ago have been unearthed, and are believed to be the earliest evidence of human grain cultivation. Experts posit that this place is the site of the origin of dry farming in China, the "home" of millet. The United Nations FAO has recognised the Aohan Banner as an important cultural heritage site of agriculture, as well as "the origin of dry farming in the world".

地理・物产
GEOGRAPHY AND PRODUCTS

驼绒
Camel wool

文：莫久愚

"长度胜过开司米，细度优于马海毛，防潮、阻燃、抗静电"，这是在说阿拉善驼绒。阿拉善双峰驼，无论是戈壁驼还是沙漠驼，终年生长在60℃至零下40℃的恶劣环境，造就了驼绒特殊的品质。这里的驼绒比其他地方的细2—3微米，每吨价格也高出5—8万元。各种驼绒制品温暖着国内外的人。

"Fibres longer than cashmere, thinner than mohair, moisture-resistant, nonflammable, antistatic"—this is Alxa camel wool. The two-humped camels of Alxa, be they Gobi camels or desert camels live in a harsh environment that ranges from 60 ℃ to -40 ℃ , to which they have adapted with special hair. The hairs of the camels here are 2 to 3μm thinner than those of other camels, and the price of the wool is 50,000 to 80,000 yuan higher per tonne. The products made of this wool are wonderful, warming garments for people both in China and abroad.

摄影：达楞

沙地云杉
Picea mongolica

文：姜苇

沙地云杉是一个古老的树种，也是一种高贵的树。现在全世界仅存的十几万亩，全部都生长在内蒙古，而集中连片的，只有3万多亩，都集中在克什克腾旗境内。

The spruces of the steppe, Picea mongolica, are an old species, and a precious kind of tree. Around one hundred square kilometres of land contain the world's remaining specimens, all in Inner Mongolia. There are only 20 square kilometres of contiguous forest of this tree, all in Hexigten Banner.

摄影：魏月飞

摄影：通拉嘎

行旅・体验
Travel and Experiences

微观内蒙古
INNER MONGOLIA: COLOURFUL AND MAGNIFICENT

草原情
Grassland feelings

文：王芳

到达希拉穆仁大草原，车一停，悠扬的马头琴和热情的歌声就扑面而来。我们几个女人身上的音乐细胞一下子被激活了，踩着节拍跳着舞下了车。在蓝色的天空下，在广袤的草原上，我们放肆地跳了起来。几大车的客人看着我们直乐，不一会儿也忍不住，扭着身子加入了我们。

We arrived at the Xilamuren Grassland and stopped our tourist bus to be met with the sound of horse-headed fiddles and passionate singing. The musical cells in me and my girlfriends' bodies were activated, and we twerked our way out of the bus. Underneath the blue sky, on the wide-open grassland we let loose and started dancing. A few other buses of people saw what a great time we were having, and couldn't resist jumping out of their buses too and joining us.

摄影：高雪峰

晾大佛
Sunning the Buddha

文：班澜

呼和浩特的大召寺，收藏有一幅长两丈、宽一丈半的大唐卡，绘迈达佛像，甚是精美。若要一睹法相，须在每年正月十五、六月十五这两天。其时，请出唐卡，挂于佛殿前，众僧诵经，法乐齐鸣，徒众膜拜，香烟缭绕。这是大召寺独有的法事，称"晾大佛"。

At the Grand Temple in Hohhot, there is a Thangka, i.e. Buddhist religious painting, about 6 metres long and 5 metres wide which depicts the Buddha of the Future, and it is quite beautiful. Those wishing to observe the Buddha must come on the 15th day of the first and sixth lunar months. At this time, the Thangka is brought out and hung in front of the Buddha hall, where monks read hymns, music is played, and pilgrims prostrate themselves before the Thangka amidst the fragrance of incense. This is unique to this temple, the practice of "sunning the Buddha".

行旅·体验
Travel and Experiences

达里诺尔湖观鸟
Birdwatching at Dalai Nur lake

文：姜苇

达里诺尔湖水面240多平方公里，是候鸟重要的迁徙通道。每年春秋季节，有100多种鸟类在这里聚集，白天鹅最多时达7万多只。望着洁白的天鹅在水面飞翔，你会感动、宁静，恨不得只剩了一双眼睛，身体不复存在——因为你会怕己身的浑浊破坏了那片纯白。

The lake of Dalai Nur has a surface area of more than 240 square kilometres, and is an important stop in the migration corridor of birds. Every spring and autumn, more than 100 kinds of birds come here to gather, with as many as 70,000 white swans arriving at the peak of the season. When you see these huge flocks fly above the surface of the water, you'll feel moved and calmed, wishing you could hide yourself as to not disrupt the unbroken pure white of the majestic scene.

草原上也会塞车
Grassland traffic congestion

文：莫久愚

夏天的周末，在去往卓资县北高山草原的路上，一位蒙古国来的客人感慨道：第一次见，草原上也会塞车。——来自京津冀的车辆载着拖家带口的游客堵在了赶赴"九十九泉"的路上，那里有近百个远古火山口形成的湖泊，一千多年来一直是草原贵族度夏的营地，也是今天寻常百姓避暑的去处。

On a summer weekend, on the way to the alpine grasslands north of Zhuozi County a traveller from Mongolia remarked that it was the first time seeing traffic congestion on the grasslands. People from Beijing, Tianjin and Hebei come driving, families in hand to the "Ninety-nine Springs" Road, where there are almost a hundred ancient volcanic lakes. It's been a summer vacation spot for Mongolian aristocrats in the past for more than a millennium, and is now a spot everyone can enjoy.

摄影：云国荣

微观内蒙古
INNER MONGOLIA: COLOURFUL AND MAGNIFICENT

摄影：朱骅

阿斯哈图石林
Arshihaty Stone Forest

文：姜苇

克什克腾旗的阿斯哈图石林是目前世界上唯一的花岗岩石林。远古冰川的融化、移动，刨蚀出它近乎垂直的纵向节理；数万年的冰蚀、风化又塑造了它近乎水平的横向节理，把坚硬的花岗岩切割成一层层的。这些山脊上的岩石远看就像摞起来的"天书"。

The Arshihaty Stone Forest of the Hexigten Banner is currently the world's only granite stone forest. Glaciers melted, moved, and eroded rocks to leave almost vertical structures. Tens of thousands of years of glacial denudation and wind weathering created this amazing landscape with almost horizontal structures, cutting through the granite layer after layer. Viewed from afar, it looks, as some people say, like piled "books of heaven".

大青沟漂流
Drift on Daqinggou River

文：莫久愚

科尔沁沙地南缘的一条沙漠峡谷，每值盛夏，沟外沙尘漫漫、热浪滚滚；沟内清泉聚成溪流，斗转蛇行，如一条曲径幽廊。溪水仅能浮舟，游人坐在橡皮筏上，如在绿色隧洞中穿行。浓荫翳蔽之下，乍明乍暗。两岸曲干横柯，乱枝纠结，树影斑驳，景色渐行渐幻。深邃清凉的感觉，让人忘却沟外的炎炎烈日。

At the southern margin of the Horqin Sand Land is a desert valley. Every year in summer when there's sand all over outside, and waves of heat roll across the landscape, the water of clear springs flows to form a twisting river upon which only very small watercraft can navigate. Tourists can observe this green corridor floating on rubber rafts. One can escape the intense heat in this green-covered retreat, shadowed and dark. Branches entwine on the banks, casting all kinds of shadows to create a calming ambience. One will feel profoundly cooled, forgetting the heat above.

行旅·体验
Travel and Experiences

额尔古纳河
Ergun River

文：莫久愚

额尔古纳河是中俄界河，它是内蒙古东北部一条风景长廊。河水蜿蜒曲折，沿岸不断有支流、溪水注入，遍布沙滩、河渚，风光旖旎。两岸山平野阔，植被茂密。金秋季节，色彩斑斓。远望对岸，是俄罗斯油画中常见的乡村景色：白桦林、碧绿的原野、金色的麦田。黄头发蓝眼睛的农夫在耕作、打草、垂钓，还会善意地向你挥手致意。

Ergun River is the border between China and Russia, which is also a scenic corridor in north-eastern Inner Mongolia. As the flow of the river curves back and forth gracefully, it is continually joined by smaller rivers, with beaches and small islands, forming a passage of charming and gentle scenery as it cuts through the landscape. There are flat peaks and dense vegetation along the banks. In autumn, the colours are amazing. Looking far out at the opposite bank, one sees a painting of pastoral Russia: forests of white birch, green fields, golden wheat fields. Blonde farmers will friendly wave at you as they plough, work the fields, and fish.

摄影：陈嘉磊

包子塔
Baozita Ridge

文：莫久愚

准格尔旗与山西偏关县之间的黄河，受两岸地形束缚，形成一个S形峡谷，当地人称太极湾。准格尔旗方向探向河中的"包子塔"山梁，犹如巨兽临河，点地痛饮。登上包子塔，顿觉风开云阖，气象壮阔。举目四望，流动的河水不见激湍之态，波平如镜；起伏的冈峦却似长龙腾跃，势如奔逐。

The flow of the Yellow River between the Jungar Banner and Pianguan County, Shanxi Province is constricted on either side by the banks, which form an S-shaped mountain valley, which is called Tai Ji Curve by the local people. The Baozita Ridge looks like a giant beast squatting on the river bank and drinking the water of the river. When you climb on top of the ridge, you'll be met with a feeling of a great open space, grand and majestic. Looking around, you'll see that the waters aren't tumbling about, but rather calm, and the dragon-like rolling mountain ridges seem to take off.

微观内蒙古
INNER MONGOLIA: COLOURFUL AND MAGNIFICENT

摄影：苏伟伟

达尔滨罗
Darbin Lake

文：姜苇

鄂伦春山林中有一个叫"达尔滨罗"的火山湖泊。浅浅一弯清水，滋养着绿树、石海、白雪和十里杜鹃，娇艳，洁净，高贵。来到这里，就是寻找缤纷的。它就像画家手中的调色板，每一种颜色都在静静流淌。你只能挥舞画笔，停不下来。初春，达尔滨罗，暗香浮动。

There is a volcanic lake called Darbin Lake in the Oroqen mountains. With clear water and green trees, rock-block field, white snow, and azaleas, it's a scene of purity and elegance. One comes here to see it all. The entire scene appears like a painter's palette, with all kinds of colours everywhere. One becomes caught up in it all, especially in the early spring, when deep fragrances of flowers flow across the landscape.

阿荣旗记忆
Memory of Arun Banner

文：姜苇

阿荣，是满语"清洁、干净"的意思，名字源自境内的阿伦河。夜幕深沉，灯光把夜色照射得晶莹剔透。彩虹谷，松风、涧水、清音，如空山弄琴。油然而生的惆怅，是过客的忧伤。我在离去时频频回头，试图留下更多的影像。那山、那林、那水，那时的心境，没有多余的记忆。我动了情，却迷失在这片林海中。

"Arun" means clean in Manchu language; the name of the banner comes from the Erun River within the area. In the deep of the night, light illuminates it for amazing effect. You hear all kinds of sounds in the Rainbow Valley—wind blows through pines, running stream water, etc., as if someone is playing music in a hollow valley. When leaving here, I felt a bit of sorrow, and turned my head back and tried to take the best mental snapshot I could. The mountains, forests, waters, my mood at the time—these are all wonderful memories for me. I was moved, and lost myself for a while in that place.

行旅 · 体验
Travel and Experiences

火山锥

Volcanic cones

文：姜苇

全国已经发现的火山锥近 2/3 在内蒙古。最有火山"范儿"的是察右后旗白音察干镇的火山锥群。其中几座是典型的圆锥台形，顶部边缘凸起，中间低凹，那形态就是典型的火山 logo。山下的火山灰呈灰色和黑灰色，黑色的火山石很轻。越往前走，黑色越发浓重。我渐渐放轻脚步，害怕惊醒了沉睡已久的火山。

More than two-thirds of the volcanic crater cones that have been discovered in China are in Inner Mongolia. Qahar Right Rear Banner's Baiyan Tsagaan Town is one of their most famous sites. A few of them here are typical cone-type volcanoes, with a depression at the top—a logo-like shape. The volcanic ashes below them are grey and grey-black, and the black volcanic rock is quite light in weight. As you walk upward, the black becomes deeper, and you begin to tread more softly, wary of awakening the sleeping volcanos.

摄影：张松云

公路上的敖包

Obo on the road

文：姜苇

我们去阿拉善右旗一个叫海森础鲁的地方，路边一个右转的标志，指向一个象征吉祥如意的敖包。敖包周围有一圈柏油铺就的小路，我们按照指示开着车绕了三圈。朋友说，过路的车都要在这里绕行三圈，保你一路平安。

On our way to the Alxa Right Banner, we stopped at a place called Haisen Chulu, where there is a road marker instructing us to turn right towards an obo. There's a ring of asphalt around it, upon which we encircled the obo three times as instructed. My friend explained that all cars that pass by are supposed to do this, as it ensures safety on the voyage.

微观内蒙古
INNER MONGOLIA: COLOURFUL AND MAGNIFICENT

锦山镇
Jinshan Town

文：姜苇

喀喇沁旗的锦山镇，酷似江南的小镇，青山环绕，碧水穿城，绿树掩映，洁净整齐。满城你侬我侬的软语，充满柔情。从草原归来，步入这个独具柔美气质的小镇，会融化你内心深处最敏感的地方。

In Harqin Banner, there is an endearing little town that resembles towns in south China, flanked by green mountains, with a clear river and thick forest surrounding it. The clean scenery of the town is complemented by the gentle voices of the locals. Coming back in from the grasslands and walking through this uniquely beautiful town will melt your heart.

图牧吉的"大鸟"
Birds of Tumuji

文：姜苇

兴安盟扎赉特旗的图牧吉保护区有一个野生动物救助中心，里面很多白色的大鸟，走近才看清楚，丹顶鹤！原本是冲着这里的大鸨来的，鹤的身影让我意外。丹顶鹤的体态与颜色，是那么高贵，一身的道骨仙风，在无边的草甸上、平阔的湖水边，越发洁白、优雅、大气。让这湖水、这草原也有了几分仙气。

The Tumuji Reserve in Jalaid Banner, Hinggan League has a wild animal rescue centre. In it, you'll see many large white birds, but upon approaching them up close, you'll see they are red-crowned cranes. When I visited and saw these large birds, I was quite surprised, since I had expected to see great bustard here previously. The cranes are elegant and noble in posture and colour, like angels from heaven, and when you see them on the grassy marshlands, or the wide-open flat lakes, you'll be impressed by the sight of their grace. The lakes here are truly enchanting, like a fairyland.

摄影：石玉平

行旅・体验
Travel and Experiences

摄影：张松云

岱海
Daihai Lake

文：莫久黑

内蒙古的"海"其实都是湖，"岱海"也不例外。它是乌兰察布市一个高山湖泊。南北朝时地理学家郦道元形容这里"池水潋滟，渊而不流，东西三十里，南北二十里"。湖水四面环山，景色奇特。周边山地分布着众多的古人遗迹。建立北魏王朝的拓跋珪就出生在这里。

In Mongolian, "sea" actually means lake; Daihai ("hai" in Chinese means sea) is such a case, and it is a high-altitude mountain lake in Ulan Qab City. Li Daoyuan, a geographer of the Northern and Southern Dynasties period himself described the calm and deep waters of this lake, 15 kilometres from east to west and 10 kilometres from north to south, in his writings. The lake is surrounded by mountains, and is a sight to behold. Many traces of human civilisation can be found surrounding it. The Emperor Daowu of the Northern Wei Dynasty was born in this area.

大兴安岭的灯笼
Lanterns at the Greater Hinggan Range

文：姜苇

大兴安岭的春节，白雪覆盖着整个山村，低矮的平房被厚厚的白雪掩埋了一半，像童话里的"雪屋"。白茫茫之中，家家户户高高竖起的长杆上，挂着红红的灯笼。一闪一闪，一片一片，点亮了雪夜，点亮了春节，温暖着你的眼睛，和你的心。

During the Spring Festival in the Greater Hinggan Range, snow covers every village, with the short cottages frequently halfway submerged in a thick layer of snow, making them look like snow houses out of the fairy tales. In the all-white landscape, each house raises a tall pole, upon which hangs red lanterns. They make a beautiful contrast as they illuminate the snow, brighten the festival's atmosphere, provide a pleasant sight and warm people's heart.

微观内蒙古
INNER MONGOLIA: COLOURFUL AND MAGNIFICENT

"九边第一泉"
"The Spring of the Nine Frontier Towns"

文：班澜

呼和浩特的大召寺门额上，不书寺名，却悬一块横匾上书"九边第一泉"。"九边"是明朝在北部边境设立的九个军事重镇，"泉"指寺门前的"玉泉井"，据说是康熙皇帝的御马奋蹄刨出的。匾是清代山西文人王国祯用棉团蘸墨所书，大草，有飞动气象，为书法珍品。这块匾点出了青城八景之"银佛映泉"的由来，悬于寺门，亦不谬矣。

On the gate of the Grand Temple in Hohhot, the plaque bears not the name of the temple itself, but the phrase "First Spring of the Nine Frontier Towns", and the spring refers to the Yuquan Well in front of the temple. It's said that the spring was carved out of the ground by the hooves of the Emperor Kangxi's horse, and the plaque was painted by Wang Guozhen, a well-known scholar in Shanxi Province, the Qing Dynasty, with cotton dipped in ink. This handwriting is lively and vigorous, and it's a calligraphic masterpiece which is worth appreciating. Since the words written on the palgue point out the origin of the scenery "silver Buddha reflecting itself in the spring", it is more than appropriate to hang at the gate of the temple.

翁牛特旗的玉龙沙湖
Yulong Sand and Lake of Ongniud Banner

文：姜苇

湖水、沙漠、草原、巨石，组合在一起，想想都美。来这里的人都喜欢赤脚，脚掌踏着沙子的感觉真好！细细的沙粒在脚下丝丝滑动，有些痒痒的，还有些被柔软包裹的温暖。巨石峰顶有一个很大的冰臼，里面蓄着水，竟有小鱼在游——如此高的山，如此孤独的生命。

Lake, desert, grassland, and giant rocks—all together in a single scene, they make for a wonderful arrangement. People who come here like to walk around barefoot, feeling the sand beneath their feet. The small grains glide around one's feet, a bit scratchy, yet still full of warmth. On the top of Giant Rock Peak there is a large moulin, full of water, that even has some small fish swimming in it. What a lonely life, to live so high up in the mountains.

摄影：汤军

行旅·体验
Travel and Experiences

摄影：张砾

黄河流凌
Icy flows on the Yellow River

文：刘秉忠

黄河内蒙古段的流凌是一大景观。12月封冻前，上游漂来浮冰相互碰撞、挤压，堆聚起水晶般的"雕塑"，一夜寒风吹过，水面冻结，"顿失滔滔"。远观夕阳中的河面，如飞机舷窗外的云海。4月开河时，冰面崩裂，融化中的冰块旋转着向岸边聚集，试图作最后的挣扎，随着暖风吹来，大河又恢复了往日的平静。

The icy flows on the upper reaches of the Yellow River in Inner Mongolia are quite a sight. In December before the river fully freezes, floating chunks of ice collide with each other and pile up to make crystalline "ice sculptures". On night, a cold wind comes in, and the surface freezes, flowing water coming to a halt. Looking out at the far-off setting sun over the surface of the river is like seeing the sea of clouds from the window of an airplane. When the river begins to melt in April, the icy surface cracks and the chunks of frozen water float over to the banks of the river, as if making a last stand. The warm winds melt them, and the river returns to its peaceful state.

室韦小镇印象
Impressions of Shiwei Town

文：莫久愚

额尔古纳河畔一个小镇。砂石铺就的街道，路旁多是独立的"木刻楞"，白桦木栅围成院落。院内不时飘来手风琴声和烤面包的香味，院落的主人可能是卓娅、冬妮娅或瓦西里……一队队的牛群牧归时，木刻楞也纷纷升起炊烟，高鼻梁、蓝眼睛的俄罗斯族大婶会用地道的东北话说起自己的家世。

On the bank of the Ergun River there is a small town. The roads are paved with gravel, and along them there are many mykden. White birch poles form their fences. You'll frequently hear the sound of an accordion, or smell the scent of bread baking. The owners of these houses may have names like Zoya, Tonya, or Vassili, etc. When the flocks of cattle return from the pasture, you'll see smoke rise from the mykden. With high noses and blue eyes, these Chinese of Russian descent will tell you in authentic North-eastern Chinese dialect the stories of their families.

微观内蒙古
INNER MONGOLIA: COLOURFUL AND MAGNIFICENT

南流黄河第一湾——老牛湾

Old Cow Curve, the first curve of the south flowing Yellow River

文：莫久愚

这里是黄河蒙晋陕大峡谷中一个美丽的河湾，两岸砂石崖壁如刀劈斧削，苍凉雄浑。由于下游兴修了万家寨水利枢纽，黄河不再奔腾咆哮，变得清澈湛蓝，波平如镜。登高四望，黄河由北向南蜿蜒而去，长城自东向西逶迤而来，中华民族最具象征性的两个历史符号在此相聚，旖旎的风光成就了许多优秀的摄影作品。

This is one of the beautiful river curves within the canyons of the Inner Mongolia-Shanxi-Shaanxi area, flanked on each side by sharp cliffs. The view feels both desolate and forceful. Because of the Wanjiazhai Hydroelectric Dam downstream, the water here no longer flows rapidly, and is clear and blue, flat as the surface of a mirror. When you look around from a high up place, you can see how the flow of the river flows windingly from north to south, and the Great Wall runs from east to west—the intersection of two of the symbols of China occurs here, and a pleasant sight illuminates the already beautiful scene.

摄影：石玉平

行旅·体验
Travel and Experiences

摄影：石玉平

最美的麦田
The most beautiful wheat fields

文：莫久愚

年轻的网友相约到额尔古纳探访大兴安岭仅存的一片原始森林，不意间却在一个叫老鹰嘴的地方看到了一望无际的滚滚麦浪，如童话一般，本该是森林或山地草原的地方，却出现了金色的麦田，美得让人心醉。网友的说法没错，如果不是最美的麦田，电影《麦田》和《白鹿原》怎么会在这里取景呢？

A group of young netizens went to Ergun River to explore the only virgin forest in the Greater Hinggan Range. At a place called Eagle's Beak, they saw endless fields of wheat, looking like a fairy world, where there was probably originally forest or grassland. It was an intensely beautiful and enchanting sight. They concluded that it makes sense that the films *Wheat* and *White Deer Plain* were filmed here.

特殊的界碑
Special boundary marker

文：莫久愚

满洲里边境的 1 号界碑是一个三脚架托举的三棱形界碑，三个棱面分别面向中、俄、蒙三国。据说三脚架的水泥基座是蒙古国方面浇筑的，不锈钢三脚架由俄罗斯提供，架上的大理石碑则由中国刻制。

In Manzhouli, the No.1 Boundary Marker is in the unusual shape of a tripod supporting a three-sided stone stele. One of each of the three faces of the stele point towards China, Mongolia, and Russia. It's said that Mongolia supplied the cement base, Russia supplied the metal tripod, and China supplied the carved stone that sits upon it.

微观内蒙古
INNER MONGOLIA: COLOURFUL AND MAGNIFICENT

摄影：达楞

萨拉乌苏峡谷
Sara Usu Valley

文：莫久愚

无定河上游河段在内蒙古，称萨拉乌苏河，河道是千万年冲刷出来的一条几十公里的沙漠峡谷，河水只是宽阔峡谷中的一涓细流。星星点点的农家、牧户掩映在一丛丛绿荫里。一个个沙洲、一片片草甸、一方方农田、一处处果园，还有大片的稻田……这个中国最大的沙漠峡谷犹如世外桃源。

The upper reaches of the Wuding River in Inner Mongolia are called the Sara Usu River. The flow of the river has carved out a valley in the desert over tens of millions of years, which is a few tens of kilometres long. The valley is wide, but the flow is small and narrow. The homes of farmers and nomads dot the green terrain like stars in the sky. Sandbanks, wet marshes, fields, orchards, rice paddies, etc.—this is China's largest valley in the desert, almost like a Shangri-La of sorts.

巴丹吉林沙漠印象
Impression of Badain Jaran Desert

文：莫久愚

吉普车像甲虫在巨大的沙丘上爬行，耳边只有风的呼叫和风撕扯衣衫的声音，还有自己的喘息声。世界只剩了透明的蓝和耀眼的金。偶遇的湖水，如晶莹的翡翠点缀了明黄的绸缎。沙漠，美得如此纯净。

The jeep crawled over the giant sand dune like a beetle, and all I could hear was the sound of the wind, my clothes also flapping in the wind, and my breath. The whole world was blue sky and brilliant yellow sand. Occasionally I'd see a lake, scattered like jade on fold of sand looking like so many yards of silk. It was a place of pure beauty.

行旅·体验
Travel and Experiences

月亮天池
Moon Lake on mountaintop

文：姜苇

扎兰屯柴河镇西面，1300多米的基尔果山山巅。当我耗尽了最后的体力，映入眼帘的美丽，令我晕眩。浑圆的湖廓，如一颗硕大的水滴，滴落在大兴安岭之巅。是谁的眼泪如此晶莹？是谁把翡翠遗忘于此？又是什么样的爱情，把心倾注在里面？

To the west of Chaihe Town in Zhalantun lies the 1,300-metre-high Kyalgo Peak. I was stunned when with the last of my strength I crested the summit and was met with the beautiful site. A perfectly round lake, like a giant water drop, lies upon this peak in the Greater Hinggan Range. Whose tear is so clear? Who has left this beautiful piece of jade here? What kind of love story resulted in such a perfect scene?

摄影：王建平

嘎仙洞的狐狸
The foxes of Gaxian Cave

文：张弓长

2016年10月，我与朋友前往鄂伦春自治旗阿里河镇北约10公里的嘎仙洞探秘，在洞外遇到一大群野生狐狸，还有一只狐狸如精灵般守在这个神秘的洞穴，竟然一点儿也不怕人。嘎仙洞隐匿在一座山峰的花岗岩峭壁之上，洞内有北魏太平真君四年的摩崖铭刻，证明嘎仙洞就是拓跋鲜卑的祖庙石室。

In October 2016, I went with some friends to a site about 10 kilometres north of Alihe Town in the Oroqen Autonomous Banner, that of the Gaxian Cave, to do a bit of exploring. Outside the cave was a large group of wild foxes, and at the entrance of the cave there is a single fox guarding it, as though the fox wasn't frightened at all. The cave is hidden in a granite cliff of a mountain, and bares some cliff inscriptions from the fourth year of the Taiping Zhenjun period of the Northern Wei Dynasty which prove that it was an ancestral temple of the Tuoba tribe of the Xianbei people, rulers of the Northern Wei Dynasty.

摄影：张弓长

微观内蒙古
INNER MONGOLIA: COLOURFUL AND MAGNIFICENT

北"五台"
"Mount Wutai" of the North

文：姜苹

巴林左旗林东镇南的一个山谷里，隐藏着一座始建于辽代的寺庙，还有东北地区少见的石窟群。清代增建的寺院殿房与石窟巧妙地融在一起，所以当地人称召庙石窟寺，又称北"五台"。背后的山顶似有巨石堆砌。其中一块形似仙桃，凌空欲坠，步入谷底回望，又像鸡雏玉立。寺中有六七位年逾九十的喇嘛。

South of Lindong Town in Bairin Left Banner in a mountain valley there is a temple built in the Liao Dynasty, as well as a rock grotto, a rarity in North-eastern China. In the Qing Dynasty the temple was expanded and built into the grotto, which led the locals to start referring to the temple as "Rock Grotto Temple". It's also known as "Mount Wutai" of the North. On the mountain behind it there are huge boulders. One looks like a heavenly peach hanging in the air, and when you walk down into the valley, it looks like a little chick standing there. In the temple there are seven monks all over 90 years of age.

巴丹吉林庙
Badain Jaran Temple

文：莫久愚

在巴丹吉林沙漠腹地，一路攀越过无尽的沙山沙丘后，眼前突现一个海市蜃楼般的画面：一池碧波静卧沙山间，水边一座古刹，古刹边一座白塔——疲惫焦躁的心顿时安静下来。那种瞬间产生的静谧、肃穆、圣洁的感觉，让人久久难忘。

In the hinterlands of Badain Jaran Desert, a road climbs over endless sand tunes. All of a sudden, one will see a seemingly unreal sight like mirages: an ancient temple sitting beside a clear lake in the middle of sand tunes. There is a white tower next to the temple. Looking upon it will calm any anxiety in your heart. The quietude, solemnity and purity you will feel in an instant are hard to forget.

摄影：王建平

行旅·体验
Travel and Experiences

摄影：李克

最后的蒸汽机车
The last steam train

文：莫久愚

2005年，全世界最后一批运营的蒸汽机车在内蒙古正式退役，赤峰克什克腾人保留了一辆，用于每年12月末举办国际蒸汽机摄影节。这里地处燕山和大兴安岭山脉交汇处，山势起伏，桥涵、隧道多，坡度大，弯道半径小。呈蛇形缓慢爬行其间的蒸汽机车，喷出的蒸汽形成银龙般飘逸流动的白色雾霭，画面很美。

In 2005, when the world's last operating steam trains were formally decommissioned, the people of Hexigten in Chifeng kept one of the trains to use in December of each year for the International Steam Train Photography Festival. Here, where the Yanshan Mountains and the Greater Hinggan Range meet, there are many different formations, bridges, culverts and tunnels. The inclines are steep and the turns are on tight radii. The train crawls through these features like a slithering snake, puffing out steam like a silver dragon—it's a beautiful sight.

长城在这里"打了个结"
"Knot" at the Great Wall

文：莫久愚

在清水河县"丫角山"上，可以看到不同年代修筑的明长城，四道长城在30平方公里内纵横交错，如同长龙盘结，壮阔恢弘。长城专家罗哲文说："清水河境内的明代长城遗址，无论从建筑结构到壮美程度，都可跟八达岭长城媲美。"

At the "Yajiao Mountain" of Qingshuihe County, one can see pieces of the Great Wall that were built at different times during Ming Dynasty, with all sections crisscrossing over an area of 30 square kilometres like a twisting dragon. Great Wall expert Luo Zhewen said: "The Ming-Dynasty segments of the Great Wall in Qingshuihe County, from both construction and aesthetics, can be said to rival those of Badaling Great Wall in Beijing."

微观内蒙古
INNER MONGOLIA: COLOURFUL AND MAGNIFICENT

千古壮观
Grand sight for all time

文：莫久熙

额济纳旗的戈壁长河景观一千多年前就出现在唐诗里了。诗人王维出长安到河西劳军，沿额济纳河骑行千里抵达宁寇军城。在茫茫大漠中，面对壮阔的河水、西下的落日，写下了"大漠孤烟直，长河落日圆"的诗句。王国维称之"千古壮观"。的确，诗壮美，景色更是壮观。

The scenery of the river in the Gobi desert of Ejin Banner was mentioned in a Tang poem more than a thousand years ago. Poet Wang Wei went from Xi'an to the west of the Yellow River to greet the army, riding hundreds of kilometres by the Ejin River to the camp at Ningkou. In the vast desert, facing the mighty river and setting sun in the west, he wrote a poem in which he described the scene. And later literature critic Wang Guowei called his description as "grand sight for all time". Indeed, the poem is spectacular in tone, as is the scenery it described.

"昭君故居"
"Former home of Wang Zhaojun"

文：王芳

在昭君博物院中仿建的昭君故居，小桥流水，杨柳依依，总令我忘了自己是在内蒙古，是在草原，像是回到了青山绿水的香溪河畔昭君村，亲切之感在心中荡漾。仰望昭君墓，我不由暗叹，原来上天也有悲悯之心，赐予了昭君一方灵秀之地。昭君，以及牵挂着昭君的人们，终是能放下心头的遗憾了。

In the replica of Wang Zhaojun's home in the Zhaojun Museum, water flows under small bridges, and poplars and willows sway. It makes me forget that I'm in Inner Mongolia, on the grasslands; I feel like I've returned to Zhaojun Village beside the Fragrant Stream, and viewing the green mountains and blue waters, a feeling of closeness wells up in my heart. Looking out at the Zhaojun Gravesite, I can't help but sigh. Heaven had empathy and gave Zhaojun a beautiful place. Zhaojun and those missing her were finally able to let go of the regret in their hearts.

昭君博物院　供稿

行旅·体验
Travel and Experiences

摄影：高晋峰

乌梁素海
Ulansuhai Nur

文：莫久愚

巴彦淖尔市的乌梁素海，黄河改道留下的一个狭长的河迹湖，是中国八大淡水湖之一。夏日里芦花飘荡，鹤翔鱼跃，水天一色，游船在无边无际的芦苇荡中穿行，湖畔的草原视野开阔。年末岁初的冰雪节上，湖面上会绽放出鲜艳的歌舞队、马队、造型各异的冰雕，还有冬捕的人群。

A change in the flow of the Yellow River created this oxbow lake in Bayannur City, one of the eight fresh water lakes in China. In the summer reed catkins sway as cranes fly and fish jump in the water. The sky and lake are of the same colour blue. Boats float along the lake amongst the reeds, and the grasslands that are covered in grass stretch far. At the end of the year a Snow and Ice Festival takes place on the surface of the lake, and Song and Dance and Horse Teams come to perform. Ice sculptures are everywhere, and people go ice fishing.

"塞外小北京"
"Little Beijing beyond the Great Wall"

文：莫久愚

在阿拉善左旗巴彦浩特镇北的一座小山上，有一个类似北京胡同中的院落，四合院布局，宽敞的庭院，青砖青瓦的房屋，还有花园、宫殿，这是按照清代营造规范建造的阿拉善王府，它最早的主人是清雍正年间的阿拉善多罗郡王。不知什么年代起，人们把这里称为"塞外小北京"。

Upon a hill north of Bayanhot Town in Alxa Left Banner, there is a courtyard like those in the Hutongs of Beijing, which has a quadrangle and wide yard and is constructed of deep-grey bricks and tiles. It also has a garden, and a little palace that was constructed in line with the principles of Qing-Dynasty construction by the Alxa Prince. It's earliest resident was the Alxa's Dorokun Prince, in the Emperor Yongzheng's ruling period. We don't know when people started calling it "Little Beijing beyond the Great Wall".

微观内蒙古
INNER MONGOLIA: COLOURFUL AND MAGNIFICENT

蒙古包里的节奏
Pace of life in a yurt

文：张弓长

有人说，在蒙古包里逗留了半日，太阳好像一点儿都没动。奇怪！同样的24小时，城里显得那么短暂、匆促，草原上怎么就这么充裕、从容呢？于是，你就有的是时间坐下来，喝茶，说话儿，那些火烧眉毛的事也大可不必那么着急。你发现牧民这种生活方式蛮好的。——居住环境变一下，你的价值观念也会跟着改变。

Some people say that you might spend what seems like half a day in a yurt, yet you look at the sun and it's hardly moved. 24 hours is such a short time in the city, but here it lasts a long time. When you come here, you'll find that all of the urgent matters in your head aren't so urgent anymore. You'll find it actually quite a nice lifestyle. Change your environment, and you may find your values change too.

搏克之乡
Home of "Burk" wrestling

文：姜茅

"搏克"是蒙古式摔跤。锡林郭勒盟有一句话：在乌珠穆沁草原，三个人中肯定有一个是搏克手。西乌珠穆沁旗山头有一个庞大的雕塑，那是三个搏克手，雄姿英发，威猛站立，俯视草原。那健硕的肌肉如钢铁一般，一股难言的力量震慑着我们，提示我们来到了搏克之乡。

"Burk" is traditional Mongolian wrestling. The Xilin Gol League has a saying: "On the Ujimqin Grassland, one out of three people is definitely a Burk wrestler." In the West Ujimqin Banner there is a large sculpture of three Burk wrestlers that looks impressively and mightily over the prairie. With muscles like steel, their hard-to-describe power fills us with awe, and shows us that this is the home of Burk wrestling.

摄影：高雪峰

行旅·体验
Travel and Experiences

摄影：高雪峰

白桦林
White birch forest

文：姜茸

没有树叶的装点，只有白色的躯干，白桦林就这样骄傲地直立着，于凛冽的天地之间。冬天的呼伦贝尔，天地是一片混沌的白，最抢眼，是白桦林的白，纯粹着你的心和眼睛，明亮了整个冬天。

Leafless, these white trunks stand tall and proud on the intensely cold landscape. At Hulun Buir in the winter, the landscape is entirely white. The most eye-catching sight is these white birch trees, purifying your mind and vision, and illuminating the entire winter.

雪屋
Snow house

文：姜茸

雪花，独爱着呼伦贝尔这片土地，片片飘落下来，便不再融化，一直驻足整个冬天。人们便把这厚厚的雪，雕塑成各种形态。最吸引我的，便是雪屋了。雪花层层飘落在我身上时，我幻想自己就是白雪公主。独处雪屋，洗涤内心，享受一个纯净如初的世界。如果你丢了初心，来雪屋里寻找吧。

Snowflakes especially favour the lands of Hulun Buir, and they drift softly down to rest but not melt, and spend the entire winter where they fall. People sculpt this thick layer of snow into all kinds of sculptures. What interested me most were the snow houses. I felt like Snow White as the snow fell all over me. Staying alone in the snow house, you will enjoy a completely pure world, and your heart was cleansed. If you feel down, this place will pick you up.

微观内蒙古
INNER MONGOLIA: COLOURFUL AND MAGNIFICENT

雅鲁河畔
Riverside of Yalu

文：莫久愚

扎兰屯市被称作"塞外苏杭"，多半得益于纵贯全境的雅鲁河。初夏时节，两岸老柳垂条，拂扫水面；远处青山叠翠，如屏如障。河中流清波缓，碧影婆娑，宛若江南。比起江南，少了些桨声烛影、雨色空濛，却多了几分天高野阔、风清气爽。入夜后，伴着花香，在蓝宝石一般的夜空下赏月观星，令人陶醉。

The city of Zhalantun has been referred to as the "Suzhou or Hangzhou of the North", mostly because of the prominent Yalu River that flows through it. At the start of the summer, the twigs of the old willows on the two banks of the river hang low, brushing the surface of the water. The verdant mountains in the distance look almost as if they are screens. Slow waves ripple along the river, setting off the luxuriant foliage for an effect like the scenery of midsouthern China. Compared to Suzhou or Hangzhou, there is less of the sound of oars and light of candles; the mist and rain are absent. However, there's more of a feeling of a big sky and clean, cool air. At night, the fragrance of flowers flows around one under the sapphire-like night sky; watching the stars at this time is an intoxicating experience.

摄影：吴钦华

草原魔力
Grassland's glamour

文：姜苇

都市的客人初到草原，顷刻就会为满眼的绿色和空旷陶醉。几天之后单调的辽阔也许会令你视觉疲劳，可一旦离开，你又会不舍这里的天空，不舍这里的白云，不舍这里热情的问候……不舍这里所有关于草原的记忆。

When city-dwellers first come to the grassland, they're intoxicated by the sight of wide-open green spaces. A few days later, the plain landscapes may tire you, but as soon as you leave you'll not want to let go of the blue skies, white clouds, friendly people, the memories you've formed...

行旅·体验
Travel and Experiences

"仙人柱"中的夜
Night at the hunting shack

文：莫久愚

敖长福说，在鄂伦春人的"仙人柱"中，透过白桦木的棚顶，"可以观察兴安岭的月色，可以看到如同珍珠一样镶嵌在天空中的星星，可以呼吸到新鲜的空气，可以听到林中的风声。远处和近处的禽兽的嚎叫声，接连不断地像摇篮曲似的传入耳鼓。就在这种美丽、安逸的大自然的怀抱中，鄂伦春人不知不觉沉入梦乡"。

Writer Ao Changfu said that at the hunting shack of the Oroqen, through the canopy of the white birch trees "one can see the moon of Hinggan Range, and the starry sky looking as if it were inlaid with so many pearls. One can breathe fresh air, and hear the sounds of the wind in the forest. Off in the distance and nearby one hears the sounds of beasts and birds creating a continuous melody, like a cradlesong. In the comfort of the embrace of nature, the Oroqen people thus fall asleep and have sweet dreams".

戈壁红驼之乡
Home of Gobi red camels

文：姜苿

乌拉特后旗号称"红驼之乡"，这里的戈壁红驼名气很大，还有被命名为"中国白驼"的白色双峰驼。一次参观"国际驼球邀请赛"后，不经意间走入驼群中发现，这里的骆驼出奇地高大。在戈壁滩的夕阳里，健硕的骆驼像群山一样，无论是红驼或白驼，它们的眼睛竟如人眼般含情。

The Urad Rear Banner is known as "the home of the red camel". The Gobi red camels here are quite famous. There are also a kind of white camels with two humps which are called "Chinese white camels". Observing them at the International Camel Polo Invitational, I saw that they were extremely tall and strong, different from the other camels. Under the setting sun of the Gobi desert, the flocks of these camels resemble a mountain range. Be they red or white, one can see human-like emotions in the eyes of these camels.

摄影：齐鸿雁

微观内蒙古
INNER MONGOLIA: COLOURFUL AND MAGNIFICENT

石堆的召唤
Beckoning of stone piles

文：姜苿

在额济纳旗，路边常见一座座小小的石头山，那是土尔扈特蒙古族人特意堆砌起来的，叫"招招"，表示附近有人家，远行者看见就可以找到人家，进去休息吃东西。这是游牧民族特有的传统。那一座座招招，似亲情的呼唤，还没看到人家，我已经感到温暖了。

In the Ejin Banner, one will frequently see small piles of stones along the side of the road, piled by the Torghut Mongolians. They're called "zhaozhao", and signify that someone lives nearby, in a home where travellers can rest and eat. I feel this is a unique tradition of nomadic people, with each zhaozhao being like a kind beckoning. Even before arriving at the house, I felt warm.

内蒙古的"北极"
Inner Mongolia's "North Pole"

文：莫久愚

大兴安岭北部林区铁路的终点满归镇，每年夏至前后的十几天里，黄昏过后便是黎明，曙光与晚霞相连。21时太阳才开始下山，依然霞光满天，零点之后，天色才开始变得有些昏暗，但天边仍然有一线白光，小镇的街容街景清晰可见。凌晨1时后，缕缕晚霞又瞬间幻化为黎明的曙光。

The terminus of the railway in the forested area of the Greater Hinggan Range is at Mangui Town. Every year in a 2-week period centred around the summer solstice, dawn comes right after dusk. At 9 in the evening, there's still plenty of light out, and red clouds fill the sky. After midnight the sky begins to darken, but there is still some light, and the streets are still clearly illuminated. After 1 in the morning, the clouds turn red again and dawn creeps in.

摄影：刘馥宁

行旅 · 体验
Travel and Experiences

摄影：石玉平

天鹅
Swans

文：莫久愚

巴彦淖尔的湖水多，每年过往栖息的天鹅、大雁也多，难怪那首《鸿雁》会产生于这里。这首歌第一句的"鸿嘎鲁"，实际上指天鹅。天鹅是鸟中贵族，很有风度，在草原的传说中被视为圣鸟。每年11月，湖水开始封冻，候鸟次第南飞，天鹅送走其他的候鸟，才展翅列队，向南飞去。

There are many lakes in Bayannur, and every year many swans and wild geese come here to roost. This is the birthplace of the famous song *Swan Goose*, and the bird mentioned in this song refers to the swans. The swans are noble amongst birds, and they are sacred birds in the folktales upon the grasslands. Every November, the lake begins to freeze, and the birds fly south. The swans see all the others off before they make the trip themselves.

摄影：石玉平

摄影：宝音

回望・轶事

Memories and Anecdotes

微观内蒙古
INNER MONGOLIA: COLOURFUL AND MAGNIFICENT

套马杆的威慑
The threat of the lasso pole

文：张弓长

过去，牧人骑马穿行在大雪覆盖的草原上，走累了，就在雪地里掏一个雪窝，把套马杆插在地上，铺上点野草，倒头就睡，毫不担心遭遇野狼袭击。因为草原上的野狼都领教过套马杆的威力，只要看到套马杆，它们就远远地躲开了。

In the past, when herders would be crossing the snow-covered grasslands, when they became tired, they'd dig a hole in the snow, stick their lasso pole in the ground, and cover the hole with a bit of wild grass, and go to sleep underneath. They had no need to fear that wolves would attack them. The wolves here learned long ago of the force of a swung lasso pole, and now when they see one, they flee.

摄影：何少华

外地人想象中的内蒙古
Outsider's impressions of Inner Mongolia

文：苏怀亮

内蒙古老板到南方出差，一个当地朋友问他：你们那儿的人上班骑马吗？老板说是的，骑马到单位，马去草原上吃草，人到办公室工作。朋友又问：有汽车吗？老板说有啊，开车在草原上狂奔，累了用砖头压着油门，就可以睡觉，一觉醒来车子还在路上跑呢。朋友竟信以为真，因为这就是他想象中的内蒙古。

When a businessman from Inner Mongolia went south, he was asked by a local: "Do you ride horses to work?" He replied: "Oh, for sure. Gotta ride the horse to work, then it rides off to the pasture to eat grass and I go into the office." The local asked: "Do you have a car?" He replied: "Oh, for sure. When I'm ripping it on the grasslands, if I get tired, I just put a brick on the accelerator. I can sleep, and when I wake up I'm still on the road, still ripping it." The local believed him, because this is what a lot of outsiders think of Inner Mongolia.

回望・轶事
Memories and Anecdotes

狩猎民族的基因
Genes of the hunters
文/莫久愿

鄂温克族女作家杜梅说："我的祖先是森林狩猎民族，我的先人都是神枪手。虽然时代的变迁使我们的生活有了很多的改变，我们也逐渐淡忘了自身血脉中与众不同的特性，但是，隐藏在我们血液中的基因总在悄然作祟。有一次我跟着一帮朋友去打靶场玩，我的枪法意想不到的好。"

Ewenki writer Du Mei says: "My ancestors were hunters in the forest, and they were all great shooters. Even though changing times have brought a lot of changes to our lives, and we've gradually forgotten that which makes us different from others, there's still something in our blood that occasionally shows up. One time, my friend and I went to a shooting range just to try it out. Turns out I'm a crack shot."

可以当钱用的砖茶
Pay with a tea brick
文/邓九刚

砖茶是蒙古族牧民日常生活须臾不可离开的物品，甚至可以用来当成货币进行交易。湖南、湖北所产的砖茶尤其受牧民欢迎。旧时旅蒙商贾除了用米、布直接交换牧民的皮毛以外，其他货物基本上都是用砖茶来确定它的价值，一块砖茶可以当两块银元来用。

Tea bricks are indispensable in everyday lives of Mongolian herders. They can even replace money in transactions. The tea bricks from Hunan and Hubei Provinces are especially valued. In ancient times, when merchants visited the area, in addition to rice and cloth, they also used tea bricks to buy leather from the herders. Almost all other products could have their value stated in tea bricks. One tea brick was equivalent to two coins of silver.

上海庙与"上海"无关
Shanghai Temple is unworthy of the name
文/苏怀亮

鄂尔多斯有个地方叫上海庙，这地名常让外地人困惑。上海庙与上海无关，蒙古语原是"沙亥庙"，"沙亥"是靴子的意思，这里曾有一个供奉成吉思汗的靴子的庙宇。初到这里的汉族人把"沙亥"听成了"上海"，于是有了这个名字。地下500亿吨的煤炭蕴藏量，让上海庙成了内蒙古西部著名的工业园区。

There is a place called the Shanghai Temple in Ordos which causes some confusion to people from other regions, since it has nothing to do with the Chinese port city of Shanghai. The temple was originally named "Shahai Temple" in Mongolian, "shahai" meaning boot. It was once a temple that had Genghis Khan's boots worshipped, to which people would make offerings. The Han Chinese who first came here had taken "shahai" for "Shanghai" and gave the place its current name. There are more than 50 billion tonnes of coal under the area, which has turned the Shanghai Temple area into a major industrial zone for western Inner Mongolia.

微观内蒙古
INNER MONGOLIA: COLOURFUL AND MAGNIFICENT

晋商财富的发源地
Sources of wealth of Shanxi businessmen

文：邓九刚

被誉为中国"金融之父"的山西平遥、太谷、祁县的票号、钱庄的老板们，大多数是在这条经由内蒙古西部的茶叶之路上淘得第一桶金的。散布在三晋大地上的乔家大院、常家庄园、王家大院、渠家大院……每一堵墙、每一条椽、每一根暴露的梁柱和每一块砖瓦都在张扬着财富。

Known as the fathers of banking in China, the bosses of exchange shops and private banks from Pingyao, Taigu and Qixian areas in Shanxi got their first money from the tea road in western Inner Mongolia. The Qiao, Chang, Wang, and Qu families mostly built their yards and homes with this money, and every corner of their residential compounds is displaying their wealth.

落雁崖
Falling Goose Cliff

文：苏怀亮

昭君墓西北侧是黄河故道，道上有一段长数百米高几丈的石壁，当地人祖祖辈辈称这段石壁为落雁崖。他们说：昭君娘娘当年路过此地，走得人困马乏，来到石崖下的河边洗脸，此时一群大雁路过，看见水中娘娘的倒影，竟然忘记了扇动翅膀，纷纷掉落下来。从此石崖有了正名，娘娘有了别名（昭君别名"落雁"）。

The old course of the Yellow River lies to the northwest of Wang Zhaojun's grave site. A rock wall a few hundred metres in length and over ten metres in height stretches along it, which the locals call "Falling Goose Cliff" for generations. They say that when Wang Zhaojun passed by the place, exhausted, she stopped there to wash her face, and a flock of wild geese flying by forgot how to fly and fell out of the sky when they saw her reflection in the water. This is where the formation gets its name, and is also the place from which Zhaojun's nick name, "Falling Goose" comes.

商旅云集的城市
A commercial centre

文：邓九刚

清代以归化城为中心形成了庞大的旅蒙和旅俄商人的群体，数量之多恐怕在世界商业史上都极为罕见。近十万人的商业大军把无数商品从京津地区、整个华北和东南沿海，由车倒船，再由马拉牛驮，辗转运到归化城，最后由驼队运往蒙古高原、西伯利亚，直至欧洲腹地。

During the Qing Dynasty, gathered around the city of Guihua (modern-day Hohhot), there were enormous groups of expatriate trades to Mongolia and Russia, a phenomenon seldom seen in the business history of the world. Tens of thousands of traders would bring goods on lorries, boats and horsebacks, from Beijing, Tianjin, other areas of North China, and south-eastern coastal areas, taking them by camel caravans to Guihua, then sending them to the Mongolian Plateau and Siberia, as well as the hinterlands of Europe.

回望・轶事
Memories and Anecdotes

王爱召
Wang'ai Temple

文：苏怀亮

"上房瞭一瞭，瞭见个王爱召，二妹妹捎来一句话，要和喇嘛哥哥交。"内蒙古好多地方都在传唱这首民歌。王爱召是一座藏传佛教的寺庙建筑群，据说其辉煌程度仅次于布达拉宫，人称东藏。1941年被日本侵略军焚毁，"火光冲天，一月未熄"。二妹妹和喇嘛哥哥实有其人，两人演绎了一段惊世骇俗的爱情故事。

"Go up the roof and see the Wang'ai Temple, where Second Sister goes to talk with her lover, a monk." People in many areas in Inner Mongolia sing this folk song. The Wang'ai Temple is a Tibetan Buddhist temple that was said to be second only to Potala Palace, and was sometimes called "Eastern Tibet". It was destroyed by the Japanese bombers in 1941, and the fire that followed burned for as long as one month. It is said that the heros of the song did exist in real life, and they had a deeply moving love story.

不用"三爷"
No nepotism

文：邓九刚

清代商号"大盛魁"在用人方面管理非常严格。伙计的选拔要通过严格的考试，考试内容有珠算、毛笔书法，甚至还要考外语。还有一项制度与现代企业相比非常难得，那就是——东家的子弟不得进入本号工作。掌柜的拥有用人自主权，但"三爷"——少爷、姑爷、舅爷——基本不用。

Dashengkui, a trade firm in the Qing Dynasty, had strict guidelines for the hiring of its clerks. They were tested on abacus calculation, calligraphy, and even foreign language. Their hiring practices can be served as examples for modern companies—family members of store owners were not to be hired. While each shopkeeper had freedom to select employees, his close relatives—sons, sons in law, and brothers of wives were generally not hired.

草原上的山西人
Shanxi people on the grasslands

文：邓九刚

呼和浩特郊区曾有一位名叫阎万山的汉族老商人，聊天到激动处不自觉地就换成蒙古语。他能用蒙古语熟练背诵中药药名，速度之快就像是相声里的贯口。漫长的草原生活早已改变了他的习惯，他吃羊肉，喝奶茶，讲蒙古话，思维方式也随之改变。他已不再是那个山西农民，而是一个地地道道的草原人了。

There was once an old Han businessman named Yan Wanshan who lived on the outskirts of Hohhot. When he became excited he would begin to speak Mongolian, and was able to quickly recite the names of Chinese herbal medicines in the language, like a skilful tongue-twister performer. After living on the grasslands for a long time, his customs became like those of the locals—eating mutton, drinking milk tea, and speaking Mongolian. His manner of thinking also changed. He was no longer a farmer from Shanxi, but a true grasslander.

微观内蒙古
INNER MONGOLIA: COLOURFUL AND MAGNIFICENT

摄影：韩小伟

飞将军射石处
A place where the general shoot the rock

文：张弓长

"林暗草惊风，将军夜引弓。平明寻白羽，没在石棱中。"唐代诗人卢纶的这首《塞下曲》，生动地描写了西汉飞将军李广射"虎"的故事。据《史记》载，这个故事发生在李广任右北平郡太守期间，右北平郡遗址就在赤峰宁城县境内。县城打虎石水库有一块巨石，当地盛传这巨石就是当年李广所射之石。

Tang Dynasty poet Lu Lun described in a poem: "When the forest is dark and the grass rustles in the wind, the general draws his bow. Dawn arrives and as he looks for the fletched arrow, he accidentally finds that he had shot a stone in the night." This is a description of the Western Han general Li Guang. According to *Historical Records*, this incident happened in Right Beiping Prefecture of the Han Dynasty, a place in modern Ningcheng County, Chifeng City, where Li served as the Prefecture Chief. There is a stone at the Shooting Tiger Reservoir in Ningcheng County that is widely believed to be the one described in the poem.

绿色的友谊
Green friendship

文：莫久愚

恩格贝曾是一处战场，中国军队在此与日本侵略军对峙过三天三夜。作家马利说："一位当年随着日本侵华军队到过内蒙古，在包头城楼上站过岗的日本老人，来到恩格贝，说他的心都在颤抖。当年，他是扛着枪来的；现在他是扛着树苗来的，他要栽下绿树，栽下一份忏悔；让绿色永远记住中日人民的世代友谊。"

Engebei was once a battleground, where Chinese troops confronted the invading Japanese army in a three-day, three-night conflict. Author Ma Li says: "A Japanese man who the time followed the army to Inner Mongolia stood guard at a gate tower in Baotou. When he went to Engebei again, his heart shook. Back then, he came carrying a gun. This time, he came carrying saplings. He wanted to plant them as a form of penitence, and let the green become a symbol of Sino-Japanese friendship."

回望·轶事
Memories and Anecdotes

一个"孤儿",两个妈妈
An "orphan" with two mothers

文：莫久愚

在鄂温克旗东苏木，身着蒙古袍、操着纯正鄂温克语的敖德巴拉，是上个世纪中叶三年困难时期内蒙古接受的来自上海的三千孤儿之一。她还记得第一声叫妈妈的人是当地育婴院的蒙古族阿姨。后来被一对鄂温克夫妇领养，鄂温克母亲端给她喷香的奶茶，又让她嗅到了"妈妈"的味道……两个妈妈的爱温暖着她的一生。

In Dongsumu, Ewenki Banner, Udbal speaks fluent Ewenki and wears a Mongolian robe, although she was one of the 3,000 orphans from Shanghai who were accepted by Inner Mongolia during 1959 to 1961. She remembers that the first woman she called mother was a Mongolian caregiver in an infant asylum. Later, an Ewenki couple adopted her. Her Ewenki mother gave her fragrant milk tea to drink with a benevolent smile, and she understood what it was to have a real mother… These two "mothers" who brought her up saved her from loneliness.

国宝级老艺人
National treasured old artist

文：黄鹂

阿拉善盟著名民间歌手奥·额日格吉德玛至少会唱200多首阿拉善民歌，而且完全以原生态形式演唱，是"国宝级艺人"。这位八十多岁的歌唱家最大的智慧与功绩，是完全按原汁原味去独唱、清唱、裸唱，并把自己会唱的一百多首长调和短调整理记录下来，永久流传。

O Ergjidema, a famous folk singer from Alxa, can sing at least 200 Alxa folk songs, completely naturally, and is honored as a national treasured artist. More than 80 years old, she is able to sing folk songs unaccompanied in the traditional style, and over 100 long and short songs sung by her have been recorded, for the purpose of passing down to the next generations.

摄影：张阿泉

微观内蒙古
INNER MONGOLIA: COLOURFUL AND MAGNIFICENT

摄影：张阿泉

通灵的古树
Telephathic old tree

文：张阿泉

呼和浩特市回民区东乌素图有一棵枝繁叶茂的古榆，传说此树树龄六百多年，十分通灵，树上的枯枝从不在白天掉，只在夜里掉，声音很轻；大树杈掉下来，也只掉在院里，从不砸屋和伤人。

In East Ust, in the Huimin District of Hohhot, there is an old elm with thick branches and dense leaves that is said to be more than 600 years old. It is said to be telepathic. The withered branches never fall during the day, only at night with a soft sound. They never fall on people or houses, but rather safely on the ground of the courtyard.

情义的交往
Ties of friendship

文：莫久愚

一位鄂伦春猎民经常到林业采伐点做客休息，一次看中了某位工友的烟袋嘴，主人当场就送给了他。第二天猎民回赠给工友一张貂皮，让他做皮帽子，过了几天又送来一只狍子。那显然不是一种交易，而是情义的往来。

An Oroqen hunter frequently visits the logging sites to rest. One time he saw one of the loggers' tobacco pipe, and took a liking to it, so the owner gave it to him. The next day, he came back and gave the logger a mink pelt to be used for making a hat with, and a few days later, brought him a roe deer. These were not commercial transactions, but rather signs of friendship.

回望·轶事
Memories and Anecdotes

广宗寺
Guangzong Temple

文：莫久愚

贺兰山深处的广宗寺俗称"南寺"，因供奉有六世达赖灵塔和遗物闻名。《仓央嘉措秘史》说，1706年六世达赖仓央嘉措道经青海时脱身辗转来到阿拉善弘法，64岁坐化于阿拉善。也许是拜多才多艺的仓央嘉措所赐，本寺迭斯尔德六世贾拉森既是活佛，又是大学博导、蒙古语言文字学家、蒙藏文献学者。

In the depths of the Helan Mountains lied the Guangzong Temple, commonly called the "Southern Temple". It's thus called and well-known because the temple has the Sixth Dalai Lama's pagoda and remains enshrined and worshiped. In *Chronicles of Tsangyang Gyatso*, it says that in 1706, the Dalai Lama passed through Qinghai to come to Alxa to spread his teaching. He died in Alxa at 64 years of age. Possibly because of his influence, the temple has given rise to Jalsan, who has been called a living Buddha, and who is also a doctoral advisor at a university, a Mongolian linguist, and philologist in Tibetan and Mongolian.

蒙古人与马
Mongolians and horses

文：莫久愚

蒙古语中形容骏马的词汇是最丰富的。不同的毛色、不同的岁口、不同的体态、不同的毛色搭配，都有独自的用语。旧时朋友相见，赞美几句对方的坐骑，是一种礼貌。成吉思汗的堂祖父一次遭遇袭击，逃脱时抛离了陷入泥沼的坐骑。追杀的人说，一个蒙古人失去了马，还有何用？就不再追赶，散去了。

There are many words to describe horses in Mongolian. Hair colour, age, body type, and the match of hair colours, etc. all have their own vocabulary. When friends met each other in old times, they'd compliment the other's horse. When Genghis Khan's granduncle was attacked, his mount became stuck in a bog, and he deserted it. His pursuers said that a man without a horse is useless, and not worth killing. They ceased their pursuit and scattered.

摄影：赵如意

微观内蒙古
INNER MONGOLIA: COLOURFUL AND MAGNIFICENT

摄影：汤军

蒙古族"巨人"
Mongolian giant

文：张弓长

赤峰市有个名叫鲍喜顺的蒙古族男子，身高2.361米，比姚明还高，是吉尼斯世界纪录中"世界自然生长第一高人"。2006年，抚顺皇家极地海洋世界的两只海豚因吞入异物病危，很多人尝试用手臂探取异物未果，鲍喜顺赶来，用他的长臂顺利取出异物，挽救了海豚的生命。

In Chifeng there is a man named Bao Xishun who is 236.1cm tall, which is taller than Yao Ming. He's recognised by the *Guinness Book of World Records* as "the tallest naturally grown man in the world". In 2006, at the Fushun aquarium, two dolphins ingested inedible wastes, which put their lives in danger. Others were unable to remove the offending objects, so Bao showed up, stuck his hand in the dolphin's mouths, and retrieved the junk, saving their lives.

空特乐
Kongtele

文：敖继红

"空特乐"是鄂伦春语"哭"的意思。当年她妈妈在森林里生下了她，刚落地的空特乐使劲哭使劲哭，于是得了这个名字。上学后她听说军人最光荣，就跑到自治区要求当兵，成了鄂伦春人的第一名女兵；她在军营里用鄂伦春人习惯的语言写日记，人们说那是"诗"，于是她成为鄂伦春第一位女诗人。

"Kongtele" is the Oroqen word for crying. When Kongtele's mother gave birth to her in the forest, she fell on the ground and cried very hard, and was thus given this name. When in school she heard that being enlisted in the military was honourable, so she went to the government to join up, becoming the first Oroqen female solider. When she was on the base she wrote her diary in the traditional Oroqen format, which others said looked like poems. Thus, she became the first female Oroqen poet, too.

回望·轶事
Memories and Anecdotes

老阿妈的推荐
The old lady's recommendation

文：莫久愚

一位天津知青回忆，1970年高校在牧区招生，需要牧民推荐。一天，房东老阿妈很早就骑马出门，很晚才回来，也不说去了哪里。事后他才打听到，老阿妈是自己骑马40里到公社，夸赞这位知青表现好，推荐他入选。以这位知青的出身，当时是不能上大学的。老阿妈并不知道这些，只是默默做了这事，以后也没有提起。

An educated youth from Tianjin remembers, colleges and universities were recruiting students from the pasturing areas in 1970, and required recommendations from the herders. One day, the old lady in whose house he lived left very early in the morning on her horse and came back very late, without telling him where she had gone. Only later did he find out she had ridden 20 kilometres to the local government to recommend him for admission, and sang his praises. With his family background, he had not an opportunity to attend the university. The old lady knew nothing about it, and she just did what she could quietly. She didn't even bring it up again.

摄影：崇先鸣

微观内蒙古
INNER MONGOLIA: COLOURFUL AND MAGNIFICENT

摄影：乌热尔图

一双白羊皮手套

A pair of white sheepskin gloves

文：莫久愚

每一位草原知青的记忆中，都会有一位额吉慈祥的面容。天津知青胡冀燕回忆，在草原第一个封冻的冬夜，房东老额吉一直在昏暗的煤油灯下忙乎到夜深。早上她正要去放牧，额吉叫住她，递过一双白羊皮手套。她心里一热，原来额吉连夜不睡是在为自己缝制手套，眼泪唰地就流了下来。

All the educated youths on the grasslands have memories of kind Mongolian mamas in their lives. Hu Jiyan, who was an educated youth from Tianjin, remembers the first time it froze over on the grassland, the old lady with whom she lived worked on something very late into the night under the dim light of a kerosene lamp. In the next morning when she was heading out, the woman handed her a pair of white sheepskin gloves. Her heart was warmed—the woman had been up all night sewing them for her. Looking at the gloves at that time, she was full of tears.

回望·轶事
Memories and Anecdotes

蒙古族阿妈的摇篮
Mongolian mother's cradle

文：莫久愚

上世纪六十年代三千南方孤儿来到草原。有个孩子病殁，工作人员要马上埋了，一位蒙古族老阿妈坚决不同意，大声说："啊呀，这苦命的孩子走了这么远的路，还没睡过我们蒙古人的摇篮呢，怎么能这样匆忙地埋了呢？"最后老阿妈硬是把这个死去的孩子放在摇篮里"安睡"了几天才安葬。这个故事打动了作曲家杜兆植，于是有了《摇篮曲》。

In the 1960s three thousand orphans from Southern China came to the grasslands. A child died of illness, and the workers were about to bury her immediately, but an older Mongolian woman exclaimed loudly: "This poor child came all the way here, and still hasn't slept in a Mongolian cradle. You can't just bury her in the earth!" She laid the lifeless child in the cradle to "rest" for a few days before being buried. This story moved famous composer Du Zhaozhi to write the song *Rocking Cradle*.

仪式般的亲情
Ritualised affection

文：莫久愚

草原知青定宜庄回忆一位阿妈时说：她每天放牧时，阿妈总是说："姑娘，天冷，出去小心呀！"接着会亲一下她的额头和面颊，拥抱一下。从羊圈向外赶羊，阿妈一面帮着轰羊，一面说："孩子，小心呀，早点回来喝茶！"又搂过她来，抚摸一下头。每天如此，像仪式一样。她难忘这仪式般的亲情。

Ding Yizhuang, an educated youth on the grassland, remembers the hostess of the herder family that she lived with: Every day when she'd go out to pasture, the hostess would tell her: "Girl, it's cold. Be careful out there." Then the hostess would kiss her forehead and cheeks, and give her a hug. When she headed out of the sheepfold, the hostess would help her drive the sheep, and tell her: "Dear, be careful, and hurry back for some tea!" She'd then hold her and rub her head. Every day it was like this; it's a memorable ritual of affection.

摄影：乌热尔图

微观内蒙古
INNER MONGOLIA: COLOURFUL AND MAGNIFICENT

有关长调的故事

A story about Mongolian Long Song

文：莫久愚

新巴尔虎草原长调歌手宝音德力格尔幼时与父亲相依为命。一天他们俩赶着羊群迷路了，天晚时，有群狼一直跟着他们，眼睛不好的父亲嘱咐她就地休息，然后叫女儿唱歌，自己拉琴。父女俩一直唱到天亮，狼群中有的躺着，有的坐着，像是在欣赏。天亮的时候，这些狼伸伸懒腰，离去了。

On the New Barag Grassland, Buyindelger, a famous singer of Mongolian Long Song and her father stuck together when she was a child. One day, when they were guiding their flock and became lost, as night fell, a group of wolves began to pursue them. Her father, with poor eyesight, exhorted her to rest there. He had her sing while he played his instrument. They played and sung until dawn, as the wolves lay and sat down, seemingly enjoying the music. Then, the wolves lazily wandered away.

七百年前的请柬

A 700-year-old invitation

文：莫久愚

这是额济纳旗黑城遗址出土的一张元代的请柬："谨请贤良，制造诸般品味，簿海馒头饰妆，请君来日试尝，伏望仁兄早降。今月初六至初八日。小可人马二。"那时的"馒头"就是今天的包子。刚刚开业的马二邀请朋友们三天内试吃自家诸般品味和包子，如今天的草原人一样感情真挚、恳切，的确"可人"。

In the remains of Khara-Khoto in Ejin Banner, an invitation of Yuan Dynasty was unearthed, which read: "Dear friend, I am honored to invite you to come to my restaurant to taste the newly made mantou and other dishes from 6th to 8th this month. Yours sincerely, Ma Er." Here "mantou" meant buns. From the invitation it's clear to see that the people of the time were as friendly, honest and lovely as those of today on the grasslands.

摄影：李逸友

回望·轶事
Memories and Anecdotes

名字就是地址
Just write my name on it

文：莫久愚

新巴尔虎左旗的宝音德力格尔因为长调受到牧民的喜爱，因为长调《辽阔的草原》获得了国际金奖，然后去了遥远的呼和浩特。喜爱她的牧民给她写信，信封上只写"呼和浩特宝音德力格尔收"。

Buyindelger, a famous singer of Mongolian Long Song from the New Barag Left Banner, is quite popular with the herders. When her song *Wide Open Grassland* won an international gold medal, she moved to far-away Hohhot. When her fans on the grassland write her letters, on the envelope they just write "Buyindelger, Hohhot".

守陵人
Guardians of the grave

文：莫久愚

1989年出生的金宝是成吉思汗陵最年轻的守陵人。作为达尔扈特人，能为圣主守灵，他感到很光荣。陵区的"溜圆白骏"，是一匹眼睛乌亮、蹄子漆黑、毛色纯白、全身无伤疤的"神马"。记者刘关关发现，一见到"神马"，金宝脱下帽子，讲了几句蒙古语，神马很配合地将头伸过来，头碰头地"心灵交汇"。

Born in 1989, Jin Bao is the youngest guardian of the Mausoleum of Genghis Khan. As a Darhad, it's a huge honour for him to keep vigil beside the grave of the great leader. In the area of the site, there is a "perfectly white horse", with intense dark eyes, black hooves, and pure white hair with no scars upon its body—it's considered a "sacred horse". Reporter Liu Guanguan discovered that when Jin Bao approaches the "sacred horse", he takes off his hat, says a few words in Mongolian, and the horse complacently reaches its head out to touch his—a meeting of spirits.

摄影：那森

微观内蒙古
INNER MONGOLIA: COLOURFUL AND MAGNIFICENT

最早的速冻饺子
The first frozen dumplings

文：邓九刚

旧时呼和浩特的商人经营灵活，有很多经营方式最早都是他们创造出来的。一般的商号是"你卖什么，顾客买什么"，而有实力的大商号则是"你需要什么，我就卖什么"。以"大盛魁"为例，蒙古王公们每年都要到五台山朝拜，路途遥远，大盛魁就为他们提供全程衣食供给，据说速冻饺子就是那时发明的。

In ancient times businessmen in Hohhot maintained flexible operation tactics, thus many modern business operation innovations first took place here. Whereas most stores had the operating model of "customers buy whatever we sell", really competitive stores operated by "we sell whatever you need". In the instance of Dashengkui, when the high nobility of Mongolia would make their pilgrimage to Mount Wutai every year, the store would stock up on provisions for them—this is where the first frozen dumplings come from.

不要失信于一个牧民
Keep your word to a herder

文：莫久愚

某年春节前，民俗学者郭雨桥在东乌珠穆沁旗采风，一位牧民跟他说想到呼和浩特现场观看内蒙古电视台蒙古语春节联欢晚会，他答应帮忙。回到呼市后，已经退休多年的郭雨桥多方努力，设法满足了牧民的要求。郭雨桥解释说："牧民最痛恨的就是失信和偷盗，如果你失信，就等于把自己出卖了。"

Before the Spring Festival one year, folklorist Guo Yuqiao went to the East Ujimqin Banner to collect ballads, and met a herder that said he wanted to visit Hohhot to watch the Mongolian-language Spring Festival Gala held by Inner Mongolia Television at the scene. When he returned to Hohhot, Guo, who had been retired for a number of years, made great efforts to fulfil the herder's request. He says: "What herders hate most is thieves and promise-breakers. If you don't keep your word, it's as if you've betrayed yourself."

摄影：高雪峰

回望·轶事
Memories and Anecdotes

摄影：乌热尔图

牧人与城市
Herder and the city

文：许淇

老阿爸来呼和浩特寻找他那进城的女儿，在一模一样的楼群中转了向。他沮丧，他觉得丢人。大草原上他不曾迷过路，大森林里他也不曾迷过路。他坐在路旁水泥管道上发愣，过往行人陌生的面孔，不如他的羊儿好分辨……终于有一个穿白制服的好心人，像牵着失路的羔羊，把老爷子领到他女儿家里。

An old man came to the city Hohhot to find his daughter. Walking through the maze of seemingly identical buildings, he became depressed when he lost his direction. He'd never been lost on the grassland, or even in the forest. He sat down on a cement pipe by the street in a daze, unfamiliar faces passing him by, even harder to tell apart than the sheep in his flock... Finally a kind-hearted person in a white uniform came up to him, took him by the hand as if taking a lost lamb, and guided him to his daughter's house.

山林・沙地
Mountains, Forests and Deserts

微观内蒙古
INNER MONGOLIA: COLOURFUL AND MAGNIFICENT

摄影：刘馥宁

北方的山是卧着的
Mountains are lying down in the North

文：莫久愚

鄂伦春作家在《走进鄂伦春》一文中说："提起鄂伦春，你也许会联想到高高的兴安岭，如火如荼的映山红，闻名遐迩的篝火节，骑马善射的狩猎民族……'高高的兴安岭'并不高，但它却舒缓而长远……如果说南方的山是竖着的，北方的山便是卧着的。"

An Oroqen author wrote in the essay *Walk in to Oroqen*: "When one mentions Oroqen, you may think of the high peaks of the Hinggan Range, flaming red azaleas, the famous bonfire festival, hunters on horseback...tall peaks of the Hinggan Range aren't really that tall. They're more relaxed… If the mountains of Southern China stand tall, the mountains of the North are lying down."

采山
Gathering mountain products

文：莫久愚

8月的兴安岭，有一种成熟的美。雾霭蒙蒙中山色重重，青绿、青蓝、青灰渐渐隐入天际，犹如一幅泼墨山水画。跟着当地人进山采摘，山泉叮咚，林木含笑，各种低矮的灌丛竟是浆果的乐园，五味子、蓝莓、山丁子随手可得，林中还能采到黑木耳、白蘑、猴头……那种不断发现的喜悦正是采山的乐趣。

In the Hinggan Range in August, there is a kind of ripe beauty. Mist is all around, and within it there are all kinds of colours. Greens in shades of teal, blue and grey, like a traditional ink-splash landscape painting. Springs tinkle, and the forest smiles. There's an assortment of short berry bushes—schizandra, blueberries, and Chinese crab apples, etc. One can also pick black fungus, tigertop (a white mushroom), and pompom mushroom, etc. It's like a botanical amusement park of endless delight in finding new ones.

山林·沙地
Mountains, Forests and Deserts

鄂温克山林里的一天

A day in the Ewenki mountains

文：娜仁托娅

山里，一片大雾，晌午才退去。我在树下看灰鼠忙碌，有时坐在栅栏上眺望远处的青山，找寻阿爸的身影。傍晚，我从撮罗子的缝隙里看夕阳。夜里，我躺在额妮（妈妈）的怀里，望着炉子里探出的红红的火星。突然远处传来狗的吠叫，马的鼻子发出"突突"的声音。我跳了起来，阿爸回来了。

The mountain is covered with mist which doesn't retreat until noon. I see a squirrel busying itself under a tree. I sit down sometimes on the fence and look off into the distance to try to see my father. At dusk, I see the setting sun through a crack in the hunting shack I live in. At night, I lay in my mother's embrace, and look at the red flame in the oven. Suddenly, I hear a dog barking somewhere, and a horse exhaling through its nose. I jump up. Father is home.

摄影：巴义尔

165

微观内蒙古
INNER MONGOLIA: COLOURFUL AND MAGNIFICENT

山林没有地平线
No horizon in the mountains

文：莫久愚

两位鄂伦春作家这样形容他们世代生活的山林："这里没有地平线，所有的道路都挂在树上，独行的猎人在树荫的蔽护下，行走了几千年之后，至今还在行走。在这棵树和那棵树之间，都随时可能出现想不到的惊恐或者惊喜。"

Two Oroqen authors describe their life in the mountains: "There's no horizon here, and all the roads are in the forest. Hunters have moved under the cover of shady trees for centuries and millennia, and still do so. Among trees, you may find frights and surprises you would not have thought of."

森林与花海
Forest and the sea of flowers

文：莫久愚

大兴安岭上绚丽的杜鹃花海，大多是往昔的林木采伐迹地。原始落叶松林被砍伐过后，岭上自然萌生的往往是桦木和杜鹃灌丛混生林。地下没有了落叶松强壮的根系争夺养分，空中不再有浓密的枝干遮蔽阳光，于是杜鹃花便灿烂起来，枝枝蔓蔓、无拘无束，如火如荼地红遍山涧冈峦，有火山熔岩的地方尤其茂盛。

The florid azalea seas of the Greater Hinggan Range exist mostly in areas that were previously forested, and then felled. After virgin larch forest is cut down, a mixed forest of birch trees and azaleas will grow. The plants will no longer have to compete for nutrients with the deep roots of the larches, nor deal with the heavy overhead cover they provide. Thus, the azaleas can flourish in abundance, decorating the mountains and valleys with their hues like a raging fire, and especially luxuriant in places with volcanic rocks.

摄影：高雪峰

山林·沙地
Mountains, Forests and Deserts

摄影：陈嘉磊

莫尔道嘎秋色
Autumn colours in Mordaga

文：莫久愚

中国面积最大的森林公园，占地578000公顷，是中国最具寒温带特色的原始针叶林。千松挺立，万绿参天，松香四溢，沁人心脾。进入8月后，青松依然苍翠，秋霜却已染红白桦林，与金色的原野、澄澈的河溪、湛蓝的天空构成莫尔道嘎凝重明艳的秋色。电影《紫日》中那一帧帧油画般的镜头，就是在这里拍摄的。

This is China's largest forest park, which covers an area of 578,000 hectares. It consists of primal coniferous forest uniquely grown in a cool temperate zone. Endless trees stand together, touching the sky. Fragrant breezes waft through their branches and bring refreshment to one's mind and body. Every year after August the verdant white birch trees are covered in autumn frost, taking on red hues; whilst the pine trees are still in dark green. The fields turn golden yellow, and the streams and rivers flow with clear water under the deep blue sky. This is the pallet of the autumn colours in Mordaga. The famously beautiful scenes from the film *Purple Sunset* look like paintings, which were shot here.

兴安杜鹃
Hinggan azaleas

文：莫久愚

不来兴安岭，不知北国也有如火似海的杜鹃林。每年5月第一场雨后，草木微醺，春山如笑，杜鹃花竞相绽放，一团团一丛丛挤满山坳，在北疆的蓝天丽日下，在寂静的山林中，泼洒出一片片喧闹的红艳。更北的山林中，杜鹃花开正值春水初融、冰皮乍解，或遇一场春雪，或是残雪未消，红花、蓝天、白雪、碧波，装点出一个清丽冷艳的世界。

You don't know there is a sea of azaleas in North China too until you've been to the Hinggan Range. In May each year after the first rain, a mild botanical fragrance flows through the air, and the azaleas pop up everywhere upon the beautiful mountains which are full of life, competing to show off their fragrance and colours. Under the bright sun and blue sky, in the quiet mountain forests, blooms of red burst into existence all around. Further north, as the ice just begins to melt, or maybe after a spring snow, or even against the white backdrop of the previous year's snowfall, red flowers, blue sky, white snow, and waves of green come together to create an amazing scene.

微观内蒙古
INNER MONGOLIA: COLOURFUL AND MAGNIFICENT

大兴安岭"休息"了
Resting the Greater Hinggan Range

文：莫久愚

一位大兴安岭老伐木工说："自己的年纪越来越大，伐倒的树却越来越年轻。可采伐的成熟林和过熟林越来越少了。"60多年来，大兴安岭为国家奉献了2亿多立方米的木材。如今，猎人放下了猎枪，伐木工收起了斧锯，山林静了下来，几十万砍树人变成了看树人。

An old lumberjack from the Greater Hinggan Range said: "As I get older, the trees I cut down get younger. The mature and overmature forest is more and more scarce." Over the past 60 years, the mountain has provided China with more than 200,000,000 cubic metres of lumber. In present day, hunters have laid down their shotguns, and woodcutters have laid down their axes and saws. The forest is quiet, as tens of thousands of tree cutters have become tree watchers.

撮罗子
Hunting shacks

文：莫久愚

鄂温克猎民居住的撮罗子，过去是桦树皮搭建的圆锥状小屋，后来是圆锥状帐篷。帐篷中心是一个火堆，地面上铺满松枝，松枝上平铺兽皮，白天是坐垫，晚上是睡褥。帐幕的北侧略显宽敞，是敬奉"玛鲁神"的地方，凡有尊贵的客人都要让到那里。现在鄂温克人的驯鹿喂养点仍然可见。

Ewenki hunting shacks are called "cuoluozi". In the past they were conical houses made out of birch bark; now they are conical tents. The tent has a fire pit in the middle, and has pine branches upon the ground, on top of which animal pelts are laid. They act as seat cushions during the day, and mattresses at night. The north side of the tent is always a bit wider to pay tribute to the "Maru God", and important guests are invited to sit there. Even now, one can still see these tents in Ewenki reindeer rearing centres.

摄影：白兰

山林·沙地
Mountains, Forests and Deserts

计算年龄的方式

Reckoning age

文：莫久愚

白兰采访山林中的鄂温克时注意到，一些鄂温克老人对于岁月和往事也许都模糊了，但对于山林中的草木枯荣却记得很清楚，他们不会那么准确地知道自己的出生年月日，只记得自己的生肖。"记龄的方式不是一年增一岁，而是山青了几次，草绿了几次。"

Bai Lan noticed when interviewing Ewenkis: A number of older Ewenkis aren't too clear about their precise age, but know the growing and withering of the plants and trees of the forest clearly. They don't know their birthdays, but rather only their year of birth, represented by one of the twelve amimals of Chinese zodiac. "Your age isn't about when you're born, but how many times the mountain has turned green, the grass has grown."

摄影：乌热尔图

抗拒严寒

Cold resistance

文：莫久愚

鄂伦春人从出生就要学会抵御寒冷，鄂伦春作家说："女人生下孩子后，夏天用冷水洗，冬天用雪擦身，把孩子放到叫'敖木度'的白桦木制作的摇篮里睡觉。生活在酷寒中的大兴安岭鄂伦春人之所以能抗拒严寒，是从千百年的颠沛中学来的……这是一个没有大门的森林民族，这个民族的大门挂在树上。"

The Oroqen people must learn how to resist the cold from the time they are born. An Oroqen author remarks: "After a woman has a child, she'll bathe it in cold water in the summer, or rub its body with snow in the winter. She puts it in a crib called an 'amdo' made out of white birch wood to sleep. The hardship of living in the intensely cold environment of the Greater Hinggan Range has caused the Oroqen to develop cold resistance over centuries and millennia—only natural for a group of people that live not in houses with firm doors, but among the trees."

微观内蒙古
INNER MONGOLIA: COLOURFUL AND MAGNIFICENT

奥克里堆峰
Aokelidui Peak

文：莫久愚

根河市阿龙山镇东北的奥克里堆峰是大兴安岭北部的主峰，有些类似日本富士山，山体雄伟且坡缓开阔，山脚下碧水环绕。每年9月刚到，山峰便被白雪覆盖，一直到第二年5月。当激流河畔杜鹃花盛开时，大地吐绿，草色遥看，山体斑驳，山巅白雪尚存。大兴安岭的气势脱然而出。

In Alongshan Town, Gegen Gol City lies the Aokelidui Peak, the main peak of the northern section of the Greater Hinggan Range. It resembles in a way Mount Fuji in Japan, tall and grand with gentle slopes, ringed by clear waters at its base. Every year as soon as September arrives, the peak of the mountain is covered in snow, which stays there until May the next year. When the azaleas bloom and the ground is green with grass, the body of the mountain is flecked with colour all over, but the snow cap still remains. This is the magnificent sight of this peak in the Greater Hinggan Range.

摄影：乌热尔图

山林·沙地
Mountains, Forests and Deserts

摄影：乌热尔图

鄂温克和大森林
Ewenkis and the forest

文：莫久愚

人类学家白兰访问了在大森林中生活的鄂温克人，看到他们平静地用生命面对大自然的险恶后感慨道："在鄂温克人和兴安岭之间，总让人感到有一种玄秘和矛盾的关联，像兴安岭上和额尔古纳河面笼罩着的永远穿不透的雾霭，超越了自然和宇宙的现实，从遥远的云端，一直掠过你的心头。"

Bai Lan, an anthropologist had visited the Ewenkis living in the forest, and remarked after seeing how they calmly faced the dangers of nature with their lives: "There's a kind of mysterious and contradictory relationship between the Ewenki people and the Hinggan Range. Just as the mist seems to always cover the Hinggan Range and the Ergun River, it's a kind of reality that transcends nature and the universe. From the far away clouds, it seems to flash past your mind."

火与鄂伦春人
Fire and the Oroqen

文：莫久愚

在山林中的"仙人柱"里，篝火驱走野兽，伴着鄂伦春人度过漫漫长夜。鄂伦春作家敖长福说："火神给人以生命的源泉和生活的勇气，但火神一旦发怒，又会带来巨大的灾难。因而鄂伦春人每逢春、秋大祭和过年或喜庆的日子，都要举行祭火仪式。"虽然历史已经远去，"但古老的篝火活动仍具有召唤人的力量"。

In the traditional Oroqen hunting shacks in the forest, bonfires keep away beasts, and keep the Oroqen company through the long night. Oroqen author Ao Changfu says: "Bonfires give us life and bravery, but if the fire god becomes angry, you'll be faced with a huge disaster. Every spring and autumn the Oroqen have a large fire festival, and fire festivals also happen at the new year and other holidays." Even though it's a tradition long in the past, these fire rituals still call to the people of today.

微观内蒙古
INNER MONGOLIA: COLOURFUL AND MAGNIFICENT

敖鲁古雅人
Olguyaa people

文：莫久愚

十几年前，根河市将森林中住着原始撮罗子的鄂温克猎民请下山来，住进有暖气和自来水的敖鲁古雅新村。可驯鹿不习惯，它们留恋密林中的苔藓，一些老人惦念驯鹿，怀念林子里鹿奶一般的晨雾中清脆的鹿铃声。于是根河市又辟出一些驯鹿养殖点，为了驯鹿，为了爱驯鹿的老人。

Over a decade ago, the government of Gegen Gol City invited those living in hunting shacks in the mountains to come down and move into the New Olguyaa Village, in residences with heating installation and running water. Their reindeer didn't like it there, thinking about the moss of the forest, and a number of these old people worried about their reindeer, and missed hearing the sound of reindeer bells in the early morning in the forest pervaded with mist which looks like reindeer milk. Thus, the government opened a number of reindeer rearing centres, for the reindeer, and the elderly people that loved them.

摄影：乌热尔图

山林·沙地
Mountains, Forests and Deserts

摄影：顾德清

猎民的传统
Hunter's traditions

文：莫久愚

鄂伦春猎民狩猎一直遵循着自己的传统，绝不滥杀乱砍。他们以山林为生，想得长远。怀孕的、正在交配的野兽从不猎取；也不会猎杀鸳鸯、鸿雁，因为它们总是雄飞雌绕，猎取一只，另一只会很快死去。采食林中浆果时从不损伤树木。

The hunting styles of the Oroqen are different from other people. They stick to their traditions, and never indiscriminately kill animals or fell trees. They live off the forest and desire it to last. They will never kill pregnant or mating animals, nor will they kill mandarin ducks or swan geese, as these animals mate for life, and if one is killed, the mate will die soon after. They never harm the branches of plants they pick from.

林区的新买卖
New industry in the forest

文：莫久愚

内蒙古的县级市几乎都在兴安岭林区，大多是随着林业开发兴起的美丽山城。单一的林业经济，让这些城市几乎没有污染源，空气清新，林区人戏言，外地人到这里会"醉氧"。一位出身内地的老林工操着东北方言对我说："俺们这儿现在不卖木头了，卖风景、卖空气、卖林区风味。"

Most of the county-level cities in Inner Mongolia are in the Hinggan Range forests, mostly beautiful places have emerged with the development of forestry. Since the main economic activity is forestry, the cities are almost completely free of pollution, with clean air. The people of the forest areas joke that outsiders will get drunk off the oxygen when they visit. An old forest worker told me: "We don't sell wood anymore, but scenery, clean air, and our local flavour."

微观内蒙古
INNER MONGOLIA: COLOURFUL AND MAGNIFICENT

摄影：石玉平

没有枪的猎民
Hunters without guns

文：莫久愚

山林中的鄂温克猎人已"缴枪"多年，仍被称为"猎民"。学者何群看到，他们的居住地往往是一个用碗口粗细木杆围起的院落，中心是帐篷式的撮罗子。一个很粗的树干安装着一个机关，是自己发明的"天线"，靠近它可以使用手机。没有枪了，栏杆上挂着一大串鞭炮，准备用来吓唬熊、狼等凶猛野兽。

The Ewenki living in the forest long ago gave up their arms, but are still called "hunters". Scholar He Qun saw that their living place is a courtyard fenced by thick woods, and in the centre of each yard there is a tent-style hunting shack called "cuoluozi".They also install a kind of mechanism, an "antenna" they've invented on the trunk of a big tree; standing near it one can receive mobile phone signals. Without guns, they hang a strip of firecrackers on the fence, which can be ignited to scare off bears, wolves, and other dangerous animals.

受伤的狍子
An injured roe deer

文：莫久愚

一位森林民警在山坳的草丛中发现了一只受伤的狍子，看到人后，狍子挣扎着站起来，踉跄着挪了几步又摔倒了，却仍跪地爬行，喉咙里咕咕地似乎在诉说。细看才发现，它身后的草丛蜷卧着一只刚出生的幼崽。小狍子蹒跚着奔向妈妈，一头钻进妈妈怀里吮吸乳汁。大颗的眼泪顺着母狍子的脸颊流下，它慢慢地闭上了眼睛。

A forest police officer found an injured roe deer in the grass on the mountain. It struggled to stand, and then took a few staggering steps before falling down. It crawled along the ground, making gurgling sounds. Looking closely, he saw a just-birthed young deer curled up in the thick grass just behind the mother. The little one walked haltingly over to its mother and began to nurse. Tears flowed down the mother's cheeks as she slowly closed her eyes.

山林·沙地
Mountains, Forests and Deserts

山林里的鄂伦春人拜月亮
The Oroqen in the forest worship the moon

文：莫久愚

月亮被山林里的鄂伦春猎人当作神，鄂伦春文化学者说，每年正月十五和八月十五他们都要拜月亮。如果数日打不着猎物，就要在露天放一个清洁的桦皮盒，人们在盒旁向月亮叩头，祈求月亮神让他们打到野兽……除此之外，他们还把日、星、风、雷、电、山川以及植物都作为崇拜对象。

The moon is worshipped by the Oroqen hunters of the forest as a god. An Oroqen cultural scholar says that every year on the fifteenth day of the first and eighth lunar months, there is a moon worship festival. If hunters catch no prey for a number of days on end, they will place a clean white birch box out in the open and kowtow before it under the moon, praying to the moon for a better hunt… Besides the moon, they also worship the sun, stars, wind, thunder, lightning, mountains, rivers, and plants.

摄影：孟松林

微观内蒙古
INNER MONGOLIA: COLOURFUL AND MAGNIFICENT

摄影：苏伟伟

雪爬犁
Snow sleds

文：莫久愚

大兴安岭每年有六七个月被冰雪覆盖。过去山区城镇人家，家家都有一个人力拖拽的雪爬犁。对于成人，它是运输工具，也是购物车和童车。拖着它拉粮食、拉饮水、拉烧柴，也拖着它赶集、购物，置办年货。对于孩子，它是玩具，趴在爬犁上顺势从坡上滑下又冲向另一个坡，伴着尖叫和笑声。

In the Greater Hinggan Range, the ground is covered with snow and ice for six or seven months out of the year. In the past, every family living in the mountains had a snow sled. They're transport tools, shopping trolleys, and baby carriages. They can be used to pull grain, drinking water, and firewood, as well as collect one's purchases from the market, especially purchase necessities for the Spring Festival. For kids, they're toys that can be used to slide down one slope after another, accompanied by laughter and screams of joy.

寄居的狍子
Roe deer lodging in the deer shed

文：莫久愚

根河市林区有一个驯鹿饲养点，一天，饲养员将圈养的驯鹿放到林子里吃草，不一会儿就发现多了五六只，仔细一看，是几只野生狍子混了进来，见到人就机警地夺路而去。傍晚鹿群归圈时，狍子又跟着回来了，它们似乎很迷恋鹿舍舒适的环境和可口的饲料。久而久之，就不再惊恐，心安理得地以此为家了。

At a feeding point for reindeer in the forest of Gegen Gol City, one day, the caregiver released the reindeer raised in captivity into the forest to eat some grass, and found soon there were five or six more. Looking carefully, he saw that some wild roe deer had joined the group. They looked upon the caregiver alertly, and ran out of the door immediately. At dusk, they followed the reindeer back to the pen again. They seemed to fall in love with the deer shed and the comfortable environment and tasty food. Not long after, they no longer feared humans, and were at ease in their new home.

山林·沙地
Mountains, Forests and Deserts

林区猪的"红杏出墙"
The sow had a love affair in the forest

文：莫久愚

一年春天，大杨树林业局一户人家失踪了一冬的母猪带着十几只活泼的猪崽回来了。主人高兴之余，发现这些猪崽带有明显的条纹而且凶猛。原来入冬发情时，母猪不耐寂寞，自己到山林中寻找野猪郎了。因此每到母猪发情期，主人会将它拴在林中树下，周边撒些黄豆，几年下来，猪群都成了二代野猪。

One year in spring, someone from the Big Poplar Forestry Bureau saw a sow he had lost came back with over ten bouncy piglets. He was quite happy, and discovered the piglets had strips and were a bit truculent. It turned out the pig had been in heat in the early winter and gone into the forest to find some companionship, where it met a wild boar. Thus, each time when the pig went into heat after that, its owner would tie it to a tree in the forest, and scatter some soybeans nearby. After a few years, almost all of the pigs in the herd were semi-wild pigs.

驯鹿
Reindeer

文：莫久愚

驯鹿肩高三尺多，不论雄雌均生茸角，能够穿密林，涉沼泽，负重80多斤可日行20多公里。喜食蘑菇和浆果，能在两三尺深的积雪下找到苔藓。中国只有内蒙古的鄂温克敖鲁古雅部落饲养驯鹿。一位鄂温克作家说："我们的驯鹿是洁净森林的精灵，它只适应森林，它永远无法寄生于浑浊的满是人的世界。"

Reindeer are about one-metre-tall at the shoulders, and both males and females have fuzzy antlers. They excel at passing through dense forest, and crossing marshes. A reindeer can carry a load of 40 kilograms more than 20 kilometres in one day. They like to eat mushrooms and berries, and can find moss in nearly one-metre-deep snow. The Olguyaa Ewenkis in Inner Mongolia are the only ones that raise reindeer in China. An Ewenki author says: "Our reindeer are pure spirits of the forest. They only belong in the forest, and could never survive in the muddy and turbid world of humans."

摄影：巴义尔

微观内蒙古
INNER MONGOLIA: COLOURFUL AND MAGNIFICENT

涂利利　供稿自《勇敢的鄂伦春》

"绿天"
"Green sky"

文：莫久愚

大兴安岭 10.6 万平方公里的浩瀚林海是我国最大的林区，它和南美洲亚马孙热带雨林被称为地球的"两大肺叶"。作家叶圣陶第一次进入这里的密林时说："只觉得在林绿之中穿行异常新鲜，神清气爽。古人栽了几棵梧桐或者芭蕉，作诗就要用上'绿天'，未免夸张。这时候我倒真有'绿天'的实感。"

The Greater Hinggan Range hosts a vast forest of 106 thousand square kilometres, the largest forested area in China, which is called together with the Amazon Rainforest of South America one of the world's two "lungs". Author Ye Shengtao recalled when he first entered the dense forest: "You just think how the air is unusually fresh in crossing the green forest, and you feel great. The ancient poets planted a few parasol trees or hardy bananas, to which they would use grandiose phrases like 'green sky' to describe; obviously they were a bit too narrow. However, I did have a feel of 'green sky' when I went there in person."

"草原小警察"
"Grassland mini-cops"

文：姜苇

经过大兴安岭南麓的一个林场时，我们看见马路上有几只小黄鼠互相追逐，样子乖巧，调皮可爱。当地人说，这种小黄鼠在这里很多，它们不怎么怕人，常在路上跑，偶尔看到车或人，就会把前爪抬起来，像是敬礼的样子。所以，当地人把这种小黄鼠诙谐地称为"草原小警察"。

When passing through a forest on the southern reaches of the Greater Hinggan Range, we saw that beside the road there were a number of weasels chasing each other around. They were cute and well-behaved. A local said that there are many weasels in the area, and that they're not especially afraid of people. They frequently run around on the road, and when they see a car or a man, they'll stand up and raise their claws as if saluting. Thus, locals jokingly call them "grassland mini-cops".

山林・沙地
Mountains, Forests and Deserts

看看自己的心
Look at your heart

文：莫久愚

鄂伦春作家敖长福谈到交出猎枪的鄂伦春猎民对山林生活的怀恋时，引用了一位猎人的话："我虽然离别了山林，但我眼里的泪水就是森林里的河流。有时到森林里走走，并不是为了猎物，而是去看看自己的心罢了。"

Oroqen author Ao Changfu, talking about the Oroqen missing their previous lifestyles of hunting after giving up their shotguns, quotes a hunter: "Even though I left the forest, the tears in my eyes are still the rivers of the forest. Sometimes I go to the forest and walk around, not to hunt, just to look at my own heart."

驯鹿、树木和人
Reindeer, trees and people

文：莫久愚

学者何群一次到鄂温克人的驯鹿喂养点采访，驯鹿正值发情期，富有攻击性。猎人提醒她不要离开树，人挨着树，驯鹿就不袭击人。她当时没来得及请教其中的原委，猜想这可能是驯鹿文化才具有的鹿、树木、人之间的关系。

Scholar He Qun once went to a reindeer feeding point to interview the Ewenkis, and discovered that reindeers were in oestrus and were quite aggressive. The hunters told her to not leave the trees—if one sticks close to a tree, the reindeer will not attack. She didn't have time to find out the reasons from the Ewenkis, and guessed it probably had to do something with reindeer culture, and the relationship between reindeer, trees and people.

摄影：德克沙

微观内蒙古
INNER MONGOLIA: COLOURFUL AND MAGNIFICENT

骆驼之乡
The land of camels

文：莫久愚

腾格里沙漠、巴丹吉林沙漠、乌兰布和沙漠在阿拉善盟聚集，全盟 27 万平方公里，只有 1 万多平方公里适合人类居住。这里却是中外闻名的骆驼之乡，拥有世界双峰驼总量的 20%，中国的 2/3。在这里随处可见大群的骆驼，几十峰几百峰聚在一起，往往无人看护。在晨曦或夕阳里，高大的驼峰就像移动的山。

The Tengger, Badain Jaran, and Ulan Buh Deserts in the Alxa League comprise 270,000 square kilometres of land area, of which only 10,000 are suitable for human habitation. The area is famous in China and abroad for being home to camels—two-thirds of China's Bactrian camels live here, constituting 20% of the total world population. You can see camels everywhere here, sometimes in groups of tens or even hundreds, unattended by humans. At dawn and dusk, seeing them walk along the sand, the tall humps on their backs look like a group of moving mountains.

驼乡人
People living on the land of camels

文：莫久愚

戈壁草原的环境是严酷的，在戈壁滩上生存下来的人一定是生活的强者，他们有资格高傲地骑在驼背上，俯视这片土地。

The environment of the Gobi grasslands is harsh, and those who manage to survive upon must be strong people. They ride proudly upon camels, looking down upon the landscape.

摄影：乌热尔图

山林·沙地
Mountains, Forests and Deserts

草原还是沙地？
Grassland or sand land?

文：莫久愚

今天的通辽市，是明代以来蒙古科尔沁部的牧场。作家和历史学者们喜欢称其为科尔沁大草原；地理和环境学者则称之为科尔沁沙地；夏秋时节，游客们看到的却是一望无际的青纱帐。再仔细观察，北边仍有一片山地草原，南部已经出现了大面积沙漠。究竟应该如何称呼这里，是一个令人深思的话题。

Modern-day Tongliao City has been a pasture of Horqin Tribe since the Ming Dynasty. Authors and historians like to refer to it as the Horqin Grassland; geologists and environmental scientists refer to it as the Horqin Sand Land. In the summer and autumn, visitors will see a green curtain of tall grass everywhere. Looking closely, the northern part still has a mountainous grassland, and the southern part already a large area of desertified land. It's a question that requires a lot of thinking, what to call it.

骆驼那达慕
Camel Nadam Fair

文：莫久愚

冬季的骆驼，毛色漂亮，形态威武。内蒙古各地冬季都有不同规模的骆驼赛，阿拉善盟和巴彦淖尔市的戈壁旗县，每年初冬季节都会举办"骆驼那达慕"。国外记载的最大规模的比赛，是几个国家联合举办的，不过二三百头骆驼。而内蒙古西部盟市动辄几百峰，阿拉善盟2013年的"骆驼那达慕"有2200峰骆驼参赛。

In the winter, the camels' coats are beautiful, and their bodies mighty. In the winter there are many camel races in all parts of Inner Mongolia. In Alxa League and Bayannur City, there are "Camel Nadam Fairs" in the Gobi banners or counties. The largest camel race outside of China was an international competition conducted by a number of countries together, with no more than two or three hundred camels. The races in Western Inner Mongolia easily gather hundreds of camels when they occur, and the 2013 Alxa League Camel Nadam Fair saw 2,200 camels competing.

摄影：高雪峰

微观内蒙古
INNER MONGOLIA: COLOURFUL AND MAGNIFICENT

摄影：乌汉毕力格

驯驼
Camel taming

文：姜苇

骆驼是很难驯服的。在很小的时候就要给它们穿上鼻栓，固定缰绳。骑手跨上刚刚穿上鼻栓的骆驼，在戈壁滩上奔跑。骆驼剧烈地摆动、腾跃，试图甩掉背上的人，直到屈服于骑手的力量和坚持。驯驼是人和骆驼的角力，是人对骆驼的征服，和骆驼对人的归顺。

Camels are hard to tame. One must give them their nose piercing and affix the halter when they are very young. Just as these have been installed, a rider takes the camel out on Gobi to run around. The camel will sway, leap up, and try to throw its rider off until it is broken by the rider's strength and perseverance. This taming process is a kind of wrestling, the human conquering the camel's will, and the camel eventually submitting.

来自日本的"治沙愚公"
A Japanese persistent in desertification control

文：莫久愚

库布齐沙漠恩格贝基地竖立着一座铜像，是一位叫作远山正瑛的日本老人。他83岁开始每年在这里待200多天，默默植了10年树。他多次在日本巡讲，号召"每人每周省下一顿饭"，支援恩格贝。多年来一批又一批的日本志愿者自购工具和树苗，自费来到这里，种下了一棵又一棵树，染绿了一片又一片沙漠。

In the Engebei Base of the Hobq Desert, there is a bronze statue of a Japanese man named Tooyama Seiei. He has laboured for ten years, staying 200 days a year here, to plant trees, since he was 83. He travelled around Japan many times delivering lectures, encouraging people to "save the money for one meal a week" to give to Engebei. Over the years waves of Japanese volunteers came, buying tools and trees, planting trees with their own hands and turning the desert greener and greener.

山林·沙地
Mountains, Forests and Deserts

给沙漠颜色看的女人
Women show the deserts of their strength

文：莫久愚

内蒙古的沙区，有许多治沙女杰。作家肖亦农称她们为"给沙漠点颜色看的女人们"。如治沙老模范宝日勒岱，每年带领 12 个姐妹在沙漠中待大半年的乌云斯庆，为治沙而辞去公职的浪腾花……在沙漠中独自植树 6 万亩的殷玉珍，还和一些国际政要一起获得诺贝尔和平奖的提名。

Many stories about heroines of desertification control take place in the sandy areas of Inner Mongolia. Author Xiao Yinong calls them "the women who show the deserts of their strength". Here are some examples: Baoriledai who is an old model worker of desertification control, Wuyun Siqing who takes twelve sisters into the desert to spend half a year in combating with the desert, Lang Tenghua who quits her job to work in the sand, and Yin Yuzhen who planted 40 square kilometres of trees in the forest alone and was nominated for Nobel Peace Prize along with international political leaders…

利用卫星放牧
Satellite herding

文：莫久愚

鄂尔多斯库布齐沙漠中的牧人们最近开始利用卫星放牧了。北斗卫星系统可以精确追踪牧群的位置和踪迹，防止牲畜走失或遭遇意外。牧民使用手机或专门的接收终端，足不出户就能实时了解牧群情况。40 岁的图门·桑每隔三四天才会出门去看一次自己的牧群。

In the Hobq Desert of Ordos people have started to use the satellite to herd. The Beidou Satellite System can accurately track herds position and past positions in order to prevent them from getting lost or having accidents. Herders can see this information on their phones or special terminals, thus obtaining real-time information about their flocks without leaving the house. 40-year-old Tumen Sang only goes out once every three or four days to check on his herd in person.

摄影：高雪峰

微观内蒙古
INNER MONGOLIA: COLOURFUL AND MAGNIFICENT

摄影：高晋峰

找骆驼
Finding camels

文：莫久愚

如蒙古马一样，骆驼也是半野放的，几天甚至十几天才照看一次。养驼人对于自家的骆驼熟悉得就跟自己的儿女一样，在一望无际的戈壁沙漠中找寻自己的骆驼时，只需看看地上的蹄印、步幅大小、印痕深浅、数量多少，寻迹而去，准能找到。

Just like Mongolian horses, the camels are raised in a semi-wild state. One only has to go out to check on them once every few or over ten days. Those that raise them are as familiar with each one as they are with their own children; when looking for their camels in the vast Gobi desert, they just need to look at their tracks in the sand. Observing the gait, depth, and number of footprints, they can easily find their flock.

最长的穿沙高速公路
Longest desert highway

文：莫久愚

2016年9月，北京—乌鲁木齐高速公路内蒙古临河至甘肃白疙瘩的全长930公里主线贯通，成为世界上穿越沙漠最长的高速公路。线路多处途经无人区，寸草不生的戈壁沙漠，施工人员形容："就像在月球表面施工。"一位老者感慨："他们是在细菌都不愿生存的地方修出了一条路啊！"

In September 2016, the segment of the Beijing-Ürümqi Highway that runs from Linhe in Inner Mongolia to Baigeda in Gansu Province was completed, with a total length of 930 kilometres, making it the longest desert highway in the world. It passes through many uninhabited areas, and much of the Gobi desert landscape is completely barren, devoid of even the smallest of grass. One of the workers on the highway described building it as "like working on the moon". An older man remarked: "Where this road runs, even bacteria don't grow."

山林·沙地
Mountains, Forests and Deserts

赛驼会
Camel race

文：姜苇

阿拉善戈壁有一户牧民，自家组织举办了一场"赛驼会"，前来参赛的人很多。不少人骑骆驼在沙漠中走了好多天才到，风尘仆仆却满脸兴致。骑手们在戈壁滩上驰骋，炫耀自己的骆驼和骑术。姑娘、小伙儿身着盛装，他们的骆驼也是一样。阳光般灿烂的笑容，在戈壁滩上醒目耀眼。

In the Alxa Gobi Desert a herder held a camel race to which many showed up. Many people rode for days on their camels to attend, and showed up very tired, but excited. The riders galloped across the sand, showing off their camels and riding skills. The decorations on the camels showed the competitive spirit of the riders, and girls and boys decked themselves and their camels out. Everyone walked around smiling. It was a wonderful scene in the Gobi desert.

摄影：高雪峰

微观内蒙古
INNER MONGOLIA: COLOURFUL AND MAGNIFICENT

农民的发明
Farmer's invention

文：苏怀亮

库布齐沙漠腹地有一条纵贯南北全长 115 公里的穿沙公路。在修路过程中，如何在路边栽种防护林是一大难题。当地一个农民发明了塑料瓶蓄水栽种法，把树苗的根浸入盛满水的瓶子，封住瓶口空隙后埋入沙中，树苗就会在瓶口外生出新根扎入沙土深处，成活率达 70% 以上。

In the inner reaches of the Hobq Desert there is a 115-kilometre road that stretches from north to south. While building the road, planning trees along the edges was a difficult problem. A local farmer worked out a method: Place a small tree in a bottle of water, then seal the top, and place the bottle underground. The tree will grow new roots outside of the bottle, and these will grow deep into the ground. The success rate is about 70%.

中国的"萨王那"
Chinese savannah

文：莫久愚

"萨王那"是指沙地疏林或疏林草原景观，常常可以在非洲的热带草原或者澳洲的乡村看到。同纬度的北美温带沙地没有树，内蒙古的四大沙地却都存在"萨王那"类型的生态系统。沙地中间隔 5—8 米稀疏的阔叶乔木，与沙生灌丛和草本植物伴生，形成沙地疏林，甚至局部的疏林草原。

Savannah refers to sparse desert forest or sparse grassland forest, and is frequently used to describe the grasslands of Africa or countryside landscapes of Australia. The temperate sand lands of the North American continent at the same latitude don't have any trees, whereas the four major sand lands of Inner Mongolia all have savannah-like ecosystem. There are 5-8 metre tall broadleaf trees along with sand land shrubs and herbage which form a sparse desert forest, or even partial sparse grassland forest.

摄影：石玉平

山林・沙地
Mountains, Forests and Deserts

摄影：刘博伦

鄂尔多斯的新亮色
New achievements of Ordos

文：莫久愚

毛乌素的沙害曾是困扰鄂尔多斯和陕北几个世纪的生态灾难。现在75%的沙区已经被绿色覆盖，沙漠或许就要消失了。作家全秉荣说："这是何等的人间奇迹……这才是鄂尔多斯最大的亮点，什么人均GDP超香港，这个世界第一，那个全国折桂，比起就要消失的毛乌素沙漠来，那只是小捏捏的事情。"

The Mu Us Desert used to cause ecological problems for Ordos and Northern Shaanxi over the centuries. But now 75% of this area is covered with green plants, therefore the desert seems to be disappearing. Author Quan Bingrong says: "This really is a human miracle. What's most striking about Ordos is neither its per-capita GDP which exceeds that of Hong Kong, nor its winning a lot of champions at home and abroad. Compared to the disappearing Mu Us Desert, however, these are just small affairs."

沙漠中寻找沙漠
Looking for a desert in the desert

文：莫久愚

50年前，诗人郭小川在乌审旗感叹："哦，简直是一片无边无际的沙海，浊浪般的沙丘一直冲向天的尽头。"七八年前，作家肖亦农多次进入乌审旗的毛乌素沙漠，寻找他曾熟悉的大起大伏的金色沙山，看到的却总是各种沙生植物如绿毯般"伸展到很远很远的天边"，不禁狐疑："这里真的存在过毛乌素沙漠吗？"

Fifty years ago, poet Guo Xiaochuan remarked in the Uxin Banner: "Wow, it's almost like an endless sea of sand, dunes ascending and descending like turbid waves as far as the eye can see." Seven or eight years ago, author Xiao Yinong visited the Uxin Banner's Mu Us Desert a number of times, trying to find scene of undulating golden sandy hills he was once familiar, but all he could see was desert plants blanketing the ground off in the desert. He couldn't help but think, was there really a Mu Us Desert in this place?

微观内蒙古
INNER MONGOLIA: COLOURFUL AND MAGNIFICENT

摄影：张朝忠

会唱歌的沙子
Singing sand

文：苏怀亮

库布齐大漠有两处响沙，它的声响需天、地、人协作。晴朗的日子，干燥的沙子，有人去触摸滑动，沙子才会赐给你奇妙的音响，三个条件缺一不可。人们一直想解开沙子唱歌的谜，然而至今只闻传说，不见谜底。

There are two places with "singing sand" in the Hobq Desert. To make the sound they need the cooperation of the sky, earth and people. On clear days, when the dry sand is touched by people, it will emit an enjoyable "singing" noise. All three of the conditions are necessary for the effect to occur. People have always tried to figure out the reason behind this, but even today there are only legends—the riddle has not been solved.

腾格里沙漠
Tengger Desert

文：莫久愚

"腾格里"在蒙古语和突厥语中，都是"天"的意思。腾格里沙漠常年刮西北风，牧民们说，是风把西北边巴丹吉林沙漠的沙子吹到了这里，所以把这片沙漠叫作天上来的沙漠，又叫"天漠"。

"Tengger" in Mongolian and ancient Turkic means "sky". A north-western wind blows year-round here. The herders say that the wind blows sand from the Badain Jaran Desert here, so the desert is called "sky desert" as the sand comes from the sky.

山林·沙地
Mountains, Forests and Deserts

沙地
Sand land

文：莫久愚

中国的浑善达克沙地、科尔沁沙地、呼伦贝尔沙地、毛乌素沙地，都在内蒙古。与沙漠不同的是，沙地降雨量可达 300 毫米以上，有短小的内流河和小湖，动植物繁茂。如浑善达克沙地就有高等植物 800 多种，远远高于沙漠的几种到几十种，也高于典型草原的 100—300 种。沙地植物的光合作用很强，是草原的三倍多。

The Onqin Daga, Horqin, Hulun Buir and Mu Us Sand Lands all lie within the borders of Inner Mongolia. What makes them different from deserts is that they have up to 300 mm of rainfall per year, with short rivers and small lakes and a large variety of plant and animal life. The Onqin Daga Sand Land has more than 800 kinds of higher plants, much more than deserts which have a few dozen or even just a few, and even more than typical grasslands which have 100-300. The photosynthetic activity here is also quite intense, more than three times that of the grasslands.

摄影：石玉平

沙漠人家
Families of the desert

文：莫久愚

神秘的巴丹吉林沙漠至今还有一万多平方公里从未出现过人类的足迹。但巴丹吉林南部有许多沙漠湖泊，每一片水域就是一片绿洲，每一片绿洲总有一户人家，几十户人家组成了一个嘎查（村）。出一次沙漠，骑行骆驼也要几天几夜。外人常常疑惑，在不断移动的不尽沙山中，他们是怎么找到"路"的？

There is an area of 10,000 square kilometres in the mysterious Badain Jaran Desert which has no traces of human activity. However, there are many desert lakes in the south of the desert, each of which is an oasis. Each oasis has a family living there, with a few tens of familes forming a "Gacha", or village. To leave the desert, one must ride a camel for a number of days and nights. Outsiders frequently are curious: Among the moving sands, how can one find a road?

攝影：高雪峰

舌尖・语言
Taste and Language

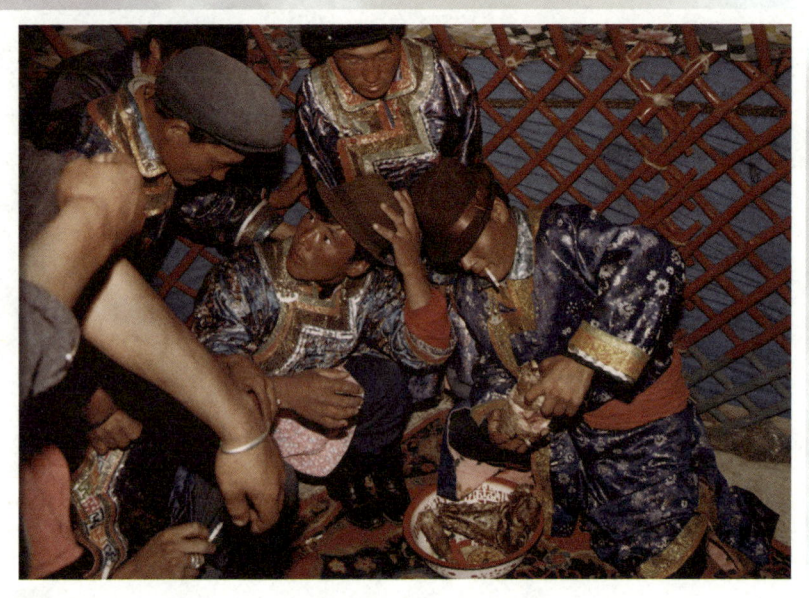

微观内蒙古
INNER MONGOLIA: COLOURFUL AND MAGNIFICENT

摄影：崇先鸣

手把肉
Hand-ripped meat

文：莫久愚

在草原上，手把肉可以款待任何身份的宾客。羊肉有千般做法，唯有手把肉才保留了最纯正的草原羊肉的鲜香。它做法简单，一个牧人，能在十几分钟内把一只刚宰杀的羊分解完毕，放入清水中煮半小时，不用盐和调料，吃时大块大块地，用手把着，蘸盐水或酱料。一些从不吃羊肉的内地朋友，吃起手把肉来却津津有味。

On the grasslands, hand-ripped meat can be used to receive and entertain guests of any status. There are thousands of ways to prepare mutton, but only this method preserves the purest and most authentic taste. It's easy to make. A herder can de-bone a freshly slaughtered lamb in about 15 minutes. After boiling it in plain water for half an hour, there's no need to add salt or spices. Chunks of meat held by hand are dipped in salt water or sauces when eaten, and even people who don't like to eat mutton will enjoy its interesting flavour.

菜包饭
Wrapped rice

文：姜苇

菜包饭是通辽人非常喜爱的食品。把白菜叶铺平，放上撕碎的葱、香菜等辅料，然后根据自己的口味加入大酱、辣椒，铺上蒸熟的米饭，大米、小米、高粱米皆可。最后将菜叶对折封底，双手握紧，即可食用。过去这道菜透着无奈的简陋，今天却是健康时尚的佳肴。

Wrapped rice is a very popular food in Tongliao. A leaf of cabbage is laid flat, and on top of it freshly crushed green onions and coriander are laid down. Then, according to one's own tastes, soy paste and peppers are added before a quantity of steamed rice, millet or husked sorghum is placed inside. The leaf is folded up, and then eaten as a package. In the past, this was a food used to make it through hard times, but now it is a healthy dish enjoyed by many.

舌尖·语言
Taste and Language

奶皮子
Milk skin

文：黄蕾

奶皮子是享用蒙餐前不可缺的佐茶品。把新鲜奶汁倒入锅中慢火熬煮，一边扬动，纯黄夹白、油渍点点、呈蜂窝状，入口奶油溢香，酥柔味美。不同地区、不同牧民家的奶皮子味道有细微差别。牧民的膳食保持着"奶食与肉食"的动态平衡，奶皮子与炒米、酸奶、奶茶、干肉一起，构成牧民的日常餐饭。

Milk skin is an essential appetiser for Mongolian cuisine. Fresh milk is slow-boiled until a skin of cream forms on top, dotted with oil, like a honeycomb, and its colour is yellow with a bit of white hue. It's soft, and delicious. In different areas, between different houses, the flavour of the skin has slight differences. The meals of the herders maintain an equilibrium between meat and milk—milk skin and fried millet, together with yoghurt, milk tea and meat jerky form an excellent everyday meal.

摄影：黄蕾　　　　　　　　　　摄影：张阿泉

羊肉吃出来的京蒙文化
Mongolian-Beijing flavour

文：邓九刚

清朝定都北京把满族人中秋吃羊肉的风俗带入了京城，而盛产肥羊的蒙古草原是京城羊肉的主要来源。京人吃羊肉上了瘾，每年农历七月八月吃"热羊"，十月十一月吃"冬羊"；吃法也变了新花样，于是著名的涮羊肉火锅"东来顺"在京城应运而生，一火就是百余年。

When the Manchu people of the Qing Dynasty came to Beijing, the capital, they brought with them the custom of eating mutton at the Mid-autumn Festival. The Mongolian grasslands produce large quantities of mutton, and thus became the mutton provider for the capital, where the people became hooked on the meat. And in the seventh and eighth months in Chinese lunar calendar people eat "hot lamb", and in the tenth and eleventh months eat "cold lamb". They created new ways of eating it, and through this process, the famous mutton hot pot restaurant of the capital "Donglaishun" was born, and has persisted as a popular brand for more than a century.

微观内蒙古
INNER MONGOLIA: COLOURFUL AND MAGNIFICENT

摄影：高雪峰

羯子羊
Gelding sheep

文：莫久愚

指去势后的成年公羊，懂得"投入产出比"的牧民很少留羯子羊了。因为吃同样多的草料，它们远不如羔羊增重快。如今内地人青睐鲜嫩而无膻味的草原羔羊肉，而牧民还是愿意用羯子羊做手把肉，肉味醇厚，香而不腻，脂肪又低。在草原做客，倘若主人为你宰杀一只三四岁的羯子羊，那你一定是被当作贵客了。

When one looks at the "input-output ratio" involved in raising a castrated sheep to adulthood, those that understand the situation know it's quite low. For the amount of feed that will be expended, it makes much more sense to raise and slaughter young lambs. Whilst people from other areas of China like the fresh and mild flavour of young lambs, the herders, for their own purposes of making some dishes, know that a mature gelding is best, with a full flavour, plentiful in fragrance yet not greasy, and a character that is low in fat. If you're a guest on the grasslands and the host slaughters a three- or four-year-old gelding for you, you are definitely a VIP.

华子鱼
Amur Ide

文：姜苧

华子鱼是生长在微碱性水域中的鱼类。达里诺尔湖的华子鱼炖出的鱼汤，味之鲜美无法形容，让人只能一直喝一直喝，从拿起勺子的那一刻，就不愿放下。久而回味，齿颊仍有余香。

The Amur Ide is a fish that lives in slightly alkaline water. Those produced in Dalai Nur lake are good materials for making fish soup which is indescribably tasty, so good that once you pick up the bowl you will not set it down. When you think about it later on, you'll still feel the fragrance and flavour of the fish in your mouth.

舌尖·语言
Taste and Language

烧卖
Shaomai

文：莫久愚

"烧卖"这个名称，很可能源自一个突厥化的蒙古语词"shirme"，本义为"皮囊"。元末一位在中国生活过的朝鲜人形容烧卖皮兜住馅儿以后撮细上部，就像皮囊口拴系后自然外翻。它曾是元代官场饭局上的一道美食，如今已遍布呼包两市的大街小巷。一壶砖茶，一两烧卖，是寻常百姓最普通的早餐。

The term "shaomai" may come from the ancient Turkic word "shirme", which originally meant "leather bag". A Korean living in China in the Yuan Dynasty described them as being filled with stuffing and then pinched at the top like one would seal a leather bag, at the top of which the inside was turned out. They used to be a delicacy for officials' banquets in the Yuan Dynasty, but now they are ubiquitous in the alleyways of Hohhot and Baotou. A pot of brick tea and an order of shaomai is a very typical breakfast for ordinary people in these cities.

摄影：张阿泉

奶茶相伴的一天
A day of milk tea

文：邓九刚

蒙古族牧民的每一天都是从喝奶茶开始的，通常一家人只在晚上放牧回家后才正式用餐一次，早、中、晚三次在外用餐也不离奶茶。牧民们经常围坐在一起，一面就着炒米、糕点细细品尝醇香的奶茶，一面谈心论事。

The Mongolian herders' day always starts with drinking milk tea. Normally a family only have one meal together in the evening when they come back from herding. When out in the fields, be it for breakfast, lunch, or dinner there will be milk tea to drink. When the herders sit around together and enjoy snacks, such as fried millet or small cakes, the smell of milk tea will waft through the air as they discuss affairs.

微观内蒙古
INNER MONGOLIA: COLOURFUL AND MAGNIFICENT

蒙古馅儿饼
Mongolian stuffed pie

文：莫久愚

草原妇女做馅儿饼，面和得很软，放在案板上几乎能"流动"。用纯羊肉或牛肉、驼肉做馅儿，拌入少量沙葱。包馅儿时，手蘸食油或干面，揪出一块面，拍成片状，包住肉馅儿后，再用手拍成饼状，入锅煎熟。饼皮薄如纸，几乎能看到里面红色的肉。著名的东苏旗肉饼，肉馅儿近1厘米厚。

When the women of the grasslands make stuffed pies, the dough is made quite soft, and can almost "flow" around the cutting board it is placed upon. Pure mutton, beef, or camel meat is used as a filling, combined with a little bit of wild onion. When making the pie, the fingers are dipped in a bit of oil or dry flour, and then a piece of dough is ripped off and pressed into a flat form upon which the filling is placed, pushed flat, sealed in, and then fried. The skin of the pie is paper-thin, so much that one can almost see the meat inside. The famous meat pies of Sonid Left Banner have filling almost 1 cm thick.

"小尾羊"餐饮集团 供稿

糕圐圙 (kūlüè)
Fried ring-shaped cake

文：苏怀亮

也叫油圐圙。用黏米面发酵蒸熟，捏成茶杯口大小的圆圈儿，用胡麻油炸成暗红色即可。家家都做，味道各异。正月里，村里邻居互相串门拜年，客人一进门就笑着说："过年好，尝一尝你家的油圐圙。"主妇满脸喜气忙下地，熬一壶茶，放一盘炒米，一盘糕圐圙。既是礼节，也是女主人茶饭手艺的展示。

It's called "gao (cake) kulüe" or "you (oil) kulüe" in the local dialect, which is a kind of fried cake made from fermented and then steamed sticky millet flour, and then pinched into little rings about the size of the mouth of a tea cup. To finish their preparation, they're fried in linseed oil until dark red. Every family makes them, and the flavour each family produces is different. During the first month of the lunar year, when people visit each other's houses, they say jokingly as they enter the door: "Happy new year! Let me try some of your youkulüe." The woman of the house will happily boil a pot of tea, bring out a plate of millet stir-fried in butter and a plate of gaokulüe. It's a holiday ritual, and also an opportunity for the woman to show off her cooking skills.

舌尖·语言
Taste and Language

呼和浩特的面食
Foods made of flour in Hohhot

文 / 邓九刚

走西口的山西人在呼和浩特占了相当大的比例，他们把山西的面食带到了这里：剔尖、擦面、拨面、猫耳朵、饸饹、拉面、刀削面、拨鱼、揪片、炝锅面、拷栳栳（kǎolǎolao）、转面、翡翠面、蛋黄面、浇肉面、打卤面、鸳鸯面……足有百十种，多由晋商推动普及。内蒙古西部人偏爱面食的习惯就是从那时候养成的。

The people of Shanxi who journeyed west to Hohhot set up a lot of businesses, and they accounted for a high proportion in the city's population. They also brought their foods made of flour with them. Pointed noodles, shaved noodles, long knife-cut noodles, "cat ears", straight noodles, pulled noodles, short knife-cut noodles, chopped noodle pieces, shrimp-flour noodles, tube noodles, turned noodles, jade noodles, egg noodles, fat-fried noodles, sauce noodles, quail noodles, etc. There are more than a hundred kinds that have been brought over by Shanxi businessmen. It's because of these that the people in the west of Inner Mongolia enjoy eating noodles so much.

面茶
Bread tea

文 / 苏怀亮

也叫油茶，既可现做现喝，也可制成半成品。将莜面炒至暗黄色，用适量羊油融化搅拌均匀，放入容器内冷却成固体的油面饼，喝时切一块面饼放入熬好的砖茶水中融开即可。这种油、面、茶三合一的稀糊汤非常好喝。奇怪的是，这种蒙汉融合的饮品却只有汉族饮用。

Also called "oil tea", it can be made and drunk fresh, or semi-prepared and stored for later consumption. First, naked oat flour is fried until dark yellow, and then a quantity of mutton fat is added, melted, and mixed in. The mixture is then placed in a container and chilled until it forms a cake. To enjoy it, simply slice off a piece and put it in a boiled cup of brick tea. This kind of pasty, soupy beverage made of tea, fat, and flour is very palatable. What's odd is that this Mongolian-Han fusion drink is only drunk by the Han Chinese.

"小尾羊"餐饮集团 供稿

微观内蒙古
INNER MONGOLIA: COLOURFUL AND MAGNIFICENT

"小尾羊"餐饮集团 供稿

碗坨儿
Jelly lump in the bowl

文：苏怀亮

荞麦糁子泡在水中反复搓擦成淀粉糊，每个碗里舀半碗蒸熟晾凉。另用盐、醋、酱油、芝麻、芥末兑入凉开水，再淋上胡麻油做成调汤。挑一担到街上只吆喝一声：碗坨儿！便有男女围拢，或站或坐。卖者取一碗在掌心，用小刀沿着碗壁利落地划成菱形块，倒入调汤，递与食客……爽嫩滑溜，美味啊！

Put some coarse buckwheat sludge in water and mix them around until a paste is formed, pour it into bowls, half-filling them, steam it, and then set them out to cool off until it becomes jellied. Then, make the sauce: take salt, vinegar, soy sauce, sesame, and mustard, and mix them into cold boiled water, and sprinkle some flaxseed oil on top for flavour. Take these to the street and yell: "I've got jelly lumps!" People will surround you, sitting or standing, as you carve each bowl up with a knife, cutting the jelly into rhombus-shaped chunks, and dump the ready made sauce into the bowl to serve. What a delicious food!

南屯牛排
Nantun steak

文：莫久愚

鄂温克旗政府所在地巴彦托海镇又称"南屯"，紧邻海拉尔市区。南屯向南的几十公里，有一百多个养牛场。那里的牛肉出奇地好吃，牛排的做法独特，有一种淡淡的乳香。一次到海拉尔，分别约几个朋友叙旧，他们都说要让我品尝当地最好吃的东西，于是我一天之内吃了三次南屯牛排。

Bayan Tuohai Town, the seat of the government in Ewenki Banner, is also known as "Nantun". It is near the Hailar City area. A few dozen kilometres south of Nantun are more than 100 cattle farms. The beef there is unusually delicious. There is also a special way of preparing steaks there, which gives them a light milky flavour. When I went to Hailar, I met up with a few different groups of friends to swap stories, and they all insisted I try the best the area had to offer. Thus, I had three meals of Nantun steak in one day.

舌尖·语言
Taste and Language

农家黄酒
Countryside yellow liquor

文：苏怀亮

临近过年时，西部一些农家的热炕头上常常放一个小瓷坛子，里面装着兑有烧酒的熟米面糊糊，坛子外包裹着棉被，这是正在发酵的黄酒。揭开坛盖，浓郁的酒香扑鼻而来。若是来了客人，锅里放适量的水，舀一勺糊糊搅匀烧开，便成了热腾腾、金灿灿的黄酒，喝上一碗，暖身暖胃。

Towards the end of each year, dropping into some farmers' houses in the west, you'll frequently see a small porcelain jar on the heatable brick bed. Within there will be a mixture of liquor and fried millet flour, and the jar will be wrapped in a quilt—this is yellow liquor in the process of fermenting. When you open the lid of the jar, you'll be met with an intense fragrance of liquor. When guests come, a bit of water will be placed in the pot, and a bit of the sticky substance from the jar will be added and boiled. When it bubbles, the stuff is ready. The bright golden liquid will warm your insides when you take a sip.

米凉粉
Millet jelly

文：苏怀亮

夏天，你若走进内蒙古西部农家，很可能会看见院子里有阴凉的地方摆放着几块高粱秸秆制作的圆形箅子，上面摊着一层金黄的黏稠糊糊，那就是米凉粉。进屋后，主人会给你挑一碗凉粉，舀一勺汤料，筷子一挑一摆，层层分离。吃上一口，凉爽开胃。

In the summer, when you go to someone's home in western Inner Mongolia, you may see in a cool area of the yard a few round plates made out of sorghum stalks, upon which there is a layer of golden-yellow paste—this is millet jelly. When you go inside, the host will give you a bowl of the stuff, and add a spoon of seasoned soup, breaking apart the jelly into chunks for you. Try it, and you'll find it's cooling and tasty.

"小尾羊"餐饮集团 供稿

微观内蒙古
INNER MONGOLIA: COLOURFUL AND MAGNIFICENT

杀猪菜
Slaughtering-a-pig speciality

文：苏怀亮

鄂尔多斯农家杀猪是一件隆重的事。割下猪脖子肉，当地叫猪项圈（hàngquan）或槽头肉，肥肥的一大块切成一指多厚、三四寸大的肉片，土豆也切成大块，酸白菜切成细丝，做成油汪汪的烩菜，叫作杀猪菜。杀猪菜原本是杀猪的时候才吃的，请来本家长辈、兄弟姐妹和邻居，齐聚同享，既是风味也是习俗。

In Ordos, slaughtering a pig is a big deal. A strip of meat is cut from its neck, which is called the "pork necklace" or "trough meat". The fat chunk of meat is cut into pieces about a finger thick and three or four inches wide, and cooked with big chunks of potato and thin strips pickled cabbage. This high-fat food is called "slaughtering-a-pig speciality", originally eaten on the occasion of slaughtering a pig. One invites one's elders, siblings, and neighbours over to enjoy it—it's both a culinary pastime and a cultural tradition.

"小尾羊"餐饮集团　供稿

酸饭和酸菜
Sour congee and sour vegetables

文：邓九刚

山西人喜欢食醋，而包头及土默川、河套地区盛产糜米，煮饭极为适口，"走西口"人把二者结合，发明了酸饭，夏天食用，既解暑，又简便，成为一道独特的饮食。此外，包头地区蒙汉人民常吃腌制的酸菜，也与吃酸饭一样，都是山西"醋文化"的变体，与汉族人"走西口"有着密切的关系。

People from Shanxi like to eat vinegar and vinegared foods. The areas of Baotou, Tumd Plain and Hetao all produce white millet in large quantities, which is excellent to eat when steamed or made into congee. Those people who came to Inner Mongolia from Shanxi merged the flavours of their homeland and the local, and thus invented a unique food named "sour congee", which is easy and nice to eat in the summer and cools one off. Additionally, in the Baotou area, the Mongolian and Han Chinese like to eat pickled vegetables, which, like the "sour congee", represent a variant of Shanxi cuisine characterized by the "vinegar culture". This particular variant is closely connected with the story of those who came west to Inner Mongolia from Shanxi.

舌尖·语言
Taste and Language

酿皮那个香
Fragrance of cold sheet jelly

文：白江宏

酿皮最讲究调料功夫。白玉般软筋筋的酿皮，浇上酸咸的汤汁，调入葱花油、辣椒油、蒜汁、香菜末、花生碎，再洒上一撮麻辣肝、几块面筋，寡淡中和丰富，朴素遭遇香艳，满满一大碗端上桌，逗得人吞口水，一头扎下去，吸溜溜吃得那个香。

"Cold sheet jelly", or chopped pieces of glutinous steamed wheat flour paste with a square cross section, depends on the seasonings it is prepared with. The sticky sheet jelly, white like jade, is doused with a sour and salty soup, and then topped with large amounts of scallion oil, pepper oil, garlic juice, crushed coriander, crushed peanuts, some spicy liver, and a few chunks of gluten. The flavours balance each other out, and the dish is quite fragrant. When a big plate is laid on the table, everyone will drool, eager to take a bite and have one's world filled with flavour.

"小尾羊"餐饮集团 供稿

微观内蒙古
INNER MONGOLIA: COLOURFUL AND MAGNIFICENT

羊肉蘸糕
Mutton-dipped cake

文：苏怀亮

羊肉蘸糕大约是鄂尔多斯地区人独特的吃法，炖一锅羊肉，用素糕蘸着汤吃。这也是大小饭店的招牌菜。外地客人来鄂尔多斯，主人点菜，第一句很可能就是："来一份羊肉蘸糕！"

The practice of "mutton-dipped cake" is more or less unique to Ordos. A pot of mutton is boiled, and then fried millet cakes are dipped in the soup and eaten. This can be the signature dish at both small and large restaurants. When visitors from elsewhere visit Ordos, and the host orders for the table, the first thing out of his mouth is very likely to be "bring us an order of mutton-dipped cake"!

"小尾羊"餐饮集团　供稿

油糕的生死缘
Life begins and ends by eating fried millet cake

文：刘秉忠

油糕是用黄米面炸出来的糕点，它与河套人有着生死之缘。农民说："人一生至少要吃三顿糕，过满月一顿，娶老婆一顿，进棺材一顿。"村里有老年人去世，不说"死"，说"吃了糕啦"；庄稼没有出苗，不说"枯死"，说"下地吃油糕去了"。委婉又不失幽默。

The lives of the people of Hetao are inextricably connected with fried millet cake (literally "oil cake"). The local farmers say: "You must eat fried millet cake three times in your life: the first time when reaching a month of age, the second when marrying, and the last when you enter the casket." When someone in a village dies, they are not said to have died, but rather to have "eaten fried millet cake". When crops fail to sprout, one says "they went underground to eat fried millet cake". It's euphemistic, but also humorous.

"小尾羊"餐饮集团　供稿

舌尖·语言
Taste and Language

不吃羊肉怎么过冬？
How can we make it through the winter without mutton?

文：莫久愚

在北京人秋后忙着冬储大白菜的时代，呼和浩特市民往往是忙着储备刚刚宰杀的草原羊，无论蒙古族还是其他民族。如今市场供给已经变化了，一些老人还是念叨着储藏几只草地上的羊过冬。特别是那些曾在草原上生活过的老人，春节时要是不吃几顿地道的手把肉，总好像少了点什么。

When people in Beijing are busy storing Chinese cabbage for the winter after the autumn harvest, people in Hohhot are scrambling to stock up on freshly-slaughtered grassland lamb, be they Mongolian or of another ethnicity. Even though the market supply has changed, you will still hear old people talking on and on about how many lambs they've bought to make it through the winter. Especially those who used to live on the grasslands believe that when the Spring Festival comes, without a few good meals of hand-ripped mutton, something is missing.

摄影：张阿泉

荞麦要"笨加工"
Simple buckwheat processing

文：张阿泉

从前包头固阳人加工荞麦面粉都是自家动手，石碾、石磨是关键工具。推碾子、围磨是家家户户少不了的活儿。后来，石碾、石磨逐渐淘汰，被"小钢磨子"（小型面粉加工机）取代。当地老农说："荞面还是大石磨上围下来的有味儿；小钢磨子里面温度太高，把荞麦给烧坏了，荞面不香。"

In previous times, buckwheat processing by the people of Guyang, Baotou was done by hand at home, with a stone roller and a millstone. Using these tools was a key task for the people in these households. Later on, these tools were abandoned for the "little steel mill" (a miniature grain processor). An old local farmer says: "You need to grind the buckwheat with a mill stone to have the right flavour; these modern machines produce too high a temperature inside, they scorch the grain, and it comes out flavourless."

微观内蒙古
INNER MONGOLIA: COLOURFUL AND MAGNIFICENT

白食和红食
White food and red food

文：邓九刚

蒙古族最喜欢的两类日常食品可用"红白"颜色区分——奶制品用汉语叫作"白食"，"红食"则指牛羊肉制品。所以要是听内蒙古的人说他"爱吃白食"，可不要误以为是吃了饭不给钱的意思。

The people of Inner Mongolia like to divide their food into two categories—"white" and "red". "White food" refers to milk products, and "red" to mutton or beef products. The Chinese word for white food is "baishi", and the most common meaning of "eat baishi" is "dine and dash". Thus, in hearing a Mongolian saying "I like eat baishi", other people may mistakenly think that he does not want to pay.

喝碗杂碎才算回家
Having some entrails, and it's like coming home

文：莫久愚

内蒙古西部城镇杂碎馆多。如同北京人的豆浆油条一样，是许多人不变的早餐。这里的杂碎馆每碗的羊杂用料，往往可够内地一些小吃店做好几碗，吃着过瘾。有的吃客出门久了，早晨下了火车或飞机，先要找到一家常光顾的杂碎馆，喝上一两碗杂碎，吞下一个白焙子，才算找到回家的感觉。

Restaurants that serve a soup of mixed cooked entrails are quite common in cities of western Inner Mongolia. Just as soy milk and twisted crullers are very popular in Beijing for breakfast, this kind of "chop suey" is a breakfast staple here. In a bowl of mixed cooked entrails in any restaurant here, you'll find several times as much sheep entrails as you would find in a restaurant elsewhere in China. It's quite nice to eat. When patrons of these restaurants take trips elsewhere and arrive back home in the morning, it's common for them to visit one of these restaurants directly from the airport or train station before heading home. Pairing a bowl of the soup with a white flour bread roll is the perfect meal, only in which way can they feel at home again.

"小尾羊"餐饮集团 供稿

舌尖·语言
Taste and Language

小尾羊，大火锅
Little Lamb, big pot

文：余佳荣

"肉中人参"内蒙古草原羊，用牧民中流传的古老配方调制的"神汤"一涮，便成了绝佳的蒙式火锅——"小尾羊"。16年来，"小尾羊"把传统的蒙式涮羊肉变成连锁店，也把"欢乐牧场"和"蒙古大营"带到中国各大城市，还漂洋过海到了日本、澳大利亚、英国、美国、阿联酋……让越来越多的人体验了蒙古式的大火锅。

The mutton produced on the Inner Mongolian grasslands is considered as "ginseng" among different kinds of meats. A good way to eat is boiling the mutton slices in a hot pot, in which the soup is well prepared in a traditional way popular with the Mongolian herders for ages. Such is the mutton served by the Little Lamb, which is a Mongolian hot pot restaurant with 16 years of history, and it is one of the best chain hot pot restaurants at home and abroad. The Little Lamb also runs restaurants with different themes in Chinese cities, such as "Happy Pasture" and "Mongolian Camp", through which the Mongolian culture is transmitted. The Chinese and people from Japan, Australia, Britain, USA, United Arab Emirates, etc., have tasted the real Mongolian hot pot through dining in the Little Lamb restaurants.

"小尾羊"餐饮集团　供稿

胡麻盐
Flaxseed salt

文：苏怀尧

胡麻是内蒙古西部的重要作物，胡麻籽可榨油，也可制成胡麻盐作调味品，类似椒盐。在无菜佐餐的情况下，可以撒在米饭上拌着吃。最传统最典型的吃法是：蒸一锅土豆，一家人围坐炕上，碗里搁一撮胡麻盐，拿土豆蘸着吃。这可能就是旧时农家的一顿饭。

Flax is an important crop of western Inner Mongolia. Flaxseed can be used to make oil, or prepared with salt as a seasoning. It's made of flaxseeds and salt fried together, similar to pepper salt. When one has no accompanying dishes, it can be sprinkled over rice and mixed in. The most traditional way to eat it is to boil a pot of potatoes, and then sit around on the heatable brick bed with the family, dipping the potatoes in the flaxseed salt before eating it. This is a farmer's meal from the old days.

微观内蒙古
INNER MONGOLIA: COLOURFUL AND MAGNIFICENT

盐是食品的"德吉"
Salt is best

文：张阿泉

蒙古人崇尚盐，认为盐是食品的"德吉"，即第一位。"盐"在蒙古人的俗语里随处可见："盐放多了"形容过火，"没放盐的汤"意为不过瘾，"大海也有缺盐的时候"意思是人无完人，"要想节约的话是水，要想品尝的话是盐"意思是多说无益，"做事有终结，放盐要足够"意思是要有始有终。

The Mongolians very much like salt, and think it is the best of the foods. "Salt" in colloquial speech is commonly seen. "To put too much salt" means to overdo something or to go too far, "unsalted soup" means something is unsatisfying, and "even the sea is short of salt sometimes" means "nobody is perfect". "Essential words you want to hear taste like salt; otherwise, water" means "there's no use saying too much". "Make sure to add enough salt" means "finish what you start".

包头话里的"来来"
"Lailai" in Baotou dialect

文：张阿泉

包头固阳人在口语中表示"过去时"，习惯用"来来"结尾，第一个"来"要音正腔圆，第二个"来"发音要弱些，两个"来"的发音高低、节奏快慢要恰到好处。譬如见面问一句："去哪圪来来？"（意为"你去哪儿了？"）这种叠音给人一种亲切感和美感。

To express the past tense, the people of Guyang, Baotou add "lailai" to the end of the sentence, with the first "lai" pronounced properly, and the second a bit more weakly. For instance, when meets a friend, one will ask "where have you been" and add "lailai" at the end of his speech. This kind of speaking style sounds familiar and nice.

牛桥
Cow bridge

文：邓九刚

过去在归化商界，"桥"这个字意指"市场"。所以在呼和浩特老城区，"桥"被赋予了特殊的含义："牛桥"曾经是买卖牛的市场，依次类推，还有羊桥、马桥、驼桥等。

In the trade world of Guihua "bridge" used to denote a market. Thus, in the old quarter of Hohhot, "bridge" has a special meaning. "Niuqiao" (cow bridge) is the site of a market where cows were once sold. In a similar fashion, there is also a lamb bridge, horse bridge, camel bridge, and so on.

沙漠人指路
Directions in the desert

文：姜苹

在阿拉善沙漠中问路，阿拉善人会告诉你"在那——里"，语气拉得很长时表示这个地方很远；如果他们告诉你"在那—里"，那就表示不是很远；如果他们说"在那里"，那就表示这个地方就在跟前。而用蒙语说时也是如此。

When asking directions in the Alxa Desert, the locals will tell you "it's over theeeeeeere", the lengthening of the vowel meaning it is quite far. If they say "it's theeere", then it means it isn't far, and "it's there" means it's right in front of you. The same pattern is used in Mongolian.

舌尖 · 语言
Taste and Language

"玉米"透露的端倪
Corn reveals origins
文：庞月莲

包头的居民有不同的来历：东河区被叫作"老包头"，祖上多是"走西口"来的；昆区和青山区则是支援包头的建设者后裔。从卖玉米大妈的吆喝里就可听出端倪：昆区的叫"苞米，热苞米"，是东北味；青山区的则喊"玉米，热玉米"，略带河北口音；东河区的"玉茭茭，玉茭茭"，让山西人感到亲切。

The people of Baotou come from different areas. The Donghe District is called "old Baotou", and is populated by descendants of people who came west from Shanxi. Kun District and Qingshan District are populated by the descendants of later arrivals who built the city up. When you hear old women calling out to hawk corn, you can hear the differences between the districts. In Kun District, it's "baomi", pronounced with authentic accent of North-eastern China; in Qingshan, it's "yumi", the common word with corn, pronounced with a bit of the Hebei accent, and in Donghe, it's "yujiaojiao", with the distinctive accent of Shanxi Province.

三条舌头的商人
A trader with three tongues
文：邓九刚

在呼和浩特，人们说起商人的类别来，会以舌头而论。只会讲汉语的商人被称为"长着一条舌头"，会讲汉语又会蒙古语的被称为"两条舌头的商人"，只有"长着三条舌头的商人"——也就是既会讲汉语蒙古语，又会讲俄语的——才是最有本事的商人，也是最有钱的商人。

In Hohhot, people categorise traders by the number of "tongues" they have. Someone who only speaks Mandarin is said to have "one tongue", someone who speaks Mandarin and Mongolian has two, and someone with "three tongues" also speaks Russian—these are the most accomplished and also wealthiest merchants.

元代语言
Yuan-Dynasty language
文：莫久愚

懂内蒙古西部方言的人，读起元杂剧来会觉得亲切。《西厢记》红娘道："白令令似水，多半是相思泪，眼面前茶饭怕不待要吃。"在西部方言中"白令令"是很白的意思，"不待要"就是不愿意。此外"圪捞"（角落）"醒得"（懂得）等词汇，含义也都一致。七百多年过去了，操着元代语言的人，仍在我们身边。

Those who understand the dialects of western Inner Mongolia will have an easy time reading Yuan plays. Phrases from works such as *Romance of the West Chamber* include a number of phrases that inexperienced readers might have to consult footnotes for, yet many of these phrases are still prevalent in the everyday speech of the people of this region. Even after 700 years, the language of the Yuan Dynasty still lives on.

微观内蒙古
INNER MONGOLIA: COLOURFUL AND MAGNIFICENT

房子
House
文：邓九刚

在呼和浩特，如果你听到一些老年人在谈话中说"房子"一词，千万别误解为人住的房子。彼时在归化商界，"房子"一词不是通常意义上人住的房子，而是特指商队远行时用的帐篷。这种房子分驼房子、羊房子、马房子，分别指驼队用的和赶运羊或者马时住的帐篷。

In Hohhot, when you hear old people talking about a "house", don't make the mistake of thinking they actually mean a house. Previously, in the trade world of the city "house" was commonly used to mean where someone lived—a tent carried with a trade caravan, rather than the house in its common sense. There are also "camel houses", "lamb houses", and "horse houses" which just mean the tents of the trade caravan, who drove these animals on the road.

"板申"
"Banshen", a settlement or village
文：邓九刚

呼和浩特地区的村落名中，带"板"或"板申"的很多，如攸攸板、察汗板。蒙古语中"板申"一词原是汉语"百姓"的音译借词，是蒙古族对早期逃亡至此的内地移民的称呼。由于内地移民习惯建造房屋、聚落而居，"板申"便有了房子的意思，引申为聚居点或村落。再回到汉语中时，就指聚居点或村落了，简称"板"。

In the names of the villages of Hohhot, there are many that end in "ban" or "banshen", such as Yoyo Ban, Chahan Ban, and so on. "Banshen" is a Mongolian pronunciation of "baixing", Chinese for "the common people". When those from the hinterland of China first came to Inner Mongolia, they built fixed houses in which they lived in communities, and thus "banshen" came to mean a house and later a place where people live together as a group. These names were translated back into Chinese, and now "ban" means a settlement or village.

蒙古语标准音
Standard Mongolian pronunciation
文：莫久愚

蒙古人在征服欧亚大陆的过程中吸纳了许多突厥语词汇，明清以来分居各地的蒙古人，形成了不同的方言。锡林郭勒盟正蓝旗蒙古人，是蒙古最后一位大汗林丹汗直接统辖的部落后裔，保留着纯正的草原传统。所以，在内蒙古的蒙古语教学、广播电视中，都以正蓝旗语音为标准音。

As the Mongolians conquered the Asian and European continents, they received a lot of influence from the ancient Turkic, and in the Ming and Qing Dynasties Mongolians began to live in different areas, then different dialects emerged. The people of Xulun Hoh Banner in the Xilin Gol League are the last line of direct descendants of Ligdan Khan—the last great Mongolian Khan, and preserve the pure traditions of the grasslands. For this reason, in Inner Mongolia, Mongolian-language education and television broadcasts take the dialect of Xulun Hol Banner as the standard Mongolian pronunciation.

舌尖·语言
Taste and Language

尾音代表程度
End sounds show extent
文：苏怀尧

鄂尔多斯人说话基本不用"很""特别""非常""稍微"等程度副词，他们用拉长带儿化的形容词尾音来表达程度：面条细细儿——的，糕软软儿——的，小米黄黄儿——的，脸红红儿——的，你慢慢儿——走，给我少少儿——来点儿……尾音越长，程度越深。

People in Ordos don't use modifiers like "very", "especially", "quite", or "a bit", but rather extend the sound of words to show extent: these noodles are thiiiiiin, this cake is soooooft, this millet is yellooooow, your face is so reeeeeed, walk slooooowly, give me a liiiiiittle. The longer the sound, the greater the extent.

巴先生不姓巴
His surname is not "Ba"
文：张弓长

在外地，常有人在介绍蒙古族人时这样说：这位先生姓巴，那位女士姓其。其实，他不姓巴，她也不姓其，巴和其只是蒙古语名字汉译之后的第一个字而已，比如巴特尔、巴根纳、其其格、其木格，等等。不能说姓巴或姓其，因为很多蒙古族人名都与姓氏无关。可你要是喊一声"巴先生""其女士"，或者"老巴""其老师"，他们还是会笑呵呵地答应你。

Outside of Inner Mongolia, people frequently introduce a Mongolian as such: "This is Mr. Ba, this is Miss Qi." Actually, their surnames are not "Ba" or "Qi", these are just the first syllables of their names when translated into Chinese. Names like Batar, Bagan, Qiqig, Qimug get truncated into things like "Mr. Ba" or "Miss Qi", but those aren't their actual surnames. This is quite common among Mongolia, since their names have little to do with their surnames. However, even when they are called "Mr. Ba", "Miss Qi" or "Old Ba" by others, they still will reply with a smile.

我说话怎么会是这个样子呢？
Do I really sound like that?
文：张弓长

多数赤峰人的普通话都带有浓重的方言口音，会情不自禁地带出当地的俚言俗语。但很多赤峰人并未意识到自己说的有方言口音，都认为自己说的是最标准的普通话。有的人偶尔一次上了电视或广播，才会对自己的声音颇感惊诧：我说话怎么会是这个样子呢？

Many people from Chifeng have a strong local accent when speaking Mandarin, and can't help but pepper their speech with dialectical expressions and local colloquialisms. However, a lot of these people aren't aware that their speech is so locally flavoured, and think they speak very standard Mandarin. Some people will go on TV or the radio, and only then be surprised by the sound of their voice in contrast with the others, remarking: "Do I really sound like that?"

摄影：连翰

文化・交融
Culture and Interactions

微观内蒙古
INNER MONGOLIA: COLOURFUL AND MAGNIFICENT

奇妙的交流

Strange interaction

文：李倩

两个小小人儿，正是咿呀学语的时候，偶尔能蹦出几个词，一个叫"哥哥"，一个喊"胡度"（蒙语：弟弟）。大部分的时间他们是不说话的，只是一起蹲在地上用狗尾巴草追蚂蚁，或者把蒲公英吹到对方脸上，然后大笑，手舞足蹈。他们虽然语言不同，却有着同样的好奇心，探索着同一个世界。

Two boys of two years of age, just barely learning to speak, can form a few words sometimes. One says "gege" (Chinese for "elder brother"), and the other says "hud" (Mongolian for "little brother"). Most of the time they don't speak, crouching on the ground chasing ants with green foxtails, or blowing dandelions into each other's faces and then laughing as they roll around. Even though they speak different language, they're curious about each other, and explore the world together.

摄影：高雪峰

文化·交融
Culture and Interactions

摄影：吴杰

达尔扈特人
The Darhut people

文／莫久愚

他们是鄂尔多斯蒙古族中一个特殊的群体。成吉思汗生前，为他服务的亲兵宿卫都是挑选的蒙古帝国贵胄子弟；圣主去世后，他们仍然要奉守、维护宫帐，保管他的诸般器物，世世代代祭祀成吉思汗。八百年来他们一直虔诚地履行着自己的职责，并将永远继续下去。被认为是成吉思汗的职业守灵人。

They are a special group of Mongolians in Ordos. During the life of Genghis Khan, they served as his bodyguards and most trusted soldiers, chosen from the sons of nobility. After he died, they took up the task of guarding and maintaining his palace, protecting his various possessions, and offering sacrifices to him over generations. For more than 800 years they have piously carried out their duty, and prepare to do so for ever. They are believed to be the professional guardians of the spirit of Genghis Khan.

鄂温克人的敖包
Obo of the Ewenki

文／莫久愚

阿荣旗音河乡鄂温克人的敖包是在一棵大树根部堆积石块而成。遇到干旱，祭祀敖包祈雨时，要供奉一头牛或一口猪及各种果品，人们在敖包树上拴系红布条，添加石块。鄂温克作家杜国良说："祭完敖包后人们互相泼水，特别是给寡妇泼得厉害，认为这样龙王爷就会下雨了。"

The obo of the Ewenki people of Yinhe Township in Arun Banner is made of stones piled on the root of a big tree. When a drought is encountered, and they pray for rain, they will bring a cow or a pig, and a variety of fruits as sacrifices, and will tie red strips of cloth around the tree before adding stones. Ewenki author Du Guoliang says: "After people make a sacrifice to an obo, they splash each other with water, splashing extra water on widows. They believe that in this way, the Dragon King (the god of rain in China) will bring rain."

微观内蒙古
INNER MONGOLIA: COLOURFUL AND MAGNIFICENT

"八白室"
"Eight White Rooms"

文 / 莫久愚

成吉思汗陵大殿中供奉着八座白色的毡包。鄂尔多斯人习惯称成陵为成吉思汗"八白室"。按照蒙古汗国时代的传统，大汗去世后，他和后妃生前居住的宫帐都会保留下来，逐渐变成祭奠的灵宫。让鄂尔多斯人自豪的是，八个世纪来，他们一直代表所有的蒙古人守护着"圣主"的宫帐。

In the grand hall of the Mausoleum of Genghis Khan there are eight white yurts. The people of Ordos call the Mausoleum of Genghis Khan as his "Eight White Rooms". In accordance with the customs of the Mongolian Khanate, when a great khan died, the palace tents in which he lived with his empress and concubines would be preserved, and gradually took on the symbolic meaning of homes for the spirits. It makes the people of Ordos proud to be the keepers of these symbols of the great Genghis Khan on behalf of the Mongolian people since 800 years ago.

摄影：希龙道尔吉

牛鼻子的印记
The imprint made by cow nose

文 / 莫久愚

在内蒙古，到处可见一种两个未闭合的圆组成的图案纹样，那是蒙古族特有的云纹图案，多为蓝色。蒙古包、蒙古袍、门楣、厅堂、器皿、用具……凡是有蒙古人生活的地方，必定有它附丽其上，俨然是蒙古族的一个符号。牧民称其为"哈木尔"，意为"鼻子"，据说是牛鼻子触碰毡帐时留下的印记。

In Inner Mongolia, you will see a pattern everywhere composed of two unclosed circles. This is a specific Mongolian "cloud style" pattern which is usually in blue. On yurts, Mongolian robes, lintels, halls, wares, and tools, mostly everywhere in Mongolian life, you can see this pattern. It is almost a mark of the Mongolian people. They call it "hamur" which means "nose", as it is said that it's the imprint made when a cow's nose touches a yurt.

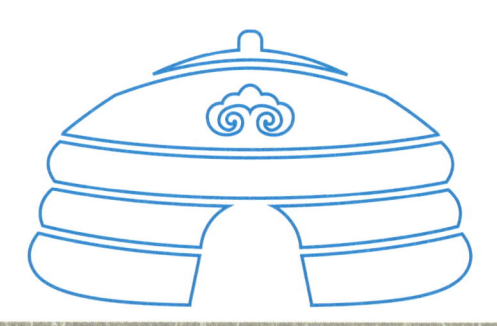

文化·交融
Culture and Interactions

生命深处的呼唤
A call from the depths of life

文：莫久愚

蒙古族民歌多是赞美山河、草木、动物，赞美慈祥的母爱、真挚的友谊和爱情。用不着翻译，不懂蒙古语的人，也能从那气息宽广、悠扬辽阔的旋律中感受到草原上生命的律动。诗人席慕蓉感叹："用原乡的语言和曲调唱出来的声音，是从生命最深处直接迸发出来的婉转呼唤，是任何事物都无法替代也无法转换的啊！"

Many Mongolian folk songs praise the beauty of the mountains, rivers, grasses, trees, and animals, the kindness and love of mothers, the virtues of friendship and romantic love… These songs sound distant, wide and melodious, and they needn't to be translated, as even those who do not understand the language can feel the rhythm of life upon the grasslands. Poet Xi Murong exclaimed: "The language of the grasslands and the melodies that accompany it are a sweet and agreeable calling out from the depths of life, something that nothing else can stand in for!"

草原人的敬畏
Awe of the grassland people

文：莫久愚

北方草原地带曾是萨满信仰的世界。萨满的时代早已过去，但这种信仰的印记却无处不在：当蒙古人端起酒杯时，当蒙古人、达斡尔人祭祀敖包时，当鄂温克人、鄂伦春人面对山林时，当他们唱起古老的歌谣时……都可以感受到那种虔诚的敬畏，敬畏苍天、敬畏大地，敬畏大自然的一草一木。

The northern grasslands used to be a shamanistic world. Although the age of shamanism has passed, these kinds of beliefs still persist: When Mongolians raise their glasses, when Mongolians and Daurs offer sacrifices to obos, when Ewenkis and Oroqens face the forest, when they sing old songs... one can feel the pious awe they feel for the sky, the earth, for nature, and every strand of grass and every tree within it.

摄影：乌热尔图

微观内蒙古
INNER MONGOLIA: COLOURFUL AND MAGNIFICENT

"多丽雅"女子合唱团
"Doria" Women's Choir

文：刘伟建

唱歌，是内蒙古人生活的一部分。正是这共同的爱好，把我们五十多个不同民族、不同职业、不同年龄的姐妹聚在了"多丽雅"女子合唱团，一唱就是二十年。"多丽雅"是蒙语"歌唱"的意思。我们开心地歌唱，去音乐厅，去工厂、学校、连队、牧区，甚至去监狱……我们用歌声传递着来自草原的真情。

Singing is a part of the life in Inner Mongolia. The common love for singing gather us together in a choir for over 20 years. There are over 50 members, who have different nationalities, ages and occupations. "Doria" is a Mongolian word for "singing". We sing happily together, and we have performed in music halls, factories, schools, armies, pastoral areas, and even prisons... We express our sincere feelings for the grasslands through our songs.

歌中的比喻
Metaphors in songs

文：殷向飞

学者顾颉刚感慨："蒙古族人民，从七八岁到七八十岁都能唱歌，所以内蒙古被称为'歌海'，到处可以听到草原的歌声……他们喜欢用马来比喻一切，如用'枣红马'来比喻勇敢的人，用'海星马'来比喻懒汉。妇女出嫁后想家，常用小羊羔来比喻自己。"

Scholar Gu Jiegang remarked: "The Mongolian people sing from seven or eight years of age to seventy or eighty, which has led to Inner Mongolia being called the 'sea of songs'. You can hear songs everywhere on the grasslands... They like to use horses as metaphors for everything, like 'russet horse' for a brave person, and 'Haixing horse' for a lazy person. When girls marry, they frequently describe themselves as 'little lambs'."

《鄂伦春舞》
Oroqen Dance

文：莫久愚

舞蹈家贾作光谈及他创作的《鄂伦春舞》时说："当时鄂伦春人的舞蹈很原生态，多是模拟狗熊的动作……另外，我观察到，因为身边（森林）的树枝子很多，所以女性们总扒来扒去，无论是从'撮罗子'里出来，还是抱柴火回来，这些动作经常出现。我把它们美化了，变成舞蹈语汇。"

Dancer Jia Zuoguang, talking about his work *Oroqen Dance*, said: "Oroqen dances were originally quite primal, mostly mimicking the movements of bears... I saw that there were many branches on the trees in the forest nearby, and that the women would frequently push them aside in order to pass through, whether they were coming out of the hunting shacks or collecting firewood, it was quite commonplace. So, I tweaked these things, beautified them, and assembled dances out of these activities."

文化·交融
Culture and Interactions

供奉"学神"
Tribute to the "God of Scholarship"

文：莫久愚

1662年，萨冈彻辰在乌审旗写出了蒙古族三大巨著之一——《蒙古源流》，述说元末到清初蒙古黄金家族的历史。他去世后家乡人在他的坟墓上立塔祭祀，后来又专门立庙，一年五次祭祀，三百多年来香火不息。每年农历五月十三大祭，方圆几百里的人们都会赶来。鄂尔多斯蒙古人是把一位学者当作神来供奉的。

In 1662, Sagang Sechen in Uxin Banner wrote one of the three great Mongolian works—*Erdeniiin Tobchi*, or *The Origin of the Mongolians*, which is a comprehensive history of Mongolia up to that point, telling the history of the Mongolian aristocracy from the end of the Yuan Dynasty to the start of the Qing Dynasty. After he died, people in his homeland erected a tower upon his grave and conducted sacrifices, and then later built a temple. Every year, 5 rites are held for him, a tradition which has continued unbroken for more than 300 years. Every year on the thirteenth day of the fifth lunar month there is a large ceremony, and people from hundreds of kilometres around come to attend. This is the story of how the people of Ordos revere an ancient scholar as a god.

摄影：莫久愚

微观内蒙古
INNER MONGOLIA: COLOURFUL AND MAGNIFICENT

筷子舞
Chopstick dance

文：苏怀亮

筷子舞是鄂尔多斯人的独创。舞者双手各持一束筷子，和着众人的歌声和各种敲击声，在跪、坐、立等姿态中，随着腿部的屈伸、身体的扭动，用筷子击打手、臂、肩、背、腰、腿、脚等部位，间以击打地面，边打边舞。动作敏捷，舒展大方，节奏感强，气氛欢快。

Chopstick dance is a unique creation of the people of Ordos. The dancer holds several chopsticks in each hand and taps them in tune to the audience's singing, while kneeling, sitting, or standing. As the dancer twists his body, he uses the chopsticks to strike the hand, arm, shoulder, back, waist, leg, foot, and other places, and in between taps the floor, tapping and dancing all through out. The motions are quick and graceful, and the pace is fast and thrilling, with a joyful atmosphere.

曲棍球之乡——莫力达瓦旗
Home of hockey – Morin Dawa Banner

文：莫久愚

在尼尔基镇大街小巷，随处可见手持曲棍球球杆的人，他们或是刚打球回来，或是在奔赴球场的路上。这个源自辽代契丹民族的游戏，在这里属于群众性体育运动，已进入中小学体育课程。中国许多优秀的曲棍球球员和教练都出自莫力达瓦旗。这里有全国最大的曲棍球运动场，每年夏季都要举办"中国莫力达瓦曲棍球节"。

In the streets and alleys of Nierji Town, one can see people with hockey sticks everywhere, either coming back from a game, or rushing to the site of a game. This game, which originated from the Khitans of the Liao Dynasty is widely popular here, and is in the curriculum at elementary and middle schools. Many of the best hockey players and famous hockey coaches in China come from this banner. This place has the largest hockey stadium in China, and every summer there is an "All-China Morin Dawa Hockey Festival" held here.

摄影：苏伟伟

文化・交融
Culture and Interactions

郭雨桥 供稿

为游牧民族吼一吼
Shout out for the herders

文：莫久愚

他是汉族，却能说地道的蒙古语，15 年来几乎走遍了国内外蒙古族聚居区，住牧人的毡房、盖羊皮被、吃奶食，几句话就能和牧民打得火热，写出一本又一本蒙古民俗著作。如今，70 多岁的郭雨桥仍然在走，怀揣的名片上写着："在牧民家中坐一坐，在大自然里走一走，在历史遗址上想一想，为游牧民族吼一吼。"

He's Han Chinese, but can speak authentic Mongolian. Over the course of 15 years, he has been all over areas inhabited by the Mongolians at home and abroad, living in herders' yurts sleeping under sheepskin blankets, eating Mongolian milk products. Just saying a few words, he can strike up a conversation with a herder. He's written a number of books on Mongolian folk customs. 70 years old, Guo Yuqiao is still travelling around. The business card keeps upon him says: "Take a seat in a herder's house, take a walk around nature, take a moment to think on historical sites, give a shout out for the herders."

羊水荡漾的声音
Music in the womb

文：李倩

一位汉族作家朋友去听蒙古语诗歌朗诵会。他不懂蒙古语却听得很享受。朗诵结束后，他说："太美了，我仿佛在母亲的子宫，听到了羊水荡漾的声音。"我想他是从蒙古语中感受到了生命的律动和音韵。

A Han Chinese friend went to a reading of Mongolian poems, and while he didn't understand the language, enjoyed it very much. Afterwards he said: "It really is so beautiful. I feel like I'm in the womb, hearing the music ripple through the amniotic fluid." I think he must have felt the rhythm and harmony of life in the Mongolian language.

219

微观内蒙古
INNER MONGOLIA: COLOURFUL AND MAGNIFICENT

草原画派
Grassland Painting School

文：莫久愚

二十世纪八十年代，蒙古族画家妥木斯在北京的一次画展，展示了草原的壮阔、草原的色彩和草原的律动，传递出人与自然、人与生物的和谐与依恋，被誉为"草原画派"。这带动了一批画家去探索蒙古民族的色彩表达方式，捕捉代表民族性格和情感的笔触，寻找那绿色的家国情怀……

In the 1980s, Mongolian painter Tuomus had a show in Beijing where exhibited the stalwart nature of the grassland, it's colours, and rhythms. He depicted the harmony and attachment between man and nature, and between man and other living beings, and his paintings were considered as a new school—the "Grassland Painting School". This motivated a number of painters to go to Inner Mongolia to see how colours are expressed by the Mongolians, and capture the character and feelings of these people with their brushes as they search for the familial feelings of these green landscapes…

摄影：吴运生

蒙古象棋没有象
Mongolian chess

文：张弓长

你动哈萨嘎，我走骆驼，一场厮杀就此开始。这是两个人在玩蒙古象棋。蒙古象棋历史悠久，对阵双方有诺颜（王爷）、哈昙（王后）各一个，哈萨嘎（车）、骆驼、马各二枚，厚乌八个，相当于卒和兵。玩法与国际象棋类似，但蒙古人把象刻成了骆驼，把兵刻成了猎狗，增添了游牧生活的情趣。

You move your hazag, I move my camel…This is how the war begins; this is two people playing Mongolian chess. The game has a long history. Each side has a nuoyan (king), hatan (queen), two hazag (rooks), camels, and horses (knights), and eight houwu (pawns). It's similar to western chess, except the bishops are carved as camels and the pawns as hounds—a bit of nomadic flavour.

文化·交融
Culture and Interactions

摄影：高雪峰

蒙古族长调
Mongolian Long Song

文：莫久愚

长调源自草原古老的生活节奏，是千百年来牧人面对苍天大地的倾诉。尽管一般只有几句歌词，却如草原上的河流般悠长舒缓、曲折徘徊、跌宕起伏，让人融化在白云悠悠、绿地茫茫的画卷中，充溢着一种顺乎自然的自由气息。散文家鲍尔吉·原野说聆听长调，会听见蒙古人那绸子一样柔软的心肠……

Mongolian Long Songs originate from the old pace of life on the grasslands, a reflection of the confiding of herders over centuries and millennia under the vast sky. Even though they only have a few lines of lyrics, they flow long and slowly like the rivers on the grasslands, back and forth with bold and unconstrained character. It makes one think of the white clouds and green plains in a painting, gives one a feeling of being free and in line with nature. Essayist Borjigin Yuanye says that when he hears these songs, he hears the hearts of the Mongolian people, as soft as silk...

呼麦，天地与心灵的交响
Hoomei, a chorus of heart, heaven and earth

文：黄蕾

一位蒙古族音乐专家说："如果雪域高原离太阳最近的话，蒙古族的呼麦、长调和马头琴是离心灵最近。"呼麦是源自蒙古高原的古老的演唱形式，单人发出多声部的唱法是特殊的喉音艺术。声乐专家形容呼麦是"高如登苍穹之巅，低如下瀚海之底，宽如于大地之边"。呼麦已有千年历史，唱出的是时间的记忆。

A Mongolian musical expert says: "If the Qinghai-Tibet Plateau is closest to the sun, then Mongolian hoomei, Long Song and the horse-headed fiddles are closest to the heart." Hoomei is a traditional form of singing originated from the Mongolian Plateau in which one emits multiple notes from the throat simultaneously. An expert of vocal music describes it as "high as the sky and deep as the ocean, wide as the land". It has more than a millennium of history, and the memories of time are contained within its notes.

微观内蒙古
INNER MONGOLIA: COLOURFUL AND MAGNIFICENT

《诺恩吉雅》
Nuoenjiya

文：莫久愚

"老哈河岸上，老马拖着缰，性情温柔的诺恩吉雅，嫁到遥远的地方……"唱的是奈曼旗贵族道尔吉的女儿远嫁乌珠穆沁草原，不到一年抑郁而终，陪送她的一匹枣红马托着缰绳，徘徊在老哈河畔。故事虽已久远，但每当听到这凄婉的叙事和旋律，都会勾起远嫁他乡的女儿对家乡、对母亲的思恋。

"On the banks of the Laoha River, a horse drags a halter, and the sweet-tempered Nuoenjiya is married off to a far-away place..." This is the story of the daughter of the noble Dorzh of Naiman Banner, who was married off to the far-away Ujimqin Grassland. Within a year she died of sadness, and the russet horse that took her there wandered around dragging its halter through the lands on the banks of the Laoha River. The story is quite old, but when a girl married off to a distant place hears its sadly moving melody, it's hard for her not to think of her homeland and mother.

劝奶歌
Lactation song

文：莫久愚

蒙古人称其为"哒咕"，是唱给生灵的歌，没有歌词，只是以叹词哒咕缓缓诉说的不固定旋律，哀婉绵长。接羔时节遇到母驼、母羊无端弃养初生幼羔时，蒙古族妇女便会伴着马头琴哼唱起这样的旋律。直唱到母畜含着眼泪去给幼羔喂奶。学者巴·苏和说："谁能说动物听不懂音乐？唯有蒙古长调能使草原的生灵彻悟。"

Mongolians call this "taigoo". It's a song sung to the spirits of life, with no lyrics, but simple sounds that accompany an unfixed rhythm, sorrowful and long. When an ewe or camel gives birth to a calf but abandons it, a Mongolian woman will play this melody on the horse-headed fiddles while humming along to it, until the dam is moved to tears and goes to nurse its offspring. Scholar Ba Suhe says: "Who says that animals don't understand music? Only these Mongolian Long Songs can enlighten the spirits of the grassland."

摄影：高雪峰

文化·交融
Culture and Interactions

摄影：乌热尔图

乌拉特蒙古人的名片——《鸿雁》

Urad's name card—*Swan Goose*

文：张铁良

悠扬，苍凉，辽远，高亢，乌拉特民歌《鸿雁》诞生于阴山脚下的呼勒斯太苏木，原创者是一位活佛。"酒喝干，再斟满……"饮下的是年华，沉淀的是永不辜负的真情。极具感染力的旋律，令人回味无穷。歌声里有蒙古人的乡愁和成长，唱出了每个人心底最柔软最深沉的缱绻。

Swan Goose, a song that is melodious, resounding and profound comes from Hulesitaisumu at the foot of Yinshan Mountains in Urat, and was written by a living Buddha. Downing a glass of liquor and filling it back up, drinking the years and weight away is a kind of true feeling that will never let one down. The song has an infectious, unforgettable melody. Within the song are the nostalgic feelings of the Mongolian people as well as the story of their growth. Anyone who hears the song will develop a tender attachment to it deep in the heart.

漫瀚调

Manhan Ditty

文：莫久愚

蒙古族"短调"融入了晋北山曲和陕北信天游的旋律，鄂尔多斯无论男女老幼，几乎人人会唱。在待客的欢宴中，往往还据来客的身份即兴编词、对唱，或庄或谐。过去唱"三十里的明沙二十里的水，五十里的路上来眊亲亲你……眊亲亲把哥哥跑成个罗圈腿"，那是因交通不便，现在则唱"想我你就给我打手机"。

In the "short tunes" of the Mongolian people, elements of the folk songs of Northern Shanxi and Shaanxi have crept in. Young or old, male or female, all the people in Ordos know how to sing these songs. When receiving guests, they will frequently improvise lyrics relevant to them, or singing in an antiphonal style, sometimes serious, sometimes humorous. In the past, songs would sound like "Over thirty li (Chinese length unit, equals to 500 metres) of bright sand and twenty li of water, I take a fifty-li path just to see you. Just to see you, I travel until my legs give out." A song like this described the difficulties of travel at the time. Now, people sing songs like "If you miss me, call me on my mobile".

微观内蒙古
INNER MONGOLIA: COLOURFUL AND MAGNIFICENT

摄影：陈慕菲

脑阁
"Naoge" performance

文：张弓长

是一种流传在土默川平原上的民间艺术，演出时把特制的铁架子固定在一成年男子身上，架上站立一至三名儿童。脑阁的演出道具以马鞭、弓、箭、哈达、狼头、鹿角等居多。演出时还伴以安代舞曲或时尚乐曲，辅以锣鼓、唢呐、钹镲等乐器，在大型场地演出时还加入扭秧歌、跑旱船、舞龙狮等，蒙汉风情兼备。

This is a kind of folk performance upon the Tumd Plain. A specially made metal frame is placed upon an adult male, upon which one to three young children stand. The props include horse whips, bows, arrows, khatags, wolf heads, deer horns, and other such objects. The performance will be set to traditional andai music or modern popular music, and accompanied by gongs, drums, suona, cymbals, and other musical instruments, and at big performances, there may also been yangko dance, land boat dance, dragon and lion dance, or other elements of both Mongolian and Han art.

沙漠诗人
Desert poets

文：莫久愚

毛乌素沙漠近代以来出诗人，诗人和诗影响着牧民的生活。牧人婚丧嫁娶，都会有诗人献上诗作。作家肖亦农说："在乌审旗大地上行走，你常会见到这样的情景：在一个月圆之夜，牧户的草地前停满汽车、摩托车，院内诗情迸发的牧人们正在大声朗读自己新创作的诗篇……"

The Mu Us Desert has produced a number of poets in modern times, and poets and poems have influenced the lives of herders there. At important occasions for a family, such as weddings and funerals, a poet will always be invited to compose poems. Author Xiao Yinong said: "In Uxin Banner, walking around you'll frequently find this kind of scene: On the night of a bright moon, people will park their cars and motorcycles on the grass in front of one herder's house, and people gather together in the herder's yard to read aloud the poems they have just composed…"

文化·交融
Culture and Interactions

达斡尔大轱辘车
Daur big wheel cart

文：莫久愚

达斡尔人保留了最古老的造车形式和技艺。用桦木杆撅成的车轮特别高大，整车几乎都用黑桦、柞木制成，车轴重心高，"越野"性能好，便于涉过浅滩、沟壑、草丛。结构简便、轻快耐用的木车曾是达斡尔人与草原牧民交换马匹的大宗商品。莫力达瓦旗每年都要举行达斡尔车比赛，追念那已经逝去的时光。

The Daur people have maintained their age-old methods of making traditional wooden carts. They bend long strips of birch into very large wheels, and make the body of the cart out of black birch and toothed oak, producing a cart with a high centre of gravity that has good "off-road" capabilities, easily crossing shoals, ravines, and thick grass. These carts, simple in construction, light, and durable used to function as a staple of exchange that the Daur would use to trade for horses with the herders of the grasslands. In Morin Dawa Banner there is a Daur cart race every year where the glory of these vehicles is showcased.

摄影：苏伟伟

巴林草原的"文化"
Bairin Grassland's "literacy"

文：姜苹

巴林右旗被认为是英雄史诗《格斯尔》的故乡，一些老人甚至能够逐一指认史诗故事的发生地。或许是英雄格斯尔那魔幻壮丽的传说哺育了巴林人的想象力，这里"盛产"文化人。一百多位在当代蒙古文学领域颇具影响的诗人，都出自这里。当地人还能说出几百位从巴林草原走出去的著名学者、记者的名字。

Bairin Right Banner is believed to be the homeland of the titular hero in *The Epic of Gesar*, and some old people can point out places where events in the epic took place. It may be the magical and majestic epic nurtured the imagination of the people in Bairin, and this area abounds with men of letters. More than a hundred influential poets in Mongolian literature circle have been born here. The locals can name hundreds of famous scholars and reporters that come from their locality.

微观内蒙古

INNER MONGOLIA: COLOURFUL AND MAGNIFICENT

摄影：高雪峰

马头琴
Horse-headed fiddles

文：莫久愚

这种奇妙的拉弦乐器具有神奇的魔力，琴声响起来，就会让人在听觉和视觉之间迅速地转换和复写。眼前叠映出这样的画面：辽阔的草原，深邃的蓝天，雪白的羊群，奔驰的骏马，喜悦或是忧伤的牧人……那是一种诉说的声音，那是带有画面的声音，柔软的琴弦似乎是在抚摸一个民族的心灵。

This wonderful string instrument is quite enticing, and when one hears it played, will feel dazzled in both vision and hearing, which exchange and overlap rapidly, seeing scenes of the wide grassland, deep blue sky, snow-white flocks of sheep, running horses, and herders both happy and melancholy… It's a kind of sound that tells a story, a song that includes images. The sounds played by the soft strings of the instrument touch the hearts of the people.

"乌力格尔"
"Ulger"

文：莫久愚

乌力格尔，蒙语意为说书，是源自游牧时代的古老的说唱艺术形式。在农家场院炕头，说书艺人讲述着蒙古民族的英雄史诗，也说三皇五帝、春秋三国，故事中充溢着对英雄和骏马的赞美。通辽市是中国蒙古族人口密度最高的地方，也是世界上从事耕作的蒙古族人最多的地方。在农耕化的蒙古人院落中，游牧民族的传统找到了新的存在形式。

"Ulger" or the monologue story-telling, is an old form of talking and singing art that originated in the nomadic era. A family sits around the heatable brick bed of the farmhouse, and a storyteller tells the tales of historical heroes of the Mongolian people, as well as stories of the Three Emperors, Five Sovereigns, The Spring and Autumn, and The Three Kingdoms, all these tales being full of praise for heroes and wonderful horses. Tongliao City has the highest concentration of Mongolians in China, and is also the city with the largest number of Mongolians participating in agriculture in the world. In these agricultural Mongolian homes, this tradition of a nomadic people still survive.

摄影：王金

微观内蒙古
INNER MONGOLIA: COLOURFUL AND MAGNIFICENT

摄影：张启民

安代舞
Andai dance

文：莫久愚

这是一种一人领唱众人应和的狂欢之舞，节奏鲜明，多顿足踏歌动作，舞姿奔放、刚劲威猛；有时又轻捷舒缓。它源于清代库伦旗一位萨满劝慰、感化精神抑郁女子的舞蹈，后来在草原上流传开来。通辽地区的城镇广场上经常有跳安代舞健身娱乐的人群，内蒙古的大型喜庆活动上，千人安代舞往往是开幕式的亮点。

Led by a leading singer and incorporating an exchange of voices with the audience, this is a dance of revelry with a clear rhythm that incorporates foot-tapping and singing. Its style is untrammelled, bold, and powerful, yet at some times also light and easy. It originated in Hure Banner in the Qing Dynasty, where a shaman used it to console a depressed girl, and then later spread across the grasslands. In the Tongliao area it's common to see groups of people dancing andai in the city squares, and at large-scale festivities in Inner Mongolia, holding a thousand-person andai dance is the highlight of the openning ceremony.

《敖包相会》
Meeting at the Obo

文：莫久愚

《敖包相会》是流传最广的一首内蒙古草原歌曲。60多年前，蒙古族作家玛拉沁夫写了《科尔沁草原的人们》，改编成电影《草原上的人们》，外景地却选在鄂温克草原，达斡尔族作曲家通福借鉴蒙古民歌的旋律谱写了影片插曲，电影中锡尼河畔主人公相会的敖包因此成了"天下第一敖包"。

Meeting at the Obo is one of the most popular songs on the grasslands of Inner Mongolia. 60 years ago, the Mongolian author Mara Qinfu wrote *The People of the Horqin Grassland* which was made into the film *People on the Prairie*, with the location shooting taken on the Ewenki Grassland. Daur composer Tong Fu used the melodies of traditional Mongolian songs to write a musical interlude for the film, and the obo at which the characters meet in the film thus became "the first obo in the world".

文化·交融
Culture and Interactions

蒙古袍的形制
Mongolian robes

文：郭雨桥

蒙古袍立领而高，袖窄而长，多接有马蹄袖，大襟而右衽，下面有底襟，腰间系有宽带。它袍里宽松，下摆肥大，整体上给人的感觉是肥大、宽松而极富封闭性。可以白天穿、黑夜盖，天阴下雨毛朝外。正如一本书里所说："它的袖子是枕头，底襟是褥子，大襟是簸箕，后摆是斗篷，怀里是口袋，马蹄袖是手套。"

The Mongolian robe has a high collar and long, thin sleeves, usually with horseshoe-shaped cuffs, and two overlapping pieces of fabric upon the chest with the buttons at the right. There is a lappet at the bottom and a wide band at the waist. It is loose, large at the bottom, and gives the person a full, wide appearance, yet it seems quite closed to outside. It can be worn during the day and used as a cover at night, and worn on rainy days with the fur turned inside out. A book described its multi-functionality: "The sleeves can be a pillow, the inner flap, a mattress, the outer flap, a dustpan, the coat-tail, a cloak, inside the front lappet, pockets, and the sleeves, gloves."

会变魔术的尤登帽
Magical Youdeng hat

文：郭雨桥

所有的部族服饰都是多功能的。比如布里亚特的尤登帽，叠在一起就是两个大小相同的四方片，外边有一道简单的滚边而已。可是只要改变戴法，通过开合耳扇、系取帽带、变样折叠、前后倒换位置，就能花样翻新，魔术般地戴出六种花样，可遮阳，可护耳，可保暖，可纳凉，适应了不同季节的需要。

All ethnic clothing is multifunctional. The Youdeng hats of Buryat made of two rectangles of the same size, and decorated with a simple embroidered border. The ear flaps and tie-strings are adjustable, and it can be worn backwards, too. In total, there are six different ways of wearing it so that it can be used to shield one from the sun, protect the ears, keep one warm, or keep one cool, making it suitable for different seasons.

摄影：郭雨桥

229

微观内蒙古
INNER MONGOLIA: COLOURFUL AND MAGNIFICENT

蒙古族的"梁祝"
Mongolia's "Butterfly Lovers"

文／莫久愚

号称"民歌之乡"的科尔沁左翼后旗流传的《达那巴拉》，是一首叙事歌曲。小伙子达那巴拉从军多年无音讯，恋人金香被家人逼迫出嫁，达那巴拉归来知道后气绝身亡，金香听说恋人已去，不久也抑郁而终。歌手伴着四胡含泪演唱，听得人跟着落泪。优美的旋律，凄美的故事，被称为蒙古族的"梁祝"。

Horqin Left Rear Banner, known as the "home of folk songs", gave birth to *Danabala*, a famous narrative song. When the young Danabala enlists in the army, he goes away for many years without any news. His love, Jin Xiang, is forced to marry by her parents, and when Danabala returns and learns of this, he becomes incredibly sad and dies. When Jin Xiang finds out, she too becomes severely depressed and dies. The song is accompanied by the "sihu", a four-stringed instrument, and is incredibly sad. When it is sung, both the singer and the audience are in tears. With a beautiful melody and beautiful yet depressing storyline, it's known as the Mongolian "*Butterfly Lovers*".

圣主在家里
The sainted Khan is in the house

文／张弓长

走进草原上的蒙古族人家，屋内最醒目的地方大多都挂着一幅圣主成吉思汗的画像。千百年来，成吉思汗那深邃的目光就这样一直注视着他的子孙，也只有心胸坦荡的子孙们才敢与圣主的目光长久对视。在蒙古人心中，成吉思汗就是一位慈祥、睿智的长者，他们容不得对这位伟大祖先的任何不敬。

When you walk into a Mongolian home, the thing you will find most noticeable is that many of them have a large portrait of Genghis Khan, their former saint Khan. For centuries, he has been watching over his descendants with a pair of deep eyes, only those with integrity can make extended eye contact with his portraits. In the hearts of the Mongolian people, Genghis Khan is a kind and wise old man, and they will allow nobody to show any disrespect to him.

白岩松眼里的蒙古人
Mongolians in Bai Yansong's eyes

文／张弓长

央视著名主持人白岩松说："蒙古族是我知道的最温和的民族。在全中国的所有民族中，我不知道哪个民族比蒙古族人更温和、更伤感、更忧郁。伤感是和自然有关系，只有游牧民族在与大自然斗争中才会感到人多么渺小。蒙古族的长调和马头琴都蕴藏着人在自然面前天然的伤感，那恰恰反映了这个民族的内心。"

Famous CCTV host Bai Yansong says: "Mongolians are the warmest people I know of. Among all the peoples of China, I don't know of a group that's warmer, more emotional, and more melancholy. Their emotionality has to do with nature—only nomadic herders who struggle with nature feel how tiny we are as human beings. The songs and melodies of the Mongolian people played by horse-headed fiddles all reflect this feeling of facing the vastness of nature, and reflect the spirit of the people."

文化・交融
Culture and Interactions

见什么唱什么
Sing what you see

文：殷向飞

学者顾颉刚说，蒙古族说书人演唱的好来宝"……是见什么唱什么，随编随唱，如果不即时记录下来，叫演唱者唱第二遍时，就和第一遍不同了，因为演唱者本人也记不住了。他们看见一个人来，就唱这个人，看见一件新鲜事物，就唱这件事物，因此随时能够吸收新的内容"。

Scholar Gu Jiegang says that when the bards of Mongolia sing holboo, "They sing about whatever they see. They compose the lyrics while singing. If one doesn't write down the lyrics sung, and tells the singer to sing again, their words will change, because the singer can not keep track of what's been sung, either. If someone shows up, they sing about that person; if an object comes into view, it is sung about. Whatever is about will be incorporated into the song immediately."

以蒙古语诵经的寺庙
Temples chanting in Mongolian

文：莫久愚

内蒙古的寺院大多是用藏语诵经，在阴山号称"塞外小华山"的大桦背脚下的梅力更召却是以蒙古语诵经。清康熙年间，这里的罗布森•丹碧•扎拉森活佛主持用蒙古文翻译了大量经卷。他还是一位作家、诗人、蒙古语文学家。通晓九种文字。如今脍炙人口的蒙古族民歌《鸿雁》的最早版本就出自他手。

Most of the temples in Inner Mongolia conduct their chants in Tibetan, but at the Meiligeng Temple at the foot of Mount Dahuabei in Yinshan Mountains—also known as the "Little Mount Huashan beyond the Great Wall", the monks chant in Mongolian. During the reign of the Emperor Kangxi in the Qing Dynasty, living Buddha Robsen Danbi Jalsan took responsibility for the translation of a large amount of sutras into Mongolian. He was an author, poet, and Mongolian linguist, proficient in nine scripts. The folk song *Swan Goose*, very popular even today, was first written by him.

摄影：白立新

微观内蒙古
INNER MONGOLIA: COLOURFUL AND MAGNIFICENT

摄影：乌热尔图

冬季那达慕
Winter Nadam

文／莫久愚

不知什么时候起，举办冬季那达慕在内蒙古各地成了时尚。篝火燃起来，乐曲响起来，身着绚丽服装的人群向着迎风招展的彩旗聚拢。在白雪的映衬中，摔跤手黝黑的皮肤、斑驳的五色骏马、棕褐色的驼群，都是那么艳丽。冬季那达慕会场就像雪原上骤然开出的花。

It isn't known when the tradition of holding Nadam in the winter became a trend throughout Inner Mongolia. Bonfires burn, music rings out, and people dressed in gorgeous clothing gather around the fluttering coloured flags. Contrasting with the white snow is the dark skin of the wrestlers, the horses of different colours, the brown camels—all appear wonderful in this scene. A winter Nadam is like a beautiful flower suddenly blooming in the snow.

"玛乃贾作光"
"Our Jia Zuoguang"

文／莫久愚

满族舞蹈家贾作光，从牧民生产生活中，从草原上的雄鹰、大雁、驰骋的骏马中，从那达慕大会上的摔跤、赛马、射箭的豪放英姿中，提炼出骑马、套马及各种肩、臂、腕、手、指动作的舞蹈语汇，他创作的《牧马舞》《马刀舞》《摔跤舞》等让牧民感到熟悉而亲切，称他是"玛乃（我们）贾作光"。

Manchu dancer Jia Zuoguang was inspired from pastoral life elements such as the eagles, wild geese, running horses on the grasslands, and wrestling, horse racing, and archery on Nadam, and the bold gestures they involve. He's incorporated the shoulder, arm, wrist, hand, and finger movements of horse riding and equestrian techniques, and taken all these to make dances such as *Horse Dance*, *Sabre Dance*, *Wrestling Dance* which are so familiar to herders of Inner Mongolia, who refer to him as "our Jia Zuoguang".

文化·交融
Culture and Interactions

额尔古纳河沿岸的村落
Villages along the Ergun River

文：莫久愚

在额尔古纳河沿岸的村落，居民多有着欧式面孔，却说着地道的东北话，妇女围着俄式花裙，头系三角巾。家家都有砖泥搭建的列巴（面包）炉，喜欢用采自林中的浆果自制果酱抹在面包上。遇到巴斯克节等俄罗斯的传统节日，人们会不约而同地聚在一起，伴着手风琴唱起熟悉的老歌，跳起欢快的舞蹈。

In the villages along the Ergun River, most of the residents have white-looking faces, but speak authentic North-eastern Chinese dialect. The women wear Russian-style flowered skirts, and tie their hair with triangular scarves. Every house has an oven made of mud and bricks in which they cook large, Russian-style bread which they eat with jam made from berries they pick themselves. At traditional Russian holidays such as Pashka (the Russian-Orthodox Easter), everyone comes together, and the singing of old songs mixes with the sound of the accordion as people dance and celebrate together.

摄影：杨毅斌

另一类酒歌
A different kind of drinking song

文：莫久愚

蒙古族的酒歌并不都是劝人畅饮的，也有劝人不要贪杯的。如《查干淖尔》酒歌，就诙谐地告诉你："查干淖尔的水呀，平日里是平静的，刮起风是咆哮的。皮囊里的奶酒呀，平日里是平静的，装到肚里是翻腾的。"另一首节奏欢快的酒歌《大老虎》幽默地提醒你："皮囊里的酒一进肚，就要变成大老虎……"

Not all Mongolian drinking songs are about encouraging one to drink—there are those that encourage moderation, such as *Qagan Nur*, which humorously chides you: "The water of Qagan Nur lake, on normal days it's calm, but when the wind blows, it roars. The alcohol in the bottle, on normal days it's calm, but when you put it in your stomach, the tides surge." Another merry song, *Big Tiger*, reminds you: "When the liquor in the bottle enters your stomach, it turns into a big tiger…"

微观内蒙古
INNER MONGOLIA: COLOURFUL AND MAGNIFICENT

"森林之神"的依恋
The attachment of "gods of the forest"

文：莫久愚

鄂伦春人号称"森林之神"，告别山林生活，交出了被视为"第二生命"的猎枪，正在经历向农耕转型的阵痛。鄂伦春族画家白英说："我小时候住猎民村。虽然政府给我们建了新房子，但人们还习惯在旁边搭个撮罗子。"他最爱画的画面，是一个身着传统狍皮衣帽的鄂伦春女人，背着猎枪，脚下是桦树皮盒。

The Oroqen are called "gods of the forest" by outside people, and when they left the forest, giving up their shotguns—what they see as their "second lives", starting the painful transition to an agricultural existence. Oroqen painter Bai Ying said: "When I was young, I lived in a hunting village. Although the government built us new houses, most of us still built our traditional hunting shacks next to them." The kind of painting he likes to paint is a woman in a roe deer skin coat and hat carrying a shotgun, with a white birch box beside her feet.

摄影：苏伟伟

文化·交融
Culture and Interactions

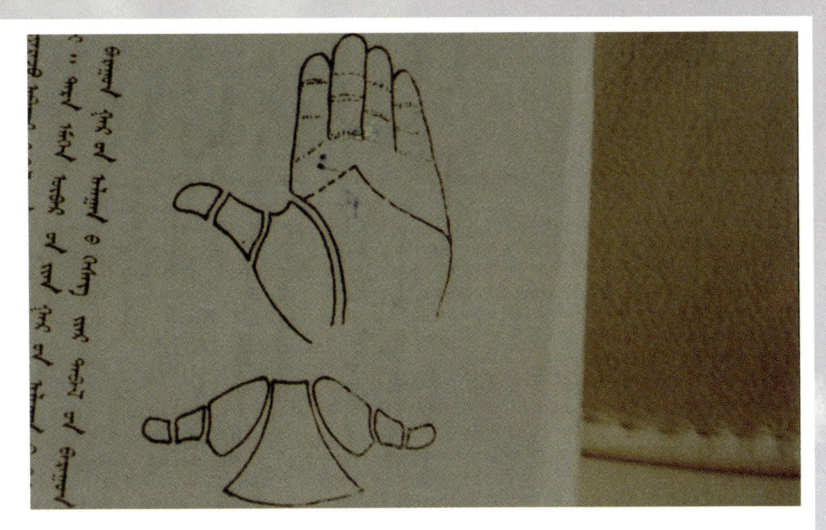

摄影：郭雨桥

用双手做裁衣样板

Patterns with hands

文：郭雨桥

蒙古族认为袍服起源于对自己肌体的模仿。布里亚特有一则传说，一对夫妇要给出嫁的女儿做衣服，苦于没有参照的样板。妻子忽然把两只手掌朝下，上下重叠起来，演示给丈夫："两个大拇指好比衣服的袖子，中间重叠的部分就是衣服的前后身子。"照着双手做出的袍，跟身体的比例正好吻合。

Mongolians believe that the shape of a Mongolian robe came originally from people's bodies themselves. There's a legend of Buryat that says when a couple were going to marry their daughter off, they had no pattern from which to make her clothing. Thus, the mother placed her hands palms facing down, one over the other, saying, "My thumbs are the sleeves, and in the middle is the front and back of the dress." They made a garment in this manner, and it fitted well.

穿袍子的讲究

How to wear a robe

文：郭雨桥

蒙古袍的领口、肩头忌讳朝里卷，因为吵架的人才这样做；忌讳袖子朝里卷，因为杀牲口的人才这样做。岳母给女婿袍子的时候，一定要把扣子全部扣好，把腰带扎好。绝对不能敞着前襟、撩着袍子、捋着袖子去别人家里。除了牧马人牧羊人，不能把袍子提得过高，看去鼓鼓囊囊，这样的人会被大家认为是吹牛匠。

One must not turn the collar of a Mongolian robe inward, as this is done by people about to fight. One must not roll the sleeves inwards, either, as this is done by those slaughtering livestock. Mothers-in-law, when giving a robe to sons-in-law, must remember to do all the buttons up and tie the waistband. One mustn't visit someone else's home with the garment open in the front, or tuck up the lappet or roll up sleeves. Except for herders of horses and sheep, one mustn't raise the garment too high up, as this will make it bulge out and make one appear to be a braggart.

微观内蒙古
INNER MONGOLIA: COLOURFUL AND MAGNIFICENT

天空之蓝，乳汁之白

Sky blue, milk white

文：郭雨桥

蒙古族自古崇拜长生天，认为天空的蓝色是最尊贵的颜色。男性喜欢穿蓝缎蒙古袍，认为它象征着永恒、坚贞与忠诚。白色也是蒙古民族喜欢的颜色，乌珠穆沁妇女一到夏天，就会穿起边缘绣有锯齿花纹的雪白长衫，对白色的喜好可能源于他们对滋养生命的乳汁的崇拜。

The Mongolian people worship Tengger, the god of the sky, and believe that sky blue is the dignified colour. Males like to wear blue satin Mongolian robes, believing it symbolises eternity, faith, and loyalty. White is also popular, and in Ujimqin in the summer, women wear snow-white gowns with embroidered saw-tooth patterns around the edges. It's possible that white has good meaning as it's associated with milk, the source of nourishment and life.

摄影：希龙道尔吉

插画

草原蓝页

敖包
obo

蒙古语意为"堆子"。以石头、土块等堆积而成,北方民族用以祭祀天地神灵,祈福许愿。

a heap of stones, earth laid out, worshipped as habitation of spirits

P17	内蒙古"王府"多	P213	鄂温克人的敖包
P104	"苏里格"	P215	草原人的敬畏
P125	公路上的敖包	P228	《敖包相会》

那达慕
Nadam

蒙古语意为"娱乐"或"游戏"。那达慕大会是蒙古族传统的节庆盛会。

a Mongolian traditional festival, typical games on which include Mongolian wrestling, horse racing, and archery

P34	草原上的街市	P232	冬季那达慕
P108	黑骏马	P232	"玛乃贾作光"
P181	骆驼那达慕		

哈(hǎ)达
khatag

藏语音译词。藏族、蒙古族等少数民族礼仪用的丝巾,表示欢迎和祝福,多为白色,也有蓝、黄等色。

ceremonial scarf usually made of silk and used as greeting gift among Tibetans and Mongolians, etc.

| P41 | 醉人的歌 |
| P224 | 脑阁 |

烧卖
shaomai

传统面食,用特制的带花褶的薄面皮兜住馅儿,撮起顶部,不封口,上笼蒸熟而成。

a type of traditional Chinese steamed dumpling with the dough frilled at the top

| P59 | 烧卖一条街 | P195 | 烧卖 |

砖茶
tea brick

压紧后形状像砖的茶叶块儿。

a block of tea leaves that have been packed in a mold and pressed into block form, shaped like a brick

| P93 | 砖茶情结 | P195 | 烧卖 |
| P147 | 可以当钱用的砖茶 | P197 | 面茶 |

草原蓝页

长调
Long Song

蒙古族独有的古老演唱形式，歌词简单，旋律悠长舒缓。

a kind of traditional Mongolian folk song, with simple lyrics and long, slow melodies

P26	草原印象	P159	名字就是地址
P32	草原是这个时代的故乡	P221	蒙古族长调
P108	黑骏马	P221	呼麦，天地与心灵的交响
P151	国宝级老艺人	P222	劝奶歌
P158	有关长调的故事	P230	白岩松眼里的蒙古人

呼麦
hoomei

蒙古语意为"咽喉"，是源自蒙古高原的古老的演唱形式，单人发出多声部的特殊喉音的艺术。

Mongolian for "throat", an old traditional form of singing originated from the Mongolian Plateau, in which one emits multiple notes from the throat simultaneously

P221　呼麦，天地与心灵的交响

好来宝
holboo

蒙古语意为"连缀""串联"，蒙古族民间说唱形式。一人自拉自唱或二人对唱，多即兴编词。

Mongolian for "couplets", a traditional Mongolian folk art form, solo or duet, mostly improvised

P231　见什么唱什么

马头琴
horse-headed fiddles

蒙古族弦乐器，有两根弦，琴柄顶端刻有马头做装饰。

Mongolian traditional two-stringed instrument, with a scroll carved like a horse's head

P120	草原情	P222	劝奶歌
P221	呼麦，天地与心灵的交响	P226	马头琴

木刻楞
mykden

俄罗斯族典型民居，木制结构，冬暖夏凉。

a kind of Russian-style wooden house, cool in the summer and warm in the winter to live in

P129　室韦小镇印象

呼伦贝尔市

1 嘎仙洞：鄂伦春自治旗
2 满洲里国门：满洲里市
3 《敖包相会》：鄂温克自治旗
4 "中国莫力达瓦曲棍球节"：
　莫力达瓦自治旗

兴安盟

5 阿尔山·柴河火山群：
　兴安盟阿尔山市—呼伦贝尔扎兰屯市
6 乌兰浩特：乌兰浩特市
7 科尔沁沙地五角枫：科尔沁右翼中旗

通辽市

8 "红干椒之都"：开鲁县

赤峰市

9 "华夏第一村"：敖汉旗
10 阿斯哈图石林：克什克腾旗

锡林郭勒盟

11 元上都：正蓝旗
12 搏克之乡：西乌珠穆沁旗

乌兰察布市

13 火山锥：察右后旗
14 神舟飞船回归处：四子王旗

呼和浩特市

15 "昭君故居"：呼和浩特市昭君博物院
16 老牛湾：呼和浩特市清水河县

鄂尔多斯市

17 "八白室" / 成吉思汗陵：
   伊金霍洛旗
18 马兰花海 / 上海庙：鄂托克前旗
19 库布齐沙漠响沙湾：达拉特旗

包头市

20 "奔鹿腾飞" 雕塑：包头市

巴彦淖尔市

21 "戈壁红驼之乡"：乌拉特后旗

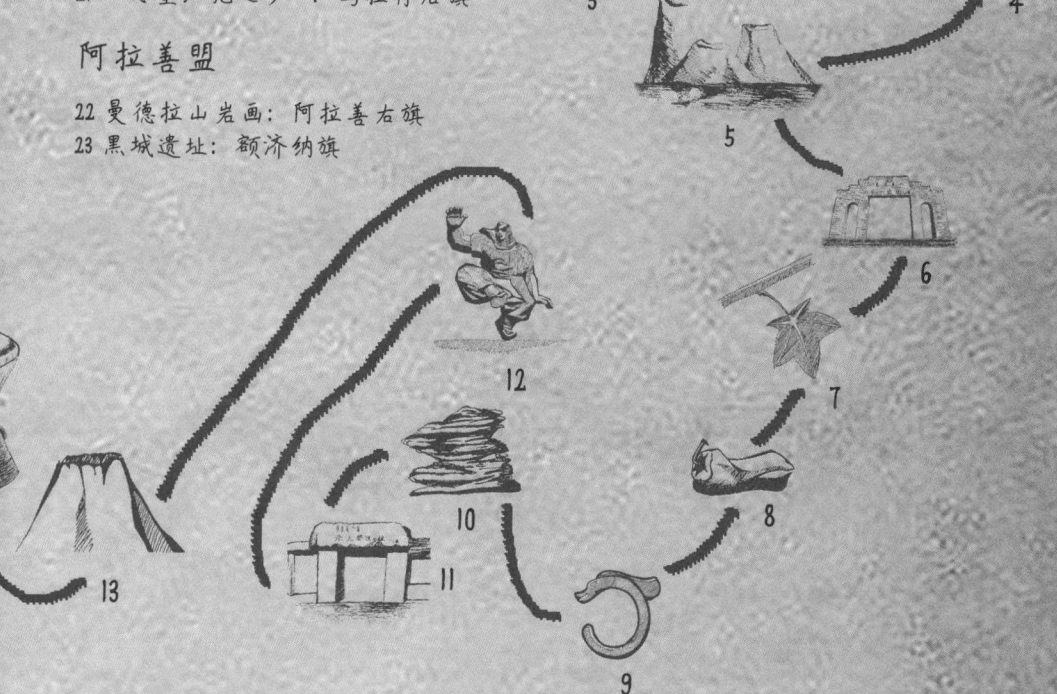

阿拉善盟

22 曼德拉山岩画：阿拉善右旗
23 黑城遗址：额济纳旗

图书在版编目(CIP)数据

微观内蒙古:汉英对照/莫久愚主编;梅皓译.—北京:
商务印书馆,2017
(微观中国)
ISBN 978-7-100-15022-4

Ⅰ.①微… Ⅱ.①莫…②梅… Ⅲ.①内蒙古—概况—汉、英 Ⅳ.①K922.6

中国版本图书馆 CIP 数据核字(2017)第 185093 号

权利保留,侵权必究。

微观内蒙古
(汉英版)

INNER MONGOLIA: COLOURFUL AND MAGNIFICENT

莫久愚 主编
梅 皓 译

商 务 印 书 馆 出 版
(北京王府井大街36号 邮政编码100710)
商 务 印 书 馆 发 行
北京中科印刷有限公司印刷
ISBN 978-7-100-15022-4

2017年8月第1版　　开本 787×1092　1/16
2017年8月北京第1次印刷　　印张 16
定价:68.00元